Understanding Prayer

The Prayer How-To Manual
Understanding
Prayer
Why Our Prayers Don't Work

R Lindemann

Aleph Publications
Wisconsin, USA

Understanding Prayer
Why Our Prayers Don't Work - The Prayer How-To Manual
Copyright 2011 - R Lindemann ©
All Rights Reserved. Published 2023

Aleph Publications
Manitowoc, WI

Paperback Edition
ISBN-13: 978-1-956814-20-0

32 31 30 29 28 27 26 25 24 23   1 2 3 4 5

Dedication

This book is dedicated to the Creator and to all those who have been seeking to have their prayers answered but have failed to see their desired results. The hurts and pains that we feel in our lives are there mostly because no one ever taught us how to properly pray.

To all of you who have suffered the torments of the troubles brought about by the lack of understanding prayer, the words in this book are here for you to better understand prayer and the Creator to which we are praying. Draw your inspiration from all good things and always seek what is true!

Disclaimer

All information, views, thoughts, and opinions expressed herein are those of the author(s) and are being presented only for your consideration and should not be interpreted as advice to take any action. Any action you take with regard to implementing or not implementing the information, views, thoughts, and opinions contained within this published work is your own responsibility. Under no circumstances are distributor(s) and/or publisher(s) and/or author(s) of this work liable for any of your actions.

Anyone, especially those who have been victim of misdirected explanation and understanding, may be best served seeking wise counsel before deciding to implement any information, views, thoughts, opinions, or anything else that is offered for your consideration in this work. All information, views, thoughts, and opinions in this work are not advice, directive, recommendation, counsel, or any other indication for anyone to take any action. All information, views, thoughts, and opinions offered herein are offered only as suggestions for your personal consideration, which is done of your own free will. Your life is your own responsibility; use it wisely.

Any use of trade names or mention of commercial sources is for informational purposes only and does not imply endorsement or affiliation.

Please note that most of the items in quotes in this book are from versions of the Bible and some quotes may have been paraphrased.

Contents

Chapter 1
Understanding Definitions for Prayer 1
   Prayer Problems and Language 11
   The Importance of Standards 12
   Measuring with Words? 14

Chapter 2
Does a Creator Exist? 19
   Measuring Our Own Existence 20
   Made In The Image Of 22
   Do you Acknowledge the Creator's Desires for You? 24
   Belief in God is Good for Your Brain 28
   Don't Try to Force God to be on Your Side 31
   "Truth" Cults 32

Chapter 3
Unneeded Competition 35
   Christian Religious Attitude 37
   Order is the Order of Matter 39
   Is Wisdom Spread Through Touch? 42
   Speaking Wisdom 43

Chapter 4
Forgiveness 47
   The Ear That Hears 50
   Why we Forgive Accidents so Easily 51
   Harsh Judgments 53
   Sympathy 55
   What Forgiveness is Not 56
   What Really is Confessing or Confession? 59
   Asking for Forgiveness 63

Chapter 5
Why Don't My Prayers Work? 69
   Praying for the Wrong Things 71
   I Want It Now! 73
   Why are We Too Blind to See It? 75
   Do You Pray Against Yourself? 78
   What to Ask for in Prayer 84
   Should We Pray for things like Weight Loss? 89
   Praying for Healing 92
   There Is a Way 95

Chapter 6
Give God Permission 101
   Wise People **Welcome** Correction 104
   Is God Superior? 106
   How do We Get God to Answer Our Prayers? 109
   Do You Dangerously Deny? 112

Chapter 7
Seeing Through the Fog of Science 117
   Always Looking for a Secret 120
   Natural "Sciences" 122
   How The Daughter of Evolution Affected You 122
   The Elite 125
   Your Faith, Evolution, and the Realm of the Wealthy ...127
   The Dawn of Enlightenment 132

The Age of Reason 132
Enlightenment is Not Magical Mystery.................................. 135
Know Me Better 137

Chapter 8

The Path to Changing Your Attitude.................... 139

Are We Machines? 142
Why Body Chemistry Matters to You 143
Can We Feel Good by Doing Good? 147
Drug Dependency... 148
Have You Thought about the Power of Your Negative Thoughts?.............150
Do You Appreciate Everything?.. 153
Showing Gratitude 156
What is the Real Power of Your Words?.............................. 158
Lifespan of Tibetan Monks 159

Chapter 9

Science, Infinity, The Unknown, and Faith 161

All Matter is Nothing 163
Does Reading More Books Make you Better?................... 167
Why Do Bad Things Happen?.. 168
From the Dead, The Raging Argument 170

Chapter 10

Being Single-Minded Versus Double-Minded 175

Are You Hedging?... 177
Are You Confused About Success?...................................... 177
Clarifying Your Needs.. 180
Clarifying Wants 181

Chapter 11

Learning How to Pray 183

Be Focused 183
Get Things In Order 185
What to Pray For.. 186
Do You Ask Questions Wrong? 188
How to Figure the Right Things to Pray For 190
Do You Make Your Own Future? 191
What about Apparent Success of Others?.......................... 195

Chapter 12

Why Do We Have Problems?........................ 197

Do You Hold On Too Tight to Your Hope?......................... 198
Recognizing Answered Prayers 199
An Answer to a Prayer is Not a Reward, It is a Result 200
Repetitious Prayer 202
Asking for Protection.. 203
Do You Accept Lies?... 204
The Four Cornerstones of Life 205

Chapter 13

Out of Our Minds and Regaining Order 207

Do You Need More, More, More? 208
Are You Suffering From Creativity Lows? 209
Are You Ashamed or Guilty?.. 211
People Who Want to Hurt You 213

Chapter 14

Do You Know Where You are Going?................ 215

Do You Know Where You Have Been?................................ 216
Do You Know Where You Are?.. 217

Do You Know Where You are Going?..218
Do You Understand Free Will?...221

Chapter 15
Religion Are You a "Religious" Person?....................................225
Do You Try to Control Others?..227
You Cannot Please the Unpleasable 228
They Will Dispose of You...229
Are You Selfish?...230
The Seed of Betrayal..231
The Dangers of Sharing your Dreams with Negative People 232

Chapter 16
Focusing on Others...237
Praying With Negativity Why Don't My Prayers Work?............................238
Negative People are Mistaken for Discerning People................................240
Leading With Negativity..242
Getting Rich with Prayer?...242
Do Your Wants Require Harm to Others?..244
Are Healings Real?..246
The Answers are there for Those Who are Willing to See 248

Chapter 17
Unkindness and Negativity 251
This is Not About Crushing Your Enemies 253
The Danger of Angry Passion 254
Protect Children from Naysayers 256
If Only We Had Passion 257

Chapter 18
Calling Down a Curse..261
If You Don't Want to Regret Your Mistakes Then… 264
Do You Give Negative Situations Power?...265
Wisdom Creates Favor 266

Chapter 19
Passion in Prayer 269
Obsession, Reward, and Compulsion 272
It Comes Down to Believing a Lie or Believing the Truth 275
Marriage Prayer Harmony..279
Where are Your Strongest Emotions?..279
Making Your Prayers Work with a New View 281
Are You in the Zone?...284
Do You Pray with Passion?...287

Chapter 20
Your Brain and Its Connection to Prayer....................................291
Is Your Thinking Organized?...295
Image of a Brain and Body 298
Your Good Addictions and Your Bad Addictions 301
Brain Waves and Mind Reading 304
Body Drugs..307

Chapter 21
True Faith is Not Surprised 311
Truth is What Builds Up 314
Truth Is a Choice 315
What is True Love?...317
Why We Cannot be Healed 321
What is The Faith of a Child?..323
Truth is a Dangerous Double-Edged Sword 327

When We Choose to Deny What is True and Good, Then We are in Error............328

When We Accept the Truth We Bind Lies, and then the Lies are Held Captive 330

Chapter 22

Clearing Your Mind to Pray Properly... **333**

Do You Know How to Weigh Information Properly?.. 334

Stop Believing Lies 336

Negative and Cruel People 339

Giving up Riches is Not a Requirement..341

Do You Hold on Tight so You Don't Lose It?...343

Pray Properly and Clear Minded 344

Introduction

Throughout your life you have likely heard scattered bits and pieces of some of what you will read here. But without the proper comprehensive organization that is required in order to deliver the information to you, those bits and pieces you have heard are of little use. This book guides you down the proper path where you can achieve effective results with your prayers.

Many people struggle with prayer. The struggle with prayer typically originates from our doubt of the existence of a supreme Creator and from our lack of understanding of what prayer actually is. We pray for things to change in our own lives. We pray in large and small groups. We pray together for years. And for many people it is all done with no apparent successes. In all of this, our prayers appear to fail to reach the heart of God and get answered. Our situations often end in dismal failure because many of us who pray about the troubling problems that we are experiencing have not been properly taught, and therefore we do not understand the key aspects about prayer that are explained in this book.

We frequently believe that our prayers are being answered whenever something common occurs, which is always there for the taking with or without prayers. It's good that we keep believing for good things to happen in our lives, but to accept lackluster events as answers to our lackluster prayers falls short of what truly can be in our lives.

It is difficult to try to explain these fundamental prayer principles during normal conversation about the subject. We fall short of having our own prayers answered until we fully understand these principles. When attempting to discuss some of the details of failed prayer versus successful prayer, the conversations often get off track or become futile exchanges of words, thus stopping delivery of the true message. We often become hostile and empty, and unnecessarily feel attacked when discussing our problems and failures. Such hostile distractions are of no help to any of us.

Unless this message can be delivered without debate during delivery, the message will continue to be obscured and misunderstood as it is being delivered, and if it is distorted or misunderstood in any way by the hearer, then it cannot be properly received.

Successful prayer is not some accidental thing that randomly occurs. Successful prayer is an *intentional* and *deliberate* action to get things right so that your mind is in the proper state, and your actions are in harmony with your proper state of mind.

Successful prayer *does* occur, and it is a truly wondrous thing when it's successful! Successful prayer is repeatable in your life when you get it right. That is to say: Get prayer right, and then you will also get the benefits that come along with praying properly.

Everyone is entitled to the privilege of having their prayers answered, but until we understand how to pray and think, we cannot expect our prayers to be answered with any certainty or consistency. You will learn a great deal about prayer in reading this book, and what you learn will allow you to take your rightful place in life—A rightful place that will teach you the true secrets of having your prayers heard and answered *when* you are able to see these Truths.

The privilege of having our prayers answered is a right of all of mankind, but that right is not without a price. We often want to do everything our own way, *and* have our prayers answered too—without a price. Does this mean that you will have to give everything up and become a preacher, monk, or nun? No, it simply means that you have a Created privileged-right that your prayers will be answered *when you* get things right. But you cannot consistently "get things right" unless you're extremely lucky, *or* you actually *understand* what causes success in prayer.

Having your prayers answered is a Right of mankind, but *understanding* is a privilege—a privilege to which everyone has a right. Only you can take away your right to the privilege of understanding. This book explains how we lose our right and what we can do to restore it. Expect your prayers to be answered and expect great things to occur in your life when you understand and apply this information about *Understanding Prayer* to your own life!

Our willingness to learn is our own choice. Within this book I have laid out, for your consideration, the information required for successful prayer. What you choose to learn from this information, and subsequently do with it, will determine your future. This book is set up in a way that will keep it comprehensive and walk you through from beginning to end. Everything you need to know about prayer is in this book. It is only your own willingness or refusal to receive, to know, and to understand this information that will determine your success or failure in your prayers and in your life. If you choose not to put forth the ambition to understand this simple, basic, and required information, then, simply put, you do not deserve to have your prayers answered reliably or have a joyful life. It's not the writer of these words who is requiring this; this is only a compact and organized collection of physical, scientific, Biblical, and real-world information that is always available to us all. It is assembled here for your benefit and understanding in order for your prayers to become effective.

Chapter 1

Understanding Definitions for Prayer

Is there actually a "God" who we can pray to who will deliver as promised when we pray? Did the fact that your prayers were not answered ever cause you to wonder if "God" even actually exists? Did the apparent lack of response from this "God" make you wonder if maybe we did evolve, rather than having been created?

Consider this as you read on: Today you have the opportunity to live a joyous life by receiving information that is hidden to most people. Or, you can choose to lag behind as you now are and continue in life's sometimes cruel toil.

At some point, most of us have looked to the heavens with our eyes and with our heart, mind, and soul, while asking and often begging for deliverance from the troubles that are in our lives. Most of us have even gone as far as to ask for things that we truly do not need, like luxury items, such as a large beautiful home or a new car. Is it right to ask for these things? Should we be asking for such luxury items and/or for deliverance from our troubles? My answer is absolutely yes, we should ask for good things. This book will be useful to you if you have ever wondered about these questions. It will be even more useful to you if you would like to create a better future for yourself and for your family by having your future prayers answered. These first few chapters are here for you to build a solid foundation of understanding before we get into the good stuff. They can appear somewhat disconnected in regard to prayer, until you realize how much deception is in our lives regarding the topics we will be discussing and how deception terribly affects your prayers. One of our problems is that we often care only about luxury items and little or nothing about what is truly in both our heart and mind.

Prayers and "miracles" are often associated in our minds due to a few miraculous events mentioned in the Bible. Events such as parting the sea, walking on water, and pillars of fire are miracles and are a topic that is better fit for scientific analysis if you are questioning their validity. In this book we are specifically addressing prayer and the subsequent answers for those prayers.

Your situation is yours alone and no one knows your circumstances as well as you do. *You* are the best person to solve your own problems, but without proper understanding you are at a severe disadvantage. *Understanding Prayer* offers many views, thoughts, and opinions for you to consider as you move forward in life, but only *you* truly know your needs, wants, and desires. The views, thoughts, and opinions in this book are here only for your consideration, and they do not tell you what you *must* do. But what you *choose* to do after reading and considering these thoughts is your own responsibility, and *no one* can do that for you. Your life and situation are unique and only you can take information and adjust it to your needs to improve your direction in life. Using a rigid step by step approach with specific instructions causes problems because it might not, and probably won't, properly fit *your specific* needs.

Our past is in the past and those errors are done, yet they often haunt us and cause our future a great deal of trouble. Most of this problem arises from our lack of understanding. Our lack of understanding primarily comes from two key sources: First is our unwillingness to learn, and second is the fact that most of us were never taught *understanding*. And the fact that we were never taught is what causes the first source to begin with.

Without understanding you will never be able to pray and *reliably* get your desired results. This book has the sole purpose to reveal the secrets of prayer to you, or better put, the mysteries that you are required to know to get consistent and reliable results when you pray.

Since *understanding* is a key part in the secrets to successful prayer, it is appropriate that we get specific about a few things. This book is not about the typical "feel-good" messages often found in sermons or in self-help books. Instead, you are going to get detailed explanations of *how* things work and *why* they work the way they do with regard to your prayers. The reason for these detailed explanations is so that you can obtain the power to cause your prayers to be effective.

Our level of understanding is lacking. I have found few people who have enough extra time in their overly busy days to take the time to do the extensive and needed research required in order to fully understand prayer, which is why I compiled this book. The reason so few of us understand prayer is mostly due to the fact that little if any details about prayer were explained to us early in life. It's also due to the fact that other than the Bible, that too few of us actually read, there really was no good place to get all of the information from one place and at one time—until now.

Often, much of the so-called "knowledge" that we are taught has been twisted and contorted to better serve the person using or selling the knowledge to promote their own agenda. Most of what is being discussed in this book is open knowledge that is free for the taking for all of mankind. It is my desire to share the truths that will allow you to be able to cut through the inaccuracies so you can better understand prayer for your own benefit and for the benefit of all of humanity.

Because prayer is a form of communication, it is important to know how to properly communicate before you pray. The fact that we don't fully understand the words we use is humanity's most common blind-spot with regard to our understanding of anything. You do not have to wonder very long whether or not this is true. For instance, what is the meaning of the word "how"? Few people have an answer to that question. For the purpose of this paragraph the meaning is not important. What I am trying to illustrate is how often we all use a word like "*how*" or "*the*", but are not readily able to explain what the word means. Yet, we believe that we know what words mean without ever thinking about what they truly mean. Some of the simplest words to understand are the most difficult for us to explain.

In truth, there are many words that, when we get down to the core of their meaning, we find we are using them somewhat incorrectly. This is typically where our prayers and communications with other people break down and where our troubles begin. In general, provided that we all have a sort of consensual agreement within society that a word is used in a certain manner, we can, for the most part, function. However, this does not mean that we are using the words properly. Improper use of a simple word is not the problem. The problem is that most words originally described something specific, and the essence of the original meanings of many words have long been forgotten, because, as a society, we have lost those meanings due to using the words incorrectly. This occurs because we use words as labels rather than as the description they were originally meant to be used as. Words become bits of trivia to us—a learned bunch of useless facts. This does not help us in our prayers

Definitions of words may be an odd way to start a book about prayer, but trying to convey the required message for successful prayer is nearly impossible without a consistent understanding of a few key words used between the person sharing the information about prayer and the person receiving that information. Your right to the privilege of understanding prayer is solely dependent upon your willingness to understand the simple words used when seeking to understand anything.

For example, if a person does not understand what a word, such as "faith", actually means, then they cannot understand what is truly being said in a discussion about faith. There are two primary ways to understand words. First is common usage: Common usage is the way we understand a word based upon our language and everyday social use. When common usage is inaccurate it causes confusion about the topic of a discussion, especially those topics that seem obscure to us.

The word "fun" is a typical example where common usage has overshadowed the true meaning of the word. The common usage of the word *fun* is often used to describe an enjoyable time, but the roots of the word "fun" mean *hoax* or to *dupe*. When we say we have had "*fun*" what we truly mean is that we have had a very enjoyable time. The word "fun" is more appropriate in a circumstance where we are referring to making fun of a person in order to mock them. The word "nice" is another word where its meaning is not what we typically think. "Nice" is more properly used in the context of "nice job!" when someone makes a foolish mistake, than it is when someone says, "Have a nice day!"

The second method of understanding words is accurate usages based upon word origin history. This is the accurate and proper way to understand words, but doing so requires a little bit of dedication. Without this understanding, some things are not able to be described properly because we have no other words to describe the underlying meaning of them. When we allow perversion of such base words, then we cannot fully understand some things regarding that word.

Most words that we use in our everyday language are reasonably well understood. If they were not understood the world would be in utter chaos. It is when we are having troubles in our communication and in our life's progress that we need to examine these definitions more closely. We should always strive to better understand. This problem is very important to address in our world. In fact, it is so important, that court cases are often specifically debated in high court about what specific meaning was actually intended in the various usages of a certain word pertaining to the particular case.

These understanding differences are critically important when we are praying. Word-usage has a two-part problem. A person can mean one thing when making a statement, but that statement could be interpreted in more than one way by the person it was intended to be heard by. Technically, the person sharing, and the person listening, could both be correct based upon the words in label form, but the *intent* can be an entirely different story. With regard to prayer, it's not that God will not understand you, but rather, it's that you yourself don't have the required clarity of *specifically* what it is that you're asking for.

No one should ever feel they are not good enough or smart enough to understand the difference between the common and accurate meanings of basic words. Since many of the lawyers and judges can't figure some words out, the rest of us will have to do it ourselves. This word definition problem runs vast and wide, but it is far simpler than it appears.

Much of the problem that people have when trying to get their prayers answered has to do with accepting the proper understanding of words. There is a recurring thought from the Bible that says ,"My people perish for lack of knowledge." This "lack of knowledge" is also true with regard to our word usage. If we are inconsistent in our understanding of what is being said, then two different people who hear the words of this book could end up coming to two entirely different conclusions about what is being said. This unfortunate and unacceptable situation commonly occurs when we hear other people's words and try to understand what they meant as we are interpreting those words.

For instance, one person's interpretation of the Bible often differs from the next person's interpretation. This most frequently occurs because of our inconsistent understanding of the meanings of the words used in the Bible. In many ways, all words are subject to each our own interpretations. This leaves anyone trying to convey a message, whether written or spoken, in a very difficult situation. The more important the topic is to peoples' lives, then the more important it is to accurately understand what the other person is actually trying to share with us.

The goal of this "Understanding Definitions for Prayer" chapter is not to get everyone to understand everything in the exact same way. Rather, it is to get everyone to understand the importance of knowing that none of us understand things in the *exact* same way as each other. Knowing that we might not specifically understand things in the same way as others, allows us to grasp that someone might not specifically understand what we are saying to them. Thus, we tend to listen more carefully when we understand this basic concept. Critical definitions will be addressed when needed throughout this book. Properly understanding them is required for your prayers to work on command. If we have the wrong understanding of the original intent of a word, then we will lack the ability to convey many of our thoughts accurately to another person when using that word. This applies to ourselves and to our prayers as well.

Words and their definitions can be thought of like a ruler or a measuring stick that we use to measure distance. For instance, a desk ruler is one foot or 12 inches long. When a reference to a foot or 12 inches is made, every person who is familiar with that measurement typically understands about how long a foot actually is. Once we reach a reasonable age we are able to approximate that distance with our hands with a relative degree of accuracy. We generally all understand that the accuracy that we display with our hands might not be exactly the same as the ruler, but we have a very good picture in our minds of that distance. With measurements we understand that when something is critical we must pick up a ruler and measure the item in order to be accurate. But when it comes to words, and especially with regard to prayer, our accuracy fails miserably. Words have a tendency to be very subjective with regard to our definitions of those words. Words are often used in a peculiar manner such as sarcastic usage and varied usage.

An example of sarcastic usage would be when someone drops something and breaks it and then another person might shout out, "good job, way to go!" when they really mean something to the order of, "you broke that and that's not good."

A varied usage example would be something on the order of "rise and shine!" where we expect the sun to rise and shine for instance, but in this case we are referring to the person whom we are waking up. They will rise up out of bed, but no particular visible light will be shining forth from them.

This seems petty on the surface, but it is very important to understand when we are trying to troubleshoot something, especially when it comes to something as abstract as our prayers. And in regard to this book, our prayers are the subject of the troubleshooting.

If someone has a different indication of what a "foot" is with regard to measurement, then when we instruct them to look ten feet to the left, then they are not likely to find what we are trying to show them. This means that they will be looking in the wrong place and will not be able to find what they are looking for because they'll be looking several feet away from where they should. Or if someone tells you to drive for two miles and then take a left, but you, instead, decide that you will drive for two kilometers and then try to turn left, you will not find the turn and might end up in a ditch because two kilometers is considerably shorter than two miles. A similar type of inaccuracy causes serious problems with our prayers.

Words are a form of measurement. Words measure communication and the meaning of the communication. When we pray, our misunderstanding a word and its actual meaning is no different than when we discuss space or distance and we misunderstand a unit of measure such as a foot or a meter, or a mile or a kilometer.

Communication is our primary means of becoming aware of anything. Everything is a form of communication—especially prayer! Everything we do is a form of a message from one being to another being.

When we verbally give someone instructions or directions, they expect us to be accurate in our delivery of that information to them. If we are not accurate, then they will not get to the destination due to our inaccuracy. A map is also an important form of communication where we expect accuracy. If a map is designed or printed inaccurately, it is likely going to be useless to anyone trying to navigate with it. It becomes a worthless piece of paper because of its inaccuracy. A map can have both measurements and language on it, plus, it has another very important visual aspect that depicts roads, rivers, and cities, thus giving us a very good idea of where things are in relationship to each other. If we have the wrong map it will not get us to our destination.

If the diagram of the streets on a map is correct, then we can *partially* navigate by that diagram. If the street names are correct, but the distances are wrong, then we can still partially navigate by the street names. If we do not understand that some of the street names may be inaccurate, then we are subject to error and we will likely end up lost and in the wrong place failing to achieve our intended goal.

Will we choose to use the distance measurements, the word measurements, or the picture measurements of the map? All of these are forms of communication and if any one of them is wrong, then it is going to be more difficult to get to our destination. Navigating life becomes more difficult when our personal word index map and personal dictionary are inaccurate. It becomes more difficult because when we don't understand words properly, then we have to sift through the inaccuracies and compare them against what we believe is true and real as we go on our journey through life. This slows us down and often has us doing things in frustration and error.

The importance of getting your information and directions about prayer from a reliable and accurate source is critical. For thousands of years mankind has been obtaining information from those who society sees as "authorities". In the more recent years of human history, "authority" has been mistakenly given to universities to hand out diplomas and degrees as they see fit. It is not the handing out of diplomas and degrees to people that is a problem. Rather, it is our unwillingness to check the accuracy of what we are taught at those schools and universities that becomes our blind-spot.

The "educated elite" have a tendency to incorrectly use *pure* words, by placing "-ism, -city, or -ity" or some other ending at the end of words in order to create bigger more important *sounding* word labels. Utilizing labels lends to a feeling of power by those who recklessly flaunt the labels. This arrogant nature is not bound only to universities; it is seen in every realm of life, including religious, scientific, political, all scholastic levels, etc. It's even found in our own homes.

As individuals, as long as we refuse to try to understand the *actual* meaning of the words in our language, we will be held captive by those who want to have authority over us and over our prayers by means of abuse of the words they use as labels.

Prayer Problems and Language

Definitions of words are critical to anything we are referring to in life any time we communicate. While words are important, it's not the words you use in your prayers that we're referring to here. When we pray, our *intentions* are known by the Creator even though we may try to fool ourselves, or God, as to what our intentions truly are. The critical definitions that I am referring to are for the pivotal words regarding prayer and everything pertaining to prayer and the entire discussion.

With regard to our beliefs there are words such as *faith, trust, love, prayer,* and other such words that have been very loosely defined in our minds. It's common to hear preachers teaching on a multitude of types of "love". While each of these various descriptions for love has a level of validity, the preachers are actually splitting hairs that need not be split. When we choose to accept complexity within simple concepts, such as "love", then we end up unnecessarily complicating our lives and we subject ourselves to a wide range of inaccuracy and distractions.

The word *prayer* is an important word to understand. Break down *prayer* into "*pray*" and "*er*," just like "*work*" and "*er*" in the word *worker*. The word we need to focus on here is "*pray*". We need to understand some basic words if we want to even begin to imagine that our prayers will be answered as per our requests. We typically use words in an accurate way, but what is often wrong is our understanding of them. In other words, we often mean something other than what actually comes out of our mouths.

Another word to understand is *praise*. The word "*praise*" is sometimes used synonymously with the word *pray*; however, there is a distinct difference between these two words, and it is a very important difference.

The word *pray* has a very specific meaning of being a request or asking for something. Where, *praise* is the exact opposite. *Praise* is to hold something in high esteem and to make an offering of appreciation. One of these words *requests* and the other word *offers*. You will find these differences to be critical to your understanding as we get further into *Understanding Prayer*.

Many of us already have the vague understanding that the two words, *pray* and *praise*, have the meanings of *request* and *offer*, but we often get hung up on other words, like the word "faith".

After you have completed this book you will have a very different and much more clear and accurate perspective about many things, especially those things pertaining to prayer. You will also have a far better understanding of prayer and how effective it can be when you properly understand these and a few other words that are critical to successful prayer.

The Importance of Standards

As already discussed, definitions of words are very important. This is the reason that people have taken it upon themselves to create *standards* throughout history. With word definitions, the standard that we use is a *dictionary*; but even with the dictionary readily at our fingertips, we still fail to take the time to actually verify the things that don't make sense to us. Setting standards for various measurements is critical to world harmony whether those standards are for time, length, width, height, or *words*. This is because standards are the units that we use to gauge everything with which we utilize the technique of comparison to these standards. Measuring is the counting or valuing of these units.

Setting standards for time, length, width, and height is extremely important for us to do in order to accurately communicate with each other. Standards are so important that agencies have been created, nationally and internationally, to address these issues in order to agree upon a set of standard measurements so that discrepancies are held to a minimum for international trade.

But sadly, when it comes to words, it is far more difficult to set up a standard as concise as we do with numbers. Numbers are as easy to understand as the ten fingers and ten toes most of us have on our bodies. So simple is this concept that the term "digit" refers to our fingers and is the reason that we count in *tens* and the cause for why we use a "digital" method for many devices. The very fact that nearly every one of us has this principle attached to our bodies, makes counting by ten easy to comprehend and a good standard for the entire world to use. Even though the western measurement system of inch, foot, and yard are somewhat obscure in units, the counting still uses the digit-al (10 "digits" on our hands) or 10 basis of counting. We simply cannot escape the utter simplicity experienced when counting with the base-ten system. It is what we are—humans have ten toes and ten fingers. Where we get into trouble with counting is in what we are counting. It is the "what" part that causes need for standards.

The Bible speaks of not using dishonest weights. Weights were used on a balance scale when selling goods. An example of a "dishonest" weight, as mentioned in the Bible, would be like going into the store to buy a pound of fruit and having it weighed on a balance with a "one pound" rock as the index, but the rock was hollowed out or of a lighter nature so that it only *appeared* to weigh one pound. Using this sort of inaccurate tactic allows a merchant to give you less material than you believe you have actually bargained for. The agencies that deal with standards for weights and measures throughout the world have been put in place to stop merchants from using dishonest weights and scales so that we are not cheated.

In many countries, merchants and manufacturers are required by law to have their scales checked periodically to assure that they are accurate so that the consumers are not cheated. But what is it that they're accurate or compared to? It is that comparison that is our standard.

Most established countries have a reference weight or will adhere to the *standard* of another country or organization that has an index weight that is used as a basis for all other weights. It is these cherished and protected weights that are the standard for all other weights within a particular weight or measurement system. If these weights were to deteriorate over time, then our standard of a kilogram or pound would change over time. Then in future generations, a pound from today would weigh more than the future pound because the index weight has partially decayed in the future. If only we took such care with our words we could live in an even better world.

Words also decay, but the decay is actually in our understanding of each of the words' original and true meanings. When we allow our words to decay and change meaning, then they are no longer pure, which allows the decayed understanding of those words to inhibit the purity of our understanding and of our prayers—Standards matter.

Measuring with Words?

Words are far more complicated than weights. We can't build the standard for words as easily as we can with measurement. It's simple with weight measurement because the items are tangible—we can touch them! With a unit of weight there are no words needed; it is its weight and only its weight that matters.

However, with words, there are *many* different units, and each word would need a standard of its very own locked away and protected for safe-keeping. The set of standards for words appears to be a relatively new thing in human history. As people migrated throughout the world they brought words, translation, and dialect along with them. Additionally, the migrating people adopted new words from the cultures that they were assimilating into. When words migrated along with the people who used those words, the primary essences of the words were often lost in translation and became nothing more than *labels*. Often, words were translated phonetically, and in doing so, the words utterly lost their essence. There was no standard for the words, and the words only had common usage meanings after the migration.

Nowadays the standards for words are generally laid out within the pages of a dictionary; with each individual definition being the standard for its word. Because words aren't concrete, like a steel weight is, they cannot be placed in a protected environment to hold their original shape and weight. Words are not a tangible substance that we can set aside and then later use to count like we can with a weight of solid metal. Words are ideas; they are concepts; they are our understanding—they are our thoughts. Unfortunately, we change word meanings at any whim for our own social acceptance.

Currently, our best way of setting and keeping standards for words is to create a paper dictionary and keep it in a safe location. While this method is not perfect, it has served as a reasonable way for us to stay relatively consistent over time with our words. But even printed dictionaries change the meanings of words to conform to society's perception of a word's meaning as each new dictionary version is prepared for print.

Prior to the twenty-first century, word standards were printed or scribed on rock, metal, leather, or some form of paper in a relatively painstaking manner. However, since the dawn of computer technology, word standards have increasingly been available in an electronic format. Ease of accessibility and repeatability in electronic format has also ushered in the ease of alteration and a rapid spreading of potentially inaccurate information.

Most of us do not have the time to dive into the needed research required to find the true meaning of all words. We could be more accurate with computer technology, but as is common with human nature, that is unlikely to happen. This leaves the task of understanding up to each one of us to try to determine what the writer actually meant when a particular word is used in its context. You will notice this as you read this book, so keep this in the forefront of your mind; doing so will be very helpful as you read on.

Often, we use words in a poetic manner and play with their meanings in analogies in an effort to better communicate an emotional thought or feeling. We also play with word meanings to make the language more fanciful or colorful in delivery for the sake of entertainment value. It's not wrong to do this, but when we lose sight of the *true* nature of a word and when or how to use that word in its proper meaning, then we lose our own ability to choose the path that we actually desire to take. For some words, our dictionaries do alter the meanings over time to accommodate popular usage. And while the underlying words still remain, we no longer are able to readily fully understand them with much clarity.

If you have been praying for solutions to problems that you're struggling with and if you have been failing to see those prayers answered then the value of understanding word standards pertaining to prayer cannot be understated. We must hold these standards in high regard and in high accuracy while we communicate with others using our words. (Communication is a form of measuring.)

If you, the reader of this book, and I, the person who is sharing these thoughts with you, do not have the same understanding of words such as *prayer* or *faith*, then it will be impossible for me to properly convey the particular information to you the way that I desire for you to understand it. This is information about how to make your prayers work, and you want to know and understand it in order to be successful with your prayers.

The fact that you want information on understanding prayer is made evident through your taking the time to acquire and read this book. It is important for us to have the *same* understanding of the simple but critical words with regard to prayer that are used in this book. If *you* try to relay the words in this book to others and share this message with other people, you cannot possibly accurately relay the intended message to them if yours and my understanding of these words do not agree.

A few basic words will be defined that are critical in our common understanding in order for you to achieve the result that you desire in your prayers. Properly understanding these words will assist you to accurately discuss this book with others.

Since this book is about prayer, there is another standard we must address that is bound tightly to the definition of words. This other standard has to do with your prayers and the God to whom you pray. Have you ever wondered if the Creator really actually exists?

Chapter 2

Does a Creator Exist?

There's another standard that has been under attack throughout all of recorded history, and that standard has much to do with our own perception of the question of whether or not a Creator exists.

At some point, nearly all of us have been exposed to people who attend church or a religious service and make requests of God in their "prayers" while at the same time believing mankind has descended from apes. Even many Church leaders have adopted the position that descending from apes can coexist with a Creator-Creation belief. This approach clearly lacks a standard of any kind since the primary book that is used by the Church specifically claims that humans are formed by the Creator.

The Bible is often regarded as a "standard" for religion , but then is refuted by some of the same people as a book of mere "fairy tales". The confusion in our minds about the Bible that has been brought on by all of the debate surrounding the Creator-standard is understandable when we consider all of the inconclusive and contradictory discussions about the Bible and a God that are offered to us by the so-called "experts".

We adopt an approach that says, "It doesn't matter! I believe there's a God, so if the first intelligent primates were Adam and Eve, then I am okay in my beliefs." This is not a standard; it is an un-standard and is inconsistent. If we want our prayers to be answered, then we best make up our mind about the *abilities* of this supposed "God", to which we are praying.

If you're going to pray at all, then for the benefit of your own mind, it is important to acknowledge the existence of a God. If you do not believe in God, but you are still going to pray, then exactly what or who are you praying to?

If you're the type who believes that if you pray to a concrete item, such as a crystal or a statue, then ask yourself: "Will an item made with human hands be able to supply all of my needs?" Often we use this sort of illogical reasoning with regard to a god where we believe in a concrete object to pray to, but we cannot find our way clear to fully believe in an unseen Creator.

For now, with regard to this book, we will be content with a mere acknowledgment that a Creator exists since it is this Creator to whom we pray. And, for the moment, we will ignore the inconsistencies in many of society's beliefs in that regard.

Measuring Our Own Existence

To understand prayer we must at least begin to try to understand our own existence. We'll do our best here to steer clear of the philosophical debates that surround religion. The topics discussed in this book are typically thought of as "philosophical" by modern standards. But, "philosophical" is another word that is commonly misused.

The science-fiction entertainment industry enjoys the idea of time travel and going back in time and changing what has already happened, or going forward in time so that we can make decisions based upon what is going to happen in order to change or guide our future. While this has entertainment value and can be enjoyable to think about, its value in reality is worthless other than it causing us to think ahead.

A portion of the community of theoretical science has embraced the possibility of time travel, believing that if one were able to surpass the speed of light, that time for them would change, and then maybe they would be able to step into their past or into their future. The reason that this is embraced in any serious manner by actual scientists is due to the lack of understanding of the *standard* of what "time" actually is.

The notion of being able to travel through time just because we can exceed the speed of light is as ridiculous as before the advent of the automobile when some people speculated that strange things would happen if we could travel at speeds exceeding 60 miles per hour. Thoughts about time travel are based on the fearful fantasies of the imaginations of people who wish things could be a certain way. It doesn't matter how much we want something to be or how afraid we are, because if it's not possible, then it's not possible. That statement might appear to be limiting in imagination, but it is not. Some people would like to time travel to alter their lives, kind of like prayer, but with no god.

What is *time*? Time is nothing more than a mere measurement of how long something has been in existence; time is an idea. Time measures how long *we* have existed. A physical example is when a baby leaves its mother's womb, the clock starts for the baby. The clock is based on the revolution of the Earth and the orbit of the Earth around the Sun. We count that child's life existence with days and years. We use this *standard* to reference when something has happened or will happen. Time is our current experience relative to what we have already seen occur.

Our ability to relate our *past* to our *present* allows us to imagine time into our future—that is to say, to think and imagine in advance, to *Hope!* And our *hope* is where our prayers begin. When it comes to you achieving success in your prayers you will find that your ability to imagine in advance is incredibly important. Our human ability to count our days and think and hope is what allows us to understand that we are alive and can direct our own future if we so choose.

Made In The Image Of

There is nothing in this world more important to you than the very fact that you exist. If you did not exist, then nothing on this Earth matters to you because you simply do not exist—you are not here and you never have been if you don't exist.

Our own existence is critically important to each of us, but we are still left with a question of—what is existence? But, do we need a body to exist? There are a few things that are required for a person to be considered alive, such as breath, blood, organs, and thoughts (brain activity).

We can temporarily remove the blood and replace it with a special solution during an operation, or we can remove the heart and replace it with a pump, or we can artificially breathe with a machine. We can even simulate knowledge contained by the brain, but we cannot duplicate the thoughts of a person. We can remove various parts of the brain and still be who we are. Many other organs or substances in the body can be eliminated to a certain extent and a person can still live for a long time. But, if you stop the heart, remove the blood, cease breathing, or do anything else to stop the flow of oxygen and other nutrients to the brain, or if the brain is destroyed, then the person will promptly come to an end. How does this issue of time and existence have anything to do with prayer?

The one part of our body that we can't seem to function without is our brain, and there seems to be no replacement for it

This is especially true of the part of our brain that connects our brain to the rest of our body. Our brain is our body's physical interface to our existence, and without it, the bodies that we utilize cannot be controlled by our *existence*—some might call it our *soul.* This is a model of our Creation and of our Creator.

We are a model of our Creator and of the Creation. We are made in the image of the Creator. This is an area that causes a great deal of difficulty for us and our understanding, and this difficulty is especially so with regard to our prayers.

We are blinded by our Creation because we see things only as they appear to be rather than as they are; for instance, when we find fossils and we make up our pretend theories about how those fossils came to be. It should be our goal to see things as they are, rather than as they appear to be. When we speculate about these fossils, we should not invent ridiculous geological theories. Nor should we blindly believe someone's inaccurate interpretations of the Bible.

As individuals, we are often soul-searching to find meaning in our lives. We seek this meaning through prayers, and even through prayer requests *for explanations* about everything. Since we have been Created in the Creator's image, our purpose is to be like the Creator.

Due to the potential differences in our understanding, it must be pointed out that we are to be *like* the Creator, we are *not* to pretend to be the Creator.

Whenever we set aside our reckless intellectual refusal to admit the possibility that there is a Creator, we begin to realize that we have no choice but to be like the Creator—it's the way we are made. It's what we were made for and *it is the foundation for being able to have your prayers answered.*

Do you Acknowledge the Creator's Desires for You?

It is only after we have chosen to accept the obviousness that we are Created by a Creator that our prayers to God can possibly become regularly effective.

There has been a movement referred to as the "thought movement" for more than the past few hundred years, which has wrongly taken basic achievement and confused it with answered prayers. The thought-movement belief system is a perverted imitation of what is taught to us throughout the four thousand years of history detailed in the Bible.

If we choose the way of the world and doubt or reject the notion of a Creator and the Creation, then can we expect to have our prayers answered? Can we really expect that a Creator will be excited to grant our requests when we speak against the Creator and doubt that this "Creator" exists?

You have likely heard or even wondered yourself about questions like, "If there is a God, then how could God allow a Stalin or Hitler?" or "Why do bad things happen to good people?" Due to our lack of insight, these questions lead the way to our doubt. Should we ignore those sorts of questions and believe in God anyway *without* answers to the questions? No, most certainly not! If there is a Creator, then we deserve access to the privilege of the answers to these and other such questions. But access to the privilege has requirements on our part.

Our problem is not in asking these questions or even getting answers to them. Our problem is that we fail to accept the answers that sit right before our very own eyes. When we do actually notice the answers, we typically don't understand what the answers mean because our doubt has excessively obscured them in our minds.

We're always looking for a focal point as a reason or cause of what happens in our life. This is true whether you believe in evolution or you believe that things were intentionally Created.

The notion of evolution implies that the cause of change through millions or billions of years is due to necessity. And through those many years and many changes, a single cell replicated and evolved into the form that we humans have come to be and the form we still are currently in.

Where the notion of Creation, on the other hand, states that, the cause of all being is that there was a deliberate and intentional effort by an intentional Creator to create things with specific purpose.

At some point a decision needs to be made in each our own minds for one of these two possibilities, or some other possibility if you can find one. But, if we are going to choose to believe anything other than an intentional Created existence, then praying to a Creator is a waste of our time. And we may as well not even bother praying because we will be praying to nothing if we choose to believe in a creatorless existence.

When we choose to understand that there is a Creator, then we must understand that because there was purpose in our Creation, that the purpose was of a constructive and good nature.

Adopting any notion that the Creator is a bully who wants to hurt everyone is counterproductive to your prayers. You need to understand the contradiction in that line of thinking: A Creator who has Created everything that exists, would not arbitrarily and deliberately torment the people who were Created with such detailed intricacy and care. Doubt has been placed into our minds and hearts with regard to the existence of a Creator. This is partially due to the mistaken view that the Creator arbitrarily and unjustly torments people.

We pray in a manner such as, "God if you really exist then answer this prayer and grant me my request, *and **then** I'll believe that you exist.*" This approach to prayer is manipulative, and it is a bully-like approach. It essentially says, "Give me my demands or I won't believe in you or love you!" Can we expect this kind of manipulation to work when we pray?

Part of the reason that we have a tendency to offer ultimatums to the Creator in this way is because we ourselves behave like this towards others. Because we don't believe in ourselves, we feel that we must prove ourselves to others, and so, we expect the Creator to offer proof to us of the Creator's existence in the same way. When you have this attitude it permeates your entire life. Everything that we do and all of the decisions that we make are affected by this inhibiting attitude and method of belief—it is a method of the belief in doubt! When we doubt and demand miraculous proof, then we cannot possibly understand that our Creator wants the very best for all of us.

The desires that the Creator has for each one of us are always good, which is where our problem in prayer really begins.

If we doubt the existence of a Creator, then we're also going to doubt that this Creator desires only good things for us as humans—humans who happen to be the handy-work of the Creator.

There is a core problem in prayer and it is that it's easy to manipulate people as follows: All that we need to do in order to manipulate someone is to do what Satan did to Eve in the Garden, which was to get her to doubt herself or to doubt in general. This common practice has been, and still is, used by every bully who has ever existed.

Doubt is a dangerous mental action, but it is also a necessary action. Without doubt we would believe anything that anyone tells us, much the way a young child believes almost anything that their parents tell them. This seems confusing, but when you understand the dangers of doubt, and a few other things that we'll discuss later, it becomes very easy to see and understand what we need to doubt versus what we need to understand as true.

This is not asking you to believe in the Creator just because it says so here in these pages, nor are these words asking you to accept the Christ as your personal Lord and Savior. The words in this book are here to shine some light on areas that most of us struggle with in our belief system and in our understanding of prayer. These struggles are the doubt and inconsistent thinking that subsequently cause our prayers to fail. Depending upon what you already know, the force of your doubt will vary. If you have not received solid information in your youth, then rereading some sections of this book can help to make things more clearly understood.

It will benefit you to understand that there is a Creator and how this is evident. But for now, just the evidence that you exist and the evidence that is all around you should suffice as evidence of a Creator with regard to your prayers and their success.

As for evidence and proof of a Creator regarding prayer, we need only to decide, is there, or is there not, a Creator? Those who insist that there is not a Creator have chosen to accept no evidence whatsoever with regard to the possibility of there actually being a Creator. This is not an honest approach. If a person has utterly disregarded any possibility of the existence of a Creator, then they cannot be believed because they have disregarded a possibility that has not been disproved. This is not saying that you should blindly accept it, but rather it is saying that you must not entirely discount the existence of a Creator. When good evidence is presented, then we should consider that new information and evidence. The all too common disregard towards the possibility of the existence of a Creator destroys virtually all of the credibility of those who promote natural-only origins of humans. Their objectivity is skewed by their *refusal* to admit to this possibility. The book series *The Science of God* offers fresh insight on the Creation topic.

The behavior of utterly rejecting the idea of a Creator blinds our perspective of the possibility of a Creator and it fouls the real evidence found while at the same time seeking to support a godless creation cause. In other words, when we have a biased agenda, we ignore *facts* that do not support our biased theories.

This causes us to concoct conclusions that are inaccurate or, at a minimum, suspect of error.

The same holds true for those who are religious with respect to a Creator. The evidence for a Creator does not need or require the Bible. The purpose and form in which everything is Created is obvious once the blinders of religious beliefs are removed. "Religious beliefs" include both Creation-origin beliefs and natural-origin beliefs. Biblical Creation and progressive evolution are, by definition, both religious belief systems, even if some people scream and shout that this is not so.

Any time a person doubts the intentional Creation of existence, then that person who doubts it is in a very difficult position with regard to their prayers being answered. If we doubt that we were Created for and with specific purpose and form, then we are obviously going to doubt that the Creator has only good intentions for us. And deep down inside, we're going to doubt that our prayers have any true value because we doubt that the Creator actually exists. Doubt causes us to not direct our prayers to their proper focus and state.

Belief in God is Good for Your Brain

Choosing to believe that a Creator exists is a choice—your choice! And it's a choice that *only you* can make for yourself. Each of us is responsible for that choice in our own mind. Making the wrong choice in this regard has ramifications that greatly impact our own lives and the lives of those around us.

Since our doubt level is the center around which the effectiveness of our prayers revolves, understanding and knowing that we are Created, and not doubting that point, is paramount to everything else in our life and existence—especially our prayers!

Anyone who is strongly opposed to a Creator, and wants to cast doubt on the very initial point of understanding truth, has the following agenda: If we do not understand that we are

Created, then we will react and behave differently than we should, causing us to be more easily turned away from the Creator. This behavior includes our reactions *and* the behavior of our thoughts—our lack of understanding causes us to be more easily manipulated.

Because you are reading this, we can assume that you want to believe in Creation and a Creator and that you want to have your prayers work as promised to you by that Creator and the Christ.

Once we have accepted that a Creator does exist, we begin to see the positive and real effects in our life that are due to that understanding and belief. Upon our own acceptance of being Created, we come to the realization that our body is Created "in the image of". It is a very important point to understand with regard to prayer that we exist "in the image of". Our religious affiliation has nothing to do with whether or not a Creator exists. Regardless of our current or prior beliefs, we all have the ability to make a choice, at any moment in time, of what we will choose to ignore with regard to establishing our beliefs. However, our personal belief has no bearing on whether or not a Creator actually exists.

A body that is Created is going to have been Created for a reason—it has purpose! If we took all of the chemicals that make up our bodies and put them in a container and shook them, then upon opening the container there would be no order or body-like organization to those chemicals. They may separate into layers due to their actual size and weight, but other than that it would just be a container of chemicals. No amount of calculating the odds of the possibility of proper chanced organization would ever change that. The chemicals will behave in a particular way because of their weight, size, and shape. Mathematicians proposing an equation stating that there is a one in 10 to the X power chances "proving" that it could occur, does not mean that it ever would occur.

It's when these chemicals are put together in a specific and orderly manner that they become what we refer to as "our bodies". This is a clear indication of purpose and intent. We can try to explain this away with natural progression, but in doing so, *purpose* is always referenced as "*adaptation*" whenever the concept of *purpose* is being deliberately avoided in the theory of evolution.

Purpose becomes very evident upon the acceptance of the possibility of a Creator. So evident is this that we must realize that **to understand the Creator** is what we are designed for.

Any time any *design* is violated, the object that embodies the design will degrade. The created item embodying the design will have a shortened life and will experience undesired results.

Our brains are a part of our Creation and are the most sensitive organ in our bodies. Violating the primary principle of design and reason of our existence is not good for our mind, brain, or body. We're going to get deeper into the importance of mind, brain, and body in regard to prayer in a later chapter, but for now consider how extremely susceptible to our thoughts our brains are. It is our thoughts that control our brain, and it is our brain that controls our body.

Having thoughts that are in harmony to that which Created you has obvious positive effects on your body. We can imagine that we are entirely empty when born, but then how do we explain the natural affinity to want to know our origin. We could say that this desire is a learned behavior, but then how did the first person come up with the question? It is a natural desire in us to want to know and to seek our origin. Reasoning through this and coming to the most likely conclusion is each our own quest. This should become easier with each generation because we should be able to learn true things from the previous generations, but humanity's perversion of truth dirties that water and sets us back with each generation. Each generation must figure things out on their own. Other than passing information on to the next generation via our *words*, there is little we can do to help them to understand. Some generations are *helped* by their current social attitude and understanding, and other generations are *hindered* by their current social attitude and understanding.

Don't Try to Force God to be on Your Side

In many religions there is a belief that what *we* believe is correct, and that God agrees with us. In fact, this horrible attitude has unleashed a multitude of troubles and untold deaths upon mankind all across the face of the globe throughout the thousands of years of human history.

We each come up with a set of understandings that is derived from what we have been told, from what we have read, and from what we believe we have seen or experienced. Then, with this information, we draw conclusions that our way is **the** way, and then we further make the claim that what *we* believe is God's will. This troublesome method is the only way we know how to make an attempt to know God. To advance, we must speculate and imagine; however, the flaws in our speculation are due to our lack of objectivity and the fact that we don't understand or accept that *we* may be *wrong*. These flaws could be in the way that we understood what we heard, or they could be in the way the evidence has been presented to us. When we insist the Creator does not exist, we suffer because of our deliberate disregard for the vast evidence indicating otherwise.

When we believe and speculate without objectivity, then we are forcing God to be on our side, and when we do this, we are wrong. To be on the side of the Creator, we only need to accept that other possibilities exist. When we accept that other possibilities exist, then, and only then, will we be able to begin to have any possibility of balance and of finding what is true.

Our quest should never be to force God to be on our side. Rather, our quest should always be to find out what is true, what is good, and to know our Creator. It is in this way that we choose to be on the Creator's side. But even the simple quest for what is true has been perverted by people who are seeking to have power over others—these are people who want to control other people.

"Truth" Cults

Earlier, the importance of having standards for words was discussed. But, even with standards, if we cannot understand the concept of a word such as *truth*, then we cannot define *truth*. It is our inability to properly define *truth* that allows us to be so easily led astray.

Various cults have thrown the word "truth" around. In fact, with humanity in general, the word truth is thrown around recklessly and has been for a very long time. If we cannot get to the bottom of what truth is, then nothing in life or in any book can ever be of any true value to us personally—including the Bible. For some of us, the word *truth* is used properly in part of a topic and in another part of the same topic we tell people information that is false, thus leading them to believe that the information is true. Sometimes this is done in innocence, but usually it is done for the purpose of controlling others. And, often, it is done in an effort to obtain their money or to keep them in submission to the cult's leaders.

At this point we're not discussing which things are true and which things are not true, but rather, we are discussing the actual meaning of the word "truth". When we allow people to redefine words to be something other than what words actually mean, then we have made ourselves subject to those people who are trying to manipulate us. When doing so, we have allowed them to become our masters, and we have made them so by not checking their "facts". Sadly, for many people who are involved in science, they have become a "truth" cult, which is made evident when we claim to seek truth, but then insist that the Bible is false and nothing more than a book of mere fairytales. There is little or nothing that has been proven false in the Bible. With each year of research that the world does, the Bible is proven more and more to be an accurate account of history.

We inherently understand what truth is, yet we still tend to gravitate towards believing lies and what is not true. If we want our prayers to ever be answered as desired, then we must take serious effort to understand one simple word—*Truth*!

From this moment forward, everything in your life is going to be viewed in reference to the word *truth* simply because you've read this sentence.

Truth is the only thing in life that matters. Truth is your existence, and without it you are not—you do not exist! Truth is to be understood by us as a natural order of our Creation, but we have allowed others to redefine our perception of truth. When we believe a lie to be true, then we have redefined, in our own minds, what *true* or *truth* means. It is this method of the redefinition of the word *truth* that cults use to get people to blindly follow their ill guided leaders—it is "the blind leading the blind". Eve followed the words of Satan and became subject to Satan, and then Adam did the same. If you follow someone's false words, you become subject to them because you put their words before the Creator's Truth.

If we follow the cult of evolution and decide in our own minds that humans have evolved, then we have put ourselves at the mercy of those whom we follow, and we will eventually submit to their belief in evolution, versus having been Created. In the end this will cause us to believe that the Creator does not exist. If you have any hope to have your prayers answered and have your circumstances change as a result, then think and reason these things through on your own to find the obvious truth regarding the Creator.

Chapter 3

Unneeded Competition

Because we have allowed others to redefine many obvious and fundamental truths about our existence, and about our Creator, we have caused ourselves to doubt. Many of us have allowed the concept of Truth to be redefined in our hearts and minds, and have subsequently allowed ourselves to doubt the existence of a Creator. When we lack a sound foundation of understanding of the beginning, then we can't have a sound foundation of ourselves. This leaves us with nothing but self-doubt. Our self-doubt is our downfall and is what destroys us and neutralizes our prayers

When we doubt things that are true, then our natural inclination is to try to compensate for that. We feel the error, but we cause ourselves to be incapable of realizing that we are doing so because of the fact that we have chosen to believe things that are not true.

One of the tactics we use in compensating for our errors is to build ourselves up beyond what we actually are—doing this is *arrogance.* Another tactic is false humility. In our false humility we try to cause others to build us up so that we can feel better about ourselves. Both of these tactics are competitive in their own right. Arrogance is a very competitive behavior. Arrogance builds up oneself beyond what the person truly is, and usually, at the same time, arrogance tries to tear others down so that the others appear to be of less value than the arrogant person feels that they themselves are. Of the two tactics, *arrogance* and *false-humility*, the one that is more obviously competitive is arrogance.

This is competition as the word "competition" is commonly used, but *competition* is the wrong word. The appropriate word here is *covetous*, and also the more commonly used term, *jealous*. However, the term "jealous" is somewhat inappropriate because what is really and truly being displayed in this sort of behavior is *covetousness*.

Covetousness is when we want something that someone else has. I am not referring to something similar or identical to what they have, but rather, to the actual things or circumstances that they have. Covetous means that we desire to take and own what belongs to someone else, and for them to not have it. And if we can't do that, then we will try to tear them down, or more rarely, actually work to become "better" than and have more than them in order to be above them.

In the erred mind of a covetous person, when they have someone else's things it makes the covetous person better than or at a higher position than those whom they want to take from. If they have what the other person once had, and the other person no longer has it, then the covetous person believes, in their own heart and mind, that they then are better than the other person from whom they have coveted.

A person who is covetous will typically try to destroy what the other person has when the covetous person cannot obtain it for themselves. Other people's possessions and status are unwanted competition for covetous people. These attempts of destruction by covetous people are common. Few of us make it through life without at least dabbling in covetous behavior at some point in our lives.

We can also covet by disregarding others rather than being in a specific competition with them. In this case we don't concern ourselves with the other people themselves, but we want what belongs to them. For your prayers to be answered you must abandon this sort of covetous thinking and behavior.

Christian Religious Attitude

Ironically, covetousness reigns supreme in religion of any kind. This sad-but-true phenomenon is so common throughout the world, that *covetousness* is the single most damaging behavior of mankind. But let us not blame religion; let us instead understand that it is some of the people within the religion.

We need not spend much time looking into historical religious matters to see covetous-arrogance rear its ugly head. Every religion claims that *it* is the way, and that *its* version of god is *the* God. The debate goes as such: "God is on my side." "No, God on *my* side." "No, God on *my* side." Is it possible that we are all correct? Is it possible that we are all *in*correct? The answer to both questions is, yes, it is *possible*, but which if either is it?

Nearly all groups, religions, sects, cults, and cultures share strikingly similar stories about the origins of mankind, but usually with a twist. These stories originated from somewhere. Was it from a common source, or did all of these cultures, by chance, randomly come upon these very similar stories of creation? Are they competing stories? Or are they the same story slightly altered through cultural bias and revision-degradation over time?

Over the centuries the inflexibility and unrelenting arrogance of some of the leaders of the Church have caused a great deal of problems in our world. The Church wisely takes its time deciding on whether to accept a change in doctrine, but in the past, the Church, or more accurately put, some of its leaders, foolishly have condemned various people for proposing accurate new theories or ideas.

It is Society's and the Church leaders' past refusal to openly and objectively examine new theories that is the damaging attitude that has caused the perpetuation of the godless theories of creation we typically hear today. These godless theories have now become commonplace in world culture. The arrogant attitude that—*we* are always right no matter what—regardless of whatever it is that we believe, is found in politics, in science, and in religion. After we pervert the truth, we further go on to either insist that God is on our side, or that there is no god at all, and that only *we* are right.

This arrogant attitude is responsible for countless deaths and the slow corruption of understanding and the rampant denial of a Creator. These bad aspects of Christian religious attitude have caused the progression of the godless naturalist evolutionary human origins belief system that emerged in the seventeenth century. This is not the Church's fault, but it is certainly the fault of many of its congregation and leaders.

Our inability, as a society, to accurately define the meanings of words or the meaning of scientific findings in a consistent manner has wrought havoc on our ability to truly believe in anything as our lies attempt to compete with truth. A fair amount of what we choose to believe *as true* is actually inaccurate. When we believe erred ideas then we inevitably encounter what appear to be anomalies in the presented data, such as the Bible. Thus, we either give up or ignore our inconsistencies and become a part of the problem.

Christians should not fight science; instead, Christians should fully and *properly* embrace *true* methods of science to prove their point. If a point cannot be proven, then it should be stated that it is speculation. Using the Bible as the "absolute authority" for all things is a foolish and baseless approach for getting others to understand what is true. Similarly, the naturalists will have many of their own inconsistencies served to them in the same way that they served the Church's inconsistencies about the Christian understanding of life origins. This arrogant competitive behavior does no one any good and only holds all of us in darkness all that much longer. We all need to better learn how to admit when we ourselves are wrong.

The problem with many people, from both the Church side and from the naturalist side of the debate (Creation versus evolution), is that they feel that if they control the argument then they are in control. This is true to an extent because they control the people who choose to blindly follow the inconsistencies that are taught within those groups. Sadly, when the Church does attempt to embrace "science", it sometimes ends badly for the discoverer of the new information, as was proven by history when critical new scientific information was presented to the Church leaders. But, it is no less damaging when the church-of-politics embraces the naturalists' views and imposes those views onto the people through the mandatory education of using the potentially erred theories and a simultaneous refusal to allow any other theories to be discussed.

Order is the Order of Matter

These first few chapters are what you must build your foundation of understanding upon, and they will allow you to see how important they are for you to know if you ever hope to see your prayers reliably answered in any consistent manner as you move forward.

Order is a very important word when trying to understand origins and cause. *Order* is a very simple truth in everything that we see. We can witness it with our very own eyes! Order is a standard of organization that groups and connects things together in a way that makes them useful.

Order shows *purpose*.

Purpose shows *design*.
Design shows *intent*.
Intent is not random—Intent is *intent*-ional.

When things work well, then they are in order. They are arranged in such a way that they work in harmony with one another. The obvious nature of the simple truth of order being everywhere is abundantly seen in everything. We deliberately have to choose to be fools in order to deny that this is true.

All the way down to the molecular level and beyond, the standards of order are incredibly consistent. If they were not, then Creation as we know it would be very different and would be utterly useless. The consistently accurate and repetitious patterns that things are Created with, at the atomic level of what we see around us, testifies to Created order.

We can argue all we want and debate the existence of a Creator, but the truth of order cannot be denied. Even in our attempts to deny a Creator, we still use an enormous amount of order in everything we do.

Order is in our writings. It's in our research. It's in our thinking. It's in the tools that we use for work. And it's also in the atoms and molecules that we are made of. The consistency of order is irrefutable and it is everywhere!

However, we must remain objective. If we take the attitude that nothing can exist without order, and then later, if a truth should be shown to demonstrate otherwise and we reject it, then we have perfected the skill to be foolish. We must remain objective and *always* allow possibilities when those possibilities are evident in the information. Yet, we must insist upon sound evidence before we fully embrace the new possibilities as true, but we need *not* denounce new possibilities in the meantime. When something seems illogical, we should, and must, question it. Our problem is that we adhere so tightly to the lies in this world that we typically miss the truth, and doing so damages our ability to believe anything, thus causing us to doubt.

We have no choice but to move forward in life with what we have before us at our disposal at any particular moment. We must build on that knowledge and understanding in order to be able to advance our own understanding. If we do not have this openness in our hearts, then we are destined for error. Even if we are correct now, we might not be correct in the future on other matters when we move ahead without openness. Our lack of objective openness to consider other ideas is an evil and unneeded rival to truth. The noise of this world makes matters even worse with its mountain of incorrect information that is spewed out upon us all in effort to keep us from hearing truth.

Order is not a law, nor is it a demand, it is *what is*. Everywhere, and in everything, we see order and organization. If something is able to be repeated at least once, then it shows that it has been duplicated, and that's admirable. When we are able to repeat something billions of times, it shows a tremendous amount of order. But, when it comes to the atomic level of order, everything is not merely billions or trillions of repetitions; it is an uncountable amount of repetitions, and it is a standard so consistent that we can depend upon it.

A "standard" is order. A standard can be relied upon. A standard that is open for correction is true! We'll get into all of this and the critical importance of it with regard to prayer in a later chapter; but for now, to understand the importance of organization, or order, is to understand how important a standard is. And without that understanding, unneeded competition will lead us astray, bringing upon us doubt and fear.

Without a reference point in life we have nothing to base anything upon, causing life to become difficult, miserable, and meaningless. When order is absent, then chaos will exist. Whatever is in a state of chaos will be destroyed until order is restored, including you and your prayers.

Chaos is the corrective nature of order. This is true for both the physical world and the world of your mind.

Is Wisdom Spread Through Touch?

"Chaos" cannot exist for long without coming back into order. Chaos is in constant competition with order and will always defeat itself. A lie or any other inaccurate information is chaos and is at odds with truth. If atoms were able to follow a lie, then you can be certain that your body would vanish instantaneously. The standards (or order) that the elements use to form your body would no longer be valid if these elements had a free will to follow the disorder of a lie. It's good for us that the elements don't have the ability to lie because we simply would not "be" without their well-structured standard of order and well-structured standard to cling together. If atoms randomly repelled or attracted, nothing could be reliably formed.

A fundamental truth to grasp is that the need and existence of **order** required in order for us to exist is reflected not only in our physical existence, but it is also reflected in our actions and lives. For our prayers to work effectively, order must be restored in our hearts and, through that ordering, in our lives as well. Chaos must no longer be allowed to compete for your life and thoughts. Only you can stop such chaos in your life.

If we don't use order in our bank accounts when calculating our bank balances, then our accounts will be in a state of disorder and chaos. Our bank balance will be incorrect and a deficit error will likely cause us to spend more than we actually have available. This will create additional disorder in our lives. For the bank's part, if *you* do not promptly restore order, they will likely freeze your account until you do. By doing so, they restore order to their bank with respect to your chaotic account balances. It is no different with the Creator: If your life is in disorder, you will be cut off until you stop using chaos to compete against order and thus restore order in your life.

In the same way that *order* affects our bank balances, it also affects our bodies and our interaction with others. A kind touch to or from another person is a form of wisdom; it is a form of compassion and love.

Wisdom is to be wise. To be wise is to be able to see. What we are "seeing" is all that is evident around us. When we see a person who is hurt, or hurting inside, and we help them or give them a hug or a touch on the shoulder in effort to comfort them, then we have wisely seen their pain and have demonstrated our wisdom in understanding their situation. We become an instrument of the answer to their prayer, thus helping them to remove themselves from the unwanted competition of chaos.

When we touch people, we're not only communicating to them that we understand and see their physical or emotional pain, but we are also changing them forever in our kindness to them. People remember this kindness and will often share it with others around them when the need arises. If you are one who has come to the understanding that people can be healed through touch, then you have likely seen or experienced this yourself. Your wisdom in this should be shared with others, so that this skill and understanding can be spread throughout all people. It is a high form of order. It is the highest form of cooperation.

Speaking Wisdom

Amongst the best ways to defeat the unwanted competition of chaos in our lives is the most common way we spread our wisdom using our voice and our words. But there is a problem in spreading wisdom, and it goes back to the definitions problem.

Even the word "*wisdom*" lacks a standard with most people because our understanding is chaotic. There are a handful of common words that are typically used in reference to prayer and the Creator. *Wisdom* is one of those words.

It's a ridiculous notion that the trivia that is taught in modern school systems is "knowledge". We can refer to the trivia as knowledge because once somebody tells us a bit of trivia then we believe we "know" it. However, if that trivia information is wrong, then it is not really **know**ledge. When we *know* something, we should recognize it as true; if we cannot recognize it as true, then we really don't "know" it. This again is the chaos that we unnecessarily compete with and must defeat and no longer allow in our lives.

Knowledge is a word that is closely related to *wisdom*, but it's different. Wisdom goes beyond knowledge. With knowledge we believe that we "know" something is true; where on the other hand, with wisdom we have the ability to look ahead and see what will occur in the future based upon that knowledge. When we are wise, then we choose to do things in a certain manner while we are on our way to our future because we can see, in advance, what will occur because of our past, current, and future choices, words, and actions.

We can also speak of the past and discuss what occurred. This is *knowledge* of the past, but when we properly use that knowledge to understand what will occur in the future, then that is called *wisdom*.

Once each of us realizes what *truth* is, then it is a requirement for us to share our wisdom with others by teaching and explaining how given consequences will occur when we make certain decisions, and then take action based upon those potentially poor decisions. Doing so allows us to avoid a great deal of pain in our lives.

If we do not share our wisdom through our words and actions, then we truly are failing our purpose for being in existence. A person who speaks something that is untrue does not have an ability to be wise as long as they hold the untrue thing as true. It is mental chaos and it challenges your truth. The ability to be wise comes only after we have obtained the skill to embrace truth.

We cannot have true knowledge without truth because you cannot "know" something that is a lie. You can know that it is a lie, but it is technically impossible to *know* the lie. A lie is a lie and it doesn't exist because it is not real. In other words, the subject of the lie cannot be real because it is not true.

Everything that we *know*, we know because it is true. And if we think we "know" something, but we are incorrect, then we do not "know" it and it is a lie—it is the competing chaos.

If we believe a lie, then we cannot ever be wise while we continue to believe that lie. Any words we speak that are in any way connected to that lie are foolish and unwise utterances unless the words that we are speaking are revealing the truth about the lie.

Speaking wisdom is a requirement for anyone who has obtained the understanding of what truth really is. The only way we can speak wisdom is to *know* things because we have balanced those things in truth. Insisting upon anything that has not been proven true as if it is fact has a high possibility of resulting in being wrong and will make us appear foolish. This doesn't mean that we cannot present our speculation about what we have observed. But, our speculation should be stated as being mere speculation, and it should only be held as a consideration of possibility until better proof is presented. Additionally, we should seek to validate our speculation in full and utter truth and honesty. *Validating* our speculation in any other way is not possible and will result in error, meaning that *we* will be *wrong* as a result of doing so.

In order for our prayers to work effectively, we must become wise and learn to *know* through testing with truth. This is the only way to defeat the unneeded competition of chaos of lies that seeks to overtake our lives and destroy our prayers.

Chapter 4

Forgiveness

Another area of life that causes us a great deal of trouble with regard to prayer is our understanding of the word "forgive." Many of us are mentally and emotionally torn when it comes to forgiving people. Some of us forgive and believe that we did not forgive the person, while others do not forgive and believe that they have forgiven someone.

The reason that there's confusion with regard to forgiveness is because we lack a *standard* in the definition of the word "forgive". Our concept of words is typically derived from common usage rather than from actually looking up the word in a dictionary and understanding it and then properly using it as per true definition. And even then, many dictionaries foolishly change the meanings to accommodate common usage.

For-give: *fore* meaning *ahead* or in *advance*—and to *give*.

Forgive is *not* something that we do *only after* someone apologizes to us. Forgiveness is something that we do **before** they apologize to us, and often we do it even before they make their

offense against us. Forgiveness is often mistaken as us
continuously and endlessly allowing others to do whatever they
want to do to us as often as they want to hurt us. This is not
forgiveness—it is ridiculous!

Here is the ultimate test of forgiveness: If someone comes to
you and apologizes, then, will you offer your trust to them? If you
have made the choice that no matter what the person does you
will refuse to *ever* trust them again, then you obviously have not
forgiven them. But, if you will trust them, even if it takes a little
time for them to regain your trust, then you have forgiven them.
Your act of allowing them to have another chance to gain your
trust shows your forgiveness, yet there are limits to the amount
of abuse we should endure before we walk away and leave it up
to them to realize their errors on their own.

We often struggle with this "forgiveness" problem because
many of us have been taught that we must "turn the other cheek"
and suffer the abuses that others repeatedly do to us. The term
"turn the other cheek" is from the words of the Christ in the
Bible. What was really meant by this statement? Did the Christ
mean that we should stand there idly by and accept all the abuse
that is thrown at us? This does not seem to be consistent with the
message that the Christ was trying to convey to us.

The "turning the other cheek" that the Christ spoke of was
not said as an instruction for us to foolishly and needlessly accept
abuse and subject ourselves to others' abuses. "Turning the other
cheek" is to get us to understand that we need not take vengeance
on the person who caused us trouble or pain, and that when we
stand firm in truth, then their lies will become apparent. We
need not run away from abusers. Instead we can turn the other
cheek and they may take another shot at us, but we can then
simply depart from them and walk away in peace knowing that,
at some point, things will be made right.

If we choose to hold onto bitterness about a situation, then we make ourselves incapable of, or unreceptive to, being able to forgive that person.

It is a self-protective nature in mankind to want to stay clear of those who inflict harm on us. Hanging around with people who regularly violate you does you no good, and it does no good for the violator either. Our moving on to a newer and better place is the best way to handle a cruel or unforgiving person. When we choose to be unforgiving, we have chosen our own self-destruction. Eventually, our choices and desire to hurt others, or to *unnecessarily* hold others apart from us, will cause our own downfall.

When you have *true* forgiveness in your heart and mind then your desire will always be for a situation to become better and for the other person to stop violating you so that you can again be close with them and once again trust them. For the person who is doing the forgiving, forgiveness is a desire, not an action. It is done in advance of someone asking for your forgiveness. Additionally, it is truly and *technically* impossible to "forgive" a person if that person does not want your forgiveness. The offer or desire to forgive is something that is done in advance, and only to that point is it up to the person doing the forgiving. The rest is up to the person who did the violating.

If, in their arrogance, the violator refuses to come forward and admit their error and violation, then the forgiveness is not being received by the violator. The impasse is on the shoulders of the violator until they repent of their errors and confess those errors to the person that they have harmed. When the violator repents and apologizes, the forgiver's desire is fulfilled and the forgiveness transaction is completed.

In general, people are very forgiving. Humanity's problem is lack of forgiving as much as it is violating and our subsequent refusal to stop violating. When we stop our habit of violating others and rebuild a reasonable track record of trust with those whom we have harmed, then we generally receive someone's forgiveness and can quickly regain their trust. It is our *repeated* violations that cause what we perceive as "unforgiveness". It is truly a ridiculous thought to expect someone to "forgive" you when you continue with the behavior that you expect to be forgiven for. We must stop our violations against others, and then receive their forgiveness in order to be forgiven. This also applies to our relationship with the Creator and to our prayers to the Creator.

The Ear That Hears

The proverb from the Bible, "He that refuses instruction despises his own soul; but he that hears reproof gets understanding", is a very profound and simple statement. Its ultimate message is this: If you won't accept the truth, then you will destroy yourself, but if you accept the truth, then you will understand.

Sometimes people say they do not want to be "corrected". It's very troubling when someone makes that statement. To be *correct* is to be accurate; it is to have a straight path to accuracy and it is to believe the thing that is true because it is evident.

If someone says "I don't want to be corrected" or "Don't correct me," then they are saying "I want to keep accepting wrong information" and "I want to be in error. Let me continue to make mistakes and believe wrong things."

Please note: we should not confuse correction with attacks and violations. Often, arrogant-covetous people will hurl insults, derogatory comments, and outright violations at others in order to get the other people to comply with their erred beliefs and demands. This arrogant-covetous attempt to get someone to change their mind, or actions, can have the appearance of correction, but it is not. Arrogance appears to people as if it is confidence, and when an arrogant person tries to get others to comply, it actually only *appears* as correction. However, the arrogant person might actually believe that they are correct. This sort of confusion is easily detected when we ask the arrogant person a question that forces them to speak words that force them to see the truth. This, of course, is in the event that they actually choose to hear and answer the question at all.

We commonly see the manipulation-method attacks and violations in news interviews where the interviewer unjustly asks a question in such a manner that the true answer will be unacceptable to the public no matter how the answer is delivered. This unjust, arrogant, and manipulative method of questioning people in a way where they cannot possibly answer honestly without with appearing to be a liar, is far different than asking a question that exposes the truth about the topic. To an observer who is not privy to the details of the topic, these two situations appear the same from the observer's perspective.

In general, we need not correct people. We only need to ask the questions that force them to see the truth for themselves. When we are asked a question, we are forced to think about and contemplate the answer. If someone has chosen to not want to see the truth, then the result is typically shown in their anger towards us. It's when we choose to close our eyes to the truth that we utter the dangerous words "I don't like to be corrected." Ask yourself: Do I allow the Creator to correct me in my own life? If you do not, then should you really expect your prayers to be answered?

Why we Forgive Accidents so Easily

Those of us who don't want to be corrected are essentially trying to say that we do not want to be wrong. This is because it is humiliating and embarrassing for us when we make a bad choice. When we choose the path of rejecting correction, we then become violators to other people who we are in contact with or who are affected by our wrongness. Those who we violate might struggle with forgiveness towards us; this is because we have made choices that are not true and honest. In making erred choices we have broken their trust in us, just as we do with the Creator.

When we are forgiven by someone, they forgive us repeatedly out of utter kindness and love, and they have chosen to give us another chance at obtaining their trust. We cannot expect others to trust us if we do not behave in a trustworthy manner. The same is true in our relationship with the Creator.

The reason that we forgive a real accident so easily is because the other person did not *deliberately* violate us. We had no expectations of trust with them in that regard. It's when we trust someone and they let us down that they have broken our *trust* and violated us. The more intimately we know a person, then the more it hurts when the trust between us and them is violated.

In the situation of an auto accident, for instance, if the brakes on your car failed and you couldn't stop in time and crashed into someone else's car, then if you pay the repairs for the damages that you caused, the person will typically be understanding and forgive you because they know that you didn't do it intentionally. We realize that if it were in the person's power to have avoided the situation, they would have done so. With an accident, we grasp the fact that the other person typically did everything they could do to avoid the collision, if they saw it coming.

It's important to note here that the word "accident" is referring to something that happened that was outside of your reasonable control. In a situation where a person was driving under the influence of mind altering substances, people are not so quick to forgive because it is completely within someone's control to *not* drive while they physically and mentally lack coordination from consuming such substances.

Our choice to forgive someone is not based on the circumstances that happened. Those circumstances may have been the end result causing the pain inflicted on us, but they are not the primary cause of violation. The primary cause of violation is the person's *intention*. It is their *intentions* that we base our forgiveness on. Now consider that in relation to the Creator.

A true "accident" is an unintentional action that happened outside of our ability to control the circumstances quickly enough to avoid a collision or problem—there is no malice intended. You will find that we become very easily offended whenever malice is intended towards us. It is the deliberate intent of harm or injury and/or the disregard of others, for one's own selfish advantage or pleasures that is the true offense or violation to another person. This is why people take issue with someone hating them for no apparent reason.

If an accident has no ill intent or malice we generally do not feel violated and therefore we truly do not need to forgive anyone because they did nothing wrong, even though we typically refer to it as *forgiveness* in such situations.

Harsh Judgments

Anytime a violation is avoidable, we tend to be more harsh in our judgment towards the violator because it was not necessary and was completely in the control of the person who violated us. The situation of a *true* accident is an obvious circumstance where the events were out of the control of the person who caused the accident.

But there is another type of situation that presents a problem and where we tend to judge very harshly. It is when someone guides us wrongly. In these cases, we need to reserve our assessment of the specific situation and reflect on their knowledge. In this situation, the events are avoidable, but because the guiding person has not been properly taught certain information, they become a blind-guide to us. The damage that their wrong information causes is not intended to harm us. It is *their* best attempt at guiding us to what they believe is a good direction or good instruction.

What we must understand is that when someone has not been taught well, and believes things wrongly, then the problem is that they can't help it and they don't know any better. In many ways this is the reason that you are reading this book. If we had all been taught, by our parents and other elders, the simple truths that we are discussing in this book, you would have no reason to read it. However, since these truths were not taught to our parents, our parents do not know, and, therefore, they were not capable of teaching it to us. There is an amount of liability on their part for being lazy because they didn't try to get to the bottom of what is true and good, and the same is true for us, but beyond that, it is each our own responsibility to overcome this particular type of blindness on our own. No one else is going to do it for us, and it is our own responsibility to regain our vision through using tools like this book.

We should reserve our judgments about the previous generation and forgive their errors and offenses against us, and then go on to correct our own errors and offences against others. If we fail to correct our own behavior, then we pass our incorrect behavior onto the next generation as well as on to those around us.

The generations that came before any current generation do not have the advantage to look back at that generation (that is to *look back* at themselves). Each subsequent generation gains a great advantage because we have the ability to look back at any previous generation and learn from their errors *when* we are wise enough to do so—Think Bible here.

While we cannot rightfully make harsh judgments against those generations, we can condemn the biases that they stand by; for instance, blindly denying the possibility of a Creator. Blindly denying the possibility of a Creator is as biased as it is to *blindly* accept a Creator. The information that is obtained from the experiences of previous generations and the information that is obtained by science allows us to better see what is true with regard to Creation. If we fail to understand how to see what is true, then we are still blind and we will judge harshly, and often wrongly, due to our blindness.

Sympathy

Sympathy is a part of forgiveness. When we are willing to look back and properly evaluate circumstances, then we can compare and weigh our experiences on the scale of truth. Truth is the ability to accurately and openly compare without bias.

We relate our current experiences and pains to other people after comparing our current experiences to our past experiences by looking back at our own lives. When we do this, we are professing *sympathy* towards those who we are sharing with. The word "*sympathy*" means to *suffer with*. *Sym* is *with* and *pathy* is *pathetic* or *suffer*. Sympathy means to look back and compare, allowing us to understand another person's pains and experiences.

Sympathy plays a huge role in forgiveness. Those who are unwilling to look back at *their own* past errors and honestly evaluate those errors, will lack the ability to be sympathetic. In turn, this unwillingness causes us to be unforgiving and unrelenting in our bitterness, which is then displayed in various degrees.

Those who are unwilling to look back at, and/or admit to, their own errors are practicing arrogance and will unjustly hold grudges against others. These same grudge holders accuse innocent people of holding grudges against them. When innocent people have become intolerant of the grudge holder's bad behavior, then those innocent people are often accused of holding a grudge. Grudge holders cannot see that it is they themselves who are being unforgiving as they hold unjust grudges against those who they have unjustly violated.

Refusing to accept someone's constant violations against you is *not* "holding a grudge". Holding a grudge is when the violator stops their bad behavior altogether, repents, and has repeatedly proven themselves worthy—*and yet* someone still refuses to forgive them for those past violations. Jealous people are holding a grudge when they unfairly treat someone with disdain and relentlessly single out an innocent person of whom they are jealous. We should be sympathetic regarding them not understanding, and then attempt to help them if we have the emotional strength without yielding to their errors. Us having sympathy does not mean we abandon our better judgement and actions.

What Forgiveness is Not

To draw a contrast, first we will summarize what forgiveness *is*: Forgiveness is to, *in advance,* allow opportunity for others to regain your trust in them *before* they ask for it. From that point forward it is up to the violator to request forgiveness through repentance and proper apology. Your ability to forgive is tested by asking yourself this one simple question: Will you allow the violator your trust if they come to you with a full confession, repentance, and they cease future violations? If you *will* allow them to regain your trust when they do so, then you have forgiven them! This is what the Creator does.

Now for "What forgiveness is not". Understanding "*what forgiveness is not*" is a very important aspect of forgiveness. Without this contrast it is difficult to see true forgiveness. Many people struggle with this problem by feeling guilty because they feel as if they have not forgiven a person who consistently violates them. They no longer want to be around the violator because they no longer care to be around someone who is constantly violating them. If you are experiencing that sort of guilt, then read very carefully: Forgiveness is *not* allowing yourself to be repeatedly abused by people who refuse to repent of, and cease, their errors and violations against you.

> ### Remember:
>
> *Forgiveness **does not*** mean allowing yourself to be repeatedly abused by people who refuse to repent of, and cease, their errors and violations against you.

A person who is too arrogant to admit to the errors that they committed against others and refuses to come to you with a full and proper apology will not accept forgiveness. It is technically impossible for *you* to force them to receive it, because receiving forgiveness occurs in the heart and mind. *They* need to do this, and it needs to originate from their own internal decisions and intentions.

If you are *willing and desire* to accept a violator's potential future apology, if it should come, along with their admission of error, then you have already forgiven them. You have done everything in your power to allow them your trust. From that point forward it's up to them to come to you with their apology and confession. Trying to force them will not bring about a true and meaningful apology and confession. A true apology and confession is something that can only be done by the violator. The violator must do it on their own as an intentional decision that they themselves have made. This is because no one can force a true and meaningful confession. The only power you have regarding their behavior is to inform them of how they are hurting you and to pray for them. The rest is up to them.

The point in time at which you have decided that you will accept their apology, if it should come in the future, is the point in time at which they have been forgiven by you.

In other words, they were fore-given *in advance* by you. But, the forgiveness transaction cannot be completed without them or without their permission.

To illustrate this point more thoroughly, consider this: You will notice that if someone is dealing with a person who is unrepentant and they go to the unrepentant person who wronged them and say to them "I forgive you", then the *unrepentant* violator will typically become angry and agitated towards them. The violator becomes angry and feels that an arrogant statement was made to them because they feel and act as if they did no wrong.

When a person feels that they themselves did no wrong, and then someone says to them "I forgive you", then the only possible conclusion that the violator can have in their mind is that the forgiver is saying that the violator is wrong. To the violator this is an accusation, and in most cases such accusations are responded to with an attack on the character of the person doing the forgiving regardless of whether or not the attack is at all true or justified.

To forgive, you only need to be voluntarily willing to give the violator another chance. If you voluntarily offer them another chance then you have forgiven them. But the action to allow them your trust again is somewhat different than forgiveness.

If they are unwilling to come to you, of their own accord, with a proper apology, then you cannot complete your forgiveness transaction because they have not offered an apology and confession for you to accept. Nor have they accepted your forgiveness. If the violator actually does confess and apologize, then to complete your forgiveness, you must accept their apology and allow them to rebuild the trust between both of you by them no longer violating you. Of course, if you are the violator, then it is you who must repent, confess, and apologize and then cease further violation against other people. However, none of this can be done if the violator will not accept the forgiveness bestowed upon them by the forgiver.

What Really is Confessing or Confession?

The word confession has gotten a tough rap within religion, mostly from the protestant sects. The attitude is that the priest cannot wipe away your sins, because only the Christ did that. While that is true, there is another point behind confession that is overlooked by those who condemn it. Hearing confession may have gone to the head of some priests of the Church over the years, as if somehow *they* have some sort of power over our lives to grant forgiveness and our entry into heaven. However, the arrogant attitude held by some clergy, as well as the people's perception of the reason behind confession, misses the mark completely. Confessing to a priest has little to do with absolving or wiping away your sins. Even many priests do not understand this.

"Sinning" is a whole lot easier to do than we imagine. Far easier than we believe it shows in the Bible or in the Ten Commandments. There are more than ten ways to sin, but not in the way most of us think.

> Any time we choose to do anything that is not true then we are, to some degree, in sin

When we *do* or *believe* things that are not true, then we are believing lies. Each one of us has the ability to weigh everything that we think and do and then balance it against reality. When we neglect to weigh things in this manner, we often do things wrongly. Our failure to balance everything on the scale of truth and our subsequent failure to then follow truth is the cause of sin.

Anyone who struggles with the concept of confession or confessing, needs to understand this: If you cannot confess, then *you* are not realizing your own errors. If you do not realize your errors, then it is technically impossible for you to properly ask for forgiveness and apologize for the violations of your errors, because either you do not see them, or you are trapped in your arrogance and cannot escape from yourself.

Confession need not be with a priest—that is optional, but confession must be made because it is in the heart that matters most to us personally. It's not for the Creator that you must confess. It is for *yourself* that you must confess! Without your own freewill ability to look back and say "**I** made a mistake", and without the ability to think and describe your mistake in detail to the Creator, or to those who you have violated, or even to yourself, you are technically incapable of being forgiven, and it's your own fault. It's your own fault because of your inability to be retrospective and look back at your own errors in an honest manner and then fully and openly admit to those errors and then change your ways.

Think of it this way, if you did something that you shouldn't have done with your vehicle and your actions broke something on the vehicle but you don't know what you did or why it broke, then it's almost certain to happen again the next time you use the vehicle while you unknowingly repeat the same innocent error.

Now, if I loan you my vehicle and you repeat the same error with my vehicle and damage it, and additionally, you do not come to me and tell me what happened, then do you expect that I should let you use it again and again? If I do allow you to use it again, but you haven't been able to describe your error in detail, then the chances are very high that you're going to damage my vehicle again in the same way *if* I allow you to use it again.

I might be willing to let you use the vehicle again, but not until after you have, of your own freewill and understanding, come to the understanding of what your errors were that caused the damage to my vehicle to begin with. If we don't realize that we're doing something wrong, it is still wrong regardless of our innocence regarding our understanding that point.

It's when you come to me and tell me what you did wrong that I will understand that you are now aware and will not repeat the same damaging behavior. In this case, you were immediately forgiven. But I'm not about to place the trust of my vehicle into your hands if you can't tell me what you did wrong, because it is obvious to me that you still do not understand what you did wrong. And it's also obvious that you will most certainly repeat the errors and damage my vehicle again and again. If someone did damage a vehicle or life in that way, then it puts the owner of the life or vehicle at risk of additional serious injury or damage or liability. And other people may also be at risk who might be hurt in a chain of events arising from the damaged vehicle. So it is the owner's responsibility *and duty* to **not** allow this to occur again without proper confession and correction from the borrower. For the owner to do so is both reckless and foolish. Most people will eventually come to this conclusion when interacting with others. The Creator is no different: You are not going to be entrusted with some of what you request in your prayers while you continue to behave irresponsibly even if you are unaware of your errors. It might be an innocent error, but it is still your own responsibility to wake up and become aware.

The reason that we do not understand our errors in our own hearts is because we refuse to look back in effort to detect our own errors, face those errors, and then correct them.

The moment you come to the full realization of your errors, I will be willing to progressively replace my trust in you because you have chosen to rebuild that trust with me. You will have rebuilt trust through your recognition and admission of your errors and through your desire to **not** continue repeating those errors. Voluntary restitution is also very helpful in regaining someone's trust in you, especially when it is the violator who initiates restitution.

We do not need to confess all of our errors or mistakes, but we do need to confess those things that we have done to those we have harmed. Our confessing is done because we have come to understand that we have violated someone and we are explaining to them that we have come upon the realization of our errors and that we will no longer make those errors. It is both a self-realization and an outward sign.

Often, when people become self-convicted about their own errors they struggle because they think that they must tell the whole world about *all* of the ills and errors that they have done. This is not necessary.

It is only necessary to make good with, confess to, and apologize to those who you have hurt for what you have done to them. When you do so, then those who have been violated by you will know that you have seen your errors and that you have seen the light and desire to, and intend to, correct your errors. They can know this because you told them in a reasonably detailed description that you understand your error and regret ever doing it, and also that you will not do it in the future. If you fail to abide by your word, then with each of your subsequent violations, you become less likely to regain someone's trust. And you do not deserve their trust in that case. There are also situations where the person you need to confess to is now dead, in such cases the best we can do is to make sure that we have confessed before our Creator and in our heart.

As for confessing all of your errors to *everyone*, that's not needed. If I have not been affected by your errors, then I do not particularly want to hear about your errors or be burdened with them. When people insist on sharing their own errors in this way, by telling others all about it, then they are being selfish by placing this burden on uninvolved bystanders who are forced to hear the sordid details of those errors. Not everything needs to be shared with everyone. Sometimes the information being shared can be damaging to other people. Doing this makes the violator guilty of harming those people who will be damaged from the unneeded and unwanted information; and for nothing more than the sake of the selfish violator's conscience. If someone does not know you violated them, then depending upon what you did, sometimes it is best to confess only to yourself and to God and not upset them with your bad behavior. To release your conscience in these situations, where it is best to leave things alone and keep quiet, you are best served to confess to only the Creator. All of the things that you confess to people who you have harmed, must also be confessed to the Creator for your own benefit.

Asking for Forgiveness

In general, the asking for forgiveness part is not what is important. It is the apology and your own realization of error that is important. But, an apology is worthless without a connected confession along with no longer violating them. Asking for forgiveness is an outward sign to others that you have seen the errors of your ways and are working to change your ways.

To understand this better, just consider two children arguing: When an adult steps in and stops the fight, demanding that children apologize to each other, the children may begrudgingly say that they are "Sorry". But in truth, they are not sorry because they refuse to realize their own errors. An apology without a voluntary self-realized confession is nearly the same as begrudged apologies; though, we do sometimes need to teach *children* to apologize and confess using this method. This applies to international politics, friendships, and even marriages.

> A confession that accompanies an un-coerced apology is critically important for full forgiveness.

There are four elements in a proper apology: First, doing it of your own free will. Second, being able to accurately confess what you did wrong. Third, apologizing, stating that you are sorry and regret what you did. And fourth, that you will no longer do it. Without any one of these four aspects of an apology, the apology is utterly worthless. Without all these aspects of a proper apology, the person apologizing will almost certainly repeat their foolish and offensive violating behavior.

Technically, forgiveness should never have to be asked for because it is already done. The only things needed for a full forgiveness exchange to actually occur are acceptance of the forgiveness offered; and then the violator returning a freewill offering of a proper apology with the confession or admission of the error and the commitment and true complete effort to no longer make the error. The apology helps ensure acceptance of your new violation-free ways.

If we come to the realization that we have harmed someone, and then, of our own freewill, we go to them to confess what we did, telling them that we are regretful and sorry for what we did and that we will no longer do it, then most people will accept our apology because their forgiveness had already been granted to us. They were just waiting for us to figure it out ourselves, and they were waiting for us to accept the forgiveness they have already given to us. However, in a case where a proper complete apology was made and forgiveness is *not* granted, then the person who is being apologized to is being unforgiving.

In cases of unforgiveness, the offender is obligated to make the effort to regain the trust of the person whom they have offended. But if over a period of time the offender has adequately shown that they are trustworthy and the other person *still* refuses to accept an apology, then the person who is being apologized to is an unforgiving person and it is unlikely that anything will sooth their bitterness. In most cases, a person who is unforgiving is also a person who frequently violates others.

It's important to be able to make the distinction between forgiveness, versus not allowing our trust in a person who *continues* to violate us.

It is not possible for you to be forgiven if you do not embrace truth. And when you do not embrace truth, then not being forgiven is your own fault.

When you violate people, they may offer you subsequent opportunities to rectify your behavior so that you can show that you are trustworthy. When someone offers you an opportunity to rectify your behavior, it is a clear display that they *have* forgiven you.

But if we are unwilling to correct our own behavior, then we technically cannot be forgiven because we have chosen to do what is not true and good.

Understanding "being forgiven" as a choice that we must make, is so important that it must be repeated in various ways to assure proper understanding. It's a technical issue of the functionality—of the concept of—*forgiveness*. It is not a matter of whether or not someone asked for forgiveness, or whether or not someone has forgiven. It is technically a matter of an inability to be able to be forgiven because of our choice to not embrace what is true.

Recall the elements of a proper apology: *forgiveness, accepting forgiveness, confessing, apologizing, and accepting an apology.* When these things have been properly done, then the forgiveness transaction has been completed and trust can and will automatically be restored. Trust in you is a sacred pact with another human being. Do not violate this by repeating your violations. Trust in you by the Creator is also a sacred pact—do not violate it!

This is such a simple concept that it is difficult to convey because it cannot be broken down to any more of a base level than this: A continued lie cannot be forgiven. The lie must be eradicated first, and then the error must be *self-realized* by the violator. Then the violator can admit to and correct the error and do restitution and receive the forgiveness that has already been bestowed upon them by the forgiver.

The forgiver is under no obligation whatsoever to allow you any more liberty when you cannot see or understand your own errors and violations against them.

As a function of the way life and truth work, if you happen to be a violator, and you do not realize that you are doing wrong or if you are too foolish, too ignorant, or too arrogant to see your own errors, then it is technically impossible for you to understand that you need to confess, repent, and apologize to those who you have hurt. If this is your case, then you have rendered yourself unforgivable, either deliberately or blindly, and the blame rests upon your own shoulders. There is little anyone can do to assist you until you begin to realize, on your own, that you have been disregarding of others and of the Creator. This is why it is important for people to take time to reflect on life. For many people this reflection is done in church and in a confessional, but it can be done anywhere.

If you have guilt regarding forgiveness then read this very carefully and remember it well:

Many people are unjustly violated and they wrongly feel tremendous guilt because, in their hearts, they feel like they are not able to forgive the violator. They want to forgive, but they believe that they have not forgiven the violator because they do not want to be around the violator any longer. This is because they misunderstand the following elements of forgiveness: *forgiveness, accepting forgiveness, confessing, apologizing,* and *accepting an apology.*

This misunderstanding has also allowed many violators to continue in their folly, harming the others while the violator plows through life in constant violation of those around them. You need to understand that if you are willing to allow a person back into your life *after* the person stops repeatedly violating you, then you have likely forgiven the violator. You do not need to allow violators to continue to hurt you or others. It is each our own right to step away from violators who won't cease their ill ways. And while the violator may try to make you feel guilty, you need not feel guilty for separating from them to protect yourself. It is your right to do so and it is wise to do so.

The necessity to properly understand *forgiveness* is important for prayer. Many of the prayers that people have are tangled in a web of connections, most of which lead to relationships that endure many repeated violations.

Understanding the forgiveness connection as discussed in this chapter will allow you to be able to make corrections in your own life and forgive others and yourself. You no longer need to unnecessarily feel guilty for wrongly believing that you have not forgiven someone who refuses to cease their constant poor behavior against you. Having your mind clear of the mess that we have been calling **un**forgiveness will help to purify your heart and prayers to the Creator, thus allowing you to better understand why your prayers have not been working as desired.

And most importantly, understand that this same thing applies to *your* offenses against the Creator. The Christ said, "Whatsoever you do to the least of my brothers, that same thing you do to me." Thus, when we hurt someone by our violations against them, we have also offended the Creator.

If our history is filled with violations against others, then can we really expect that the Creator should grant us our prayer requests and liberty from the chains that bind us, which we ourselves have forged link by link by means of our violations?

Repent of all violations first and confess them to the Creator, and then begin praying, unless of course, your prayer is to more clearly see how and *when* you have violated others. This is the beginning of making your prayers work as desired.

Chapter 5

Why Don't My Prayers Work?

Since the beginning of recorded history, mankind has been in a situation where some spiritual leaders did not know how to properly pray, leaving them unable to properly teach the people whom they led. While the Church is to be credited for bringing the calendar through thousands of years, it is also true that the Church couldn't get something as simple as the calendar right (it was changed to account for newly discovered errors, and still has issues after hundreds, even thousands, of years of effort), then can we expect that *all* Church leaders *fully* understand prayer? We must respect the Church, but realize that clergy are *people*, and it is these people who guide us, and many of those people are little, if any, more enlightened than the rest of us.

It is peculiar that after thousands of years of contemplation and study of the Bible, and philosophical discussion about the Bible and life, that many Church and community leaders have not come upon the understanding of prayer, or maybe how to convey that understanding, how it works, and why prayer sometimes does not work. This knowledge should have become a normal part of our culture, but this has not yet happened in a way that the bulk of the people can understand it.

Now as well as over the centuries, our arrogance as humans has sought to oppress others and hold ourselves as superior over them. Our arrogance causes us to ignore fact in effort to be "right." This blindness has robbed us of our ability to see prayer for what it truly is—a wonderful free gift!

Often, we pray for the wrong things and then complain that our prayers didn't work. We believe that we are righteous and deserve to have our prayers answered, even though we constantly doubt, misbehave, and ask for things that are ultimately bad for us and those around us. When our prayers are not answered, we turn against the Creator and deny the existence of the Creator just because *we* believe no answer came to us. This behavior reveals our utter lack of understanding.

If you reflect upon the last chapter, you can see how the attitude of unforgiveness can also affect our prayer requests. Because of the arrogance of the often incorrect scientific community, and with regard to the Bible and the Church, many of us have been placed in a state of mental doubt.

It's easy to see why so many of us are falling away from religion when we consider that many in the scientific community have been deliberately seeking to destroy people's belief in a Creator. Add to that, that some Church leaders intermittently fought against new science over the centuries and often failed to embrace true science. To make matters worse, some in the Church have now mistakenly decided to come into an agreement with "science" and to alter the core belief of Creation. This is a very troubling thing for us because we look to the Church for the "truth". When some in the Church concede that mankind has evolved from an amoeba, it opens the door to a great amount of doubt in our hearts. As you read you will see how our doubt renders our prayers useless.

All of this has caused centuries of decay—of the truth—in the hearts of too many of us. It has caused us to come to a point in life where we are so destitute that we pray for patches on our life, rather than understanding *why* it needs to be patched in the first place. This very troublesome snare that we are caught in causes us to pray for the wrong things.

Praying for the Wrong Things

When we pray, we often pray in a way that requests a bandage for a wound, rather than focusing on the wound being tended to and healed, or better yet, for the *cause* of the wound to be removed. Praying for a bandage is a very simple example of our inability to know that a prayer *can* be answered. Even praying for the wound to be healed, somewhat misses the point.

Because we do not have truth within us, we concede to a lie by believing that we're not worthy, or we believe that the Creator is not able to provide for our prayer in having the wound healed.

Here is a self-imposed catch to our prayer problems: If we do not embrace truth and, yet *know* that the Creator is able to supply our needs and fulfill our prayer requests, then we have, of our own accord, made ourselves unworthy to have our prayers answered.

Seldom do people pray for *good* things. We usually pray for bad things to stop, like when we say things such as, "Lord, take away my pain". Even if we are praying for something like a new car, our mind is still often focused on replacing our old used car which is often in disrepair. We do this for the tangible things in our lives, but we also do it for the bad circumstances of our lives.

In most cases, we don't even need to request anything of the Creator; we only need to do our part and trust that "it is already done". The asking part (the praying) is mostly for us, so that, in our own heads, we can lay down a plan for what we actually desire.

Our lack of understanding about prayer did not start within the last few hundred years; it has been going on since the Creation of mankind. Based upon the historical accounts reported in the Bible, we can see that people quickly and regrettably forgot about their Creator on numerous occasions.

The unfortunate theme of people losing sight of the Creator was repeated throughout the entire period of history recorded in the Bible. Historically, mankind has behaved poorly by disregarding the Creator and our fellow man. In doing so, those from the past, and us here today, have lowered the expectations of the absolute power of the Creator, ending with us turning away from the Creator, and, subsequently, turning to idolatry. Our doubtful and low expectations of the Creator have been repeated since the beginning of mankind, and it will continue until we all come to understand truth. Since this is unlikely to happen anytime soon, the best we can do is for each one of us to understand this for ourself, and then go on to do our best to share our understanding with others.

The reason that we pray for the wrong things is because of our lack of understanding. We behave poorly and then approach the Creator with passionless, half-hearted prayers. And then later, we insult the Creator by believing within our hearts that our lackluster requests and low expectations are not able to be fulfilled by the Creator. And then we go on yet further to think that the Creator should answer all of our thoughtless prayers regardless of the consequences of that occurring.

Our low expectations are the "bandages" spoken of earlier. While it is not evil to request a bandage, it completely misses the point; and most of us pray in this lackluster way. We pray to be soothed and we request for our pain to go away, rather than *knowing* that the wound itself can be healed and that the cause of the wound can be taken out of our life.

Too often, deep down inside we simply do not *believe* that prayers can be answered, yet we still pray. Then, because we do not truly believe, we set our sights lower so that we don't have to experience the disappointment of our prayers not being answered. And if we do pray for lofty things, we often expect that, of its own accord, the universe should make a pile of cash, or whatever else we want, to somehow magically appear in our hands or fall out of the sky.

If we are going to take the time to pray and expect our prayers to be answered, then doesn't it seem logical to actually *believe*, and actually *know* that what we are praying for can occur through the Creator?

I Want It Now!

Our inability to understand and pray properly causes our prayers to appear unsuccessful, which has us dealing with our own share of unwanted toil, and we want that toil instantly removed from our lives, yet we fail to see our own error. Our "I want it now!" attitude is probably the most difficult part of having our prayers answered. We humans are a very impatient group. Often, an answer to a prayer does not come quickly enough for us, if it comes at all. So how do we change this?

We do it by getting things right. Can you honestly say that you *deserve* to have things given to you when you are unwilling to see the truth about everything in life, even if you not being able to see truth is not a deliberate error on your part?

For example, consider a boss' position: Let's say that your every intention is good and you want to do your best work ever, but you have not yet come to understand certain information that is required in order to do the job that you're trying to get. Is it just and right for you to expect that a boss should hire you for the job? Wouldn't the boss be better served to give the work to someone who actually has the skills to do the job? Even if you pretended that you knew what was happening and you were actually hired immediately, then how long would it be before it is made evident that you do not know how to do the job correctly?

Once we have come to a basic understanding, then, and only then, are we qualified to receive any of what we request in prayer. Yet, even so, our prayers are often answered, but we miss seeing the answers because we lack understanding.

We truly need to be honest about our understanding of things. This means that if we want the job, then we had better acquaint ourselves with the true needs of that job. Only after we have come to understand the full nature and needs of the job, should we even begin to ask for that type of job. Of course there is always some minor on-the-job learning to do, but we ought to know and have the basic skills for the job when applying.

In much the same way that you would be demoted or fired from the job due to your lack of understanding, that is to say, lack of ability, so too is it with prayer. When we cannot do something right, we are forced to settle for the basics of just getting by. If we believe that we deserve more than a basic position at our job, and we become hostile towards our bosses while complaining and making mean or cutting remarks to others about our boss when the promotion doesn't come, is it then reasonable to expect that somehow we should not be further demoted or altogether fired?

Pray for the right things, in the right order, and at the right time. If you want a particular job, first pray that you can learn the trade. Then believe in your own heart that you can and will accomplish learning the trade. And finally, learn from a master of the trade and study it with all of your heart. You should have a desire and passion for this occupation or you will be wasting your future boss' time.

Most of us pray for the wrong things, and then we further go on to pray for those things in the wrong order. In many cases we are praying for the wrong things *because* they are in the wrong order. This error of ours causes inaction both on our part and in regard to our prayers being answered. If we want it now, then it is best to follow the instructions that have been presented to us. Doing this will best facilitate the most expedient possibility for your prayers to be answered

Why are We Too Blind to See It?

All too often people get hung up on the Bible. This includes both atheists and believers. We should not need to be dependent upon the Bible in order to prove in our own minds, or to other people, that there is a Creator. This does not mean the Bible is irrelevant. It means that the evidence of the Creator is everywhere we look.

The evidence of Creation is so overwhelming that we must choose to be deliberately blind to not see Creation's pattern.

Often, we want a sign from the Creator or some sort of visitation that will prove to our own minds that this "Creator" exists, but it never seems to be delivered to us to a point where we are satisfied. Yet, we look all around us in the environment and we see consistent repeated patterns throughout every level of life and existence. But somehow, in all of what we see, we fail to recognize the essence of that which has formed us. By choice, we are too blind and/or too ignorant to see it. In recent centuries we have made an effort to try to explain away the Creation. However, for those who are willing to take a proper and *true* scientific approach and truly look at all of Creation, they will see beautiful and unexplainable patterns that repeat and are produced with regular precision as is described in the Bible. The Bible should *not* be our basis for belief. The Bible is a historical confirmation of what we see, and it is reliably recorded over a several thousand year period.

Those of us who have lived after the beginning of the twenty-first century are especially blessed to have had a multitude of scientific research and discovery laid out before us. With this technology and information, we have the opportunity to see the inner workings of Creation. An unbiased mind that is open to all possibilities will quickly see that science confirms Creation and supports what the Bible documented about Creation and mankind so many years ago. However, there is a perversion in the way many of us have been taught and in how we choose to understand the Bible's accounts of Creation. As explained in the book series *The Science of God*, when we misinterpret the account of Creation, it is rendered useless to us—we have made *ourselves* blind.

The arrogant biases, both in religion and in the scientific world, have inhibited our ability to see the simple truth of Creation, and we have become blind because of these biases. This blindness profoundly affects our prayers.

When we pray and request a visitation, or other evidence, it is a very blind and arrogant prayer. The evidence is placed before us on a daily basis, but because we have chosen to believe lies, we have trapped ourselves in darkness. With every unexplainable beat of your heart, with every unexplainable thought of your mind, with every sensation of your body, and with every seen thing, we are constantly given evidence of the utter absoluteness in which image we have been Created. Choosing to accept or deny this overwhelming evidence is each our own choice.

If you have been asking for proof of existence of a Creator, then know that with every breath your body takes, you have been given that proof. Even your thought to ask for proof of the Creator's existence is proof of the Creators existence.

There is also another blindness that most of us experience with regard to our prayers being answered. We often get what we prayed for, but we don't understand that the answer to the prayer has already been received by us. This is because it didn't come to us how *we* expected it to, thus we do not recognize it, causing us to entirely miss seeing or realizing those answers.

To get a better grasp on the idea that we often miss the fact that our prayers are answered, we need to understand certain things. One key point to understand is that if there is a problem that we need rooted out of our life, the problem's source is often rooted more deeply than we would like to imagine, and usually more deeply than we are able to see in our blindness.

Earlier we spoke of not praying for the wrong things and not praying for a bandage. At minimum we should instead pray for the wound to be healed. While this is true, it does not mean that the prayer for a bandage will not be answered. If we are praying for a bandage, then our underlying intention is truly to have the bleeding stop, is it not? So, to dig a bit deeper, a wound is caused from something. Wounds do not usually appear spontaneously. A wound is typically there from some cause or error. If you were cut or injured at work, and this repeatedly happens over a long period of time and is difficult to avoid, then when you pray for a bandage what you are really wanting is to no longer be injured at work. The root of your cut is your job, and therefore, blindly asking for a bandage, is, at the very base of the root, asking to have a different job without you realizing you are doing so. Thus, we pray to be healed and then lose our job but are too blind to realize that the job was the cause of our problem to begin with.

Asking to have a wound healed only to return to the source of the injury so that you can be injured again is irrational behavior. It would be an irrational thought to want to go into the water wearing a typical swimsuit and hope to not get wet. Praying for a bandage is no different when the source of the problem is your job. This is not saying that you intend for a different job, but since the reason for the bandage is the job, then your prayer might be answered by giving you cause to leave that job, and possibly by you getting fired or downsized from that job, which will seem bad to you if you are too blinded to realize on your own that you needed to quit. I understand that this may initially sounds crazy to you, but this is just a small example of how prayer can work when you are not paying close attention. In other words, when you jump into the water of having the wound healed, then you will get wet by possibly having to get a different job. You cannot swim without getting wet. Getting wet is an unavoidable part of jumping in the water, and if you choose to *not* jump in the water you will never be able to swim and be refreshed by the water. When you get wet, learn to use that water to your advantage and swim to your next destination. The water is your blessing. If you panic and refuse to swim you will either tread water endlessly or you will drown. Getting wet can be a good thing and it is often the required cleansing in order for the prayer to be answered. If you are in a job and you have been putting in extra effort that has gone unnoticed for too long, it's possible that you are working at the wrong job or with the wrong people.

What we all need to realize is that we often pray for the wrong things, and we're too blind to see what we are doing because we're always looking for a solution *right now*, the way *we* imagined it.

We're always looking for the bandage to make our problems go away "right now!" We realize that it takes time for a wound to heal, but a bandage can be put on immediately. Seldom do we stop to realize that the source of the problem is actually the thing that caused the cut to begin with. This is a common issue, and it is very important for you to be aware of it. When we are too blind to see this, we end up praying against ourselves.

Do You Pray Against Yourself?

Blindness in our prayers comes from our inability to get to the most base, or deepest root, of a problem. When we have the problem of blindness in our prayers, it places us in a very peculiar position—We become unable to see our problem's root cause. And when a prayer answer is delivered to us we often fight that answer to the prayer request that we made, and then we pray again with another contradictory prayer.

We pray against ourselves on a regular basis in this way, and then with every ounce of our energy, we unwittingly fight to stop the very thing that we prayed for.

For example: If you are being physically or emotionally hurt by someone, and you want your pain to stop, then you will likely pray for your pain to be relieved. This may require situations to occur that you did not anticipate when you made your initial request in prayer.

This is similar to when a workman will have to remove many obstacles in order to repair a small problem. For instance, a cracked piston ring inside the engine on your car is a very small problem. However, to repair it, requires the entire engine to be removed and much of it dismantled in order to repair the tiny crack that is causing your car to lose some of its power—your life is no different. There are many things that our life situations are dependent upon, and in many cases we are in control but do not realize that this is so. Sometimes our problems require a major overhaul, and when we are told this then we argue and fight the answer, often by using prayers that are contrary to the best solution to the problem.

We need to define what the word "prayer" means. *Prayer* means to *request*. So if we say "when you made your *request* in *prayer*", then what we are actually saying is, "when you made your *request* in *request*".

We can just say "when you prayed" instead of saying "when you made your request in prayer". But the term *prayer* has become a label, and in that label, the word "prayer" has lost the value of what it means when we speak of prayer without using the word *request* in conjunction with it. A "*prayer*" is a *request*.

When we make requests, we should be very cautious to look at the potential ramifications of having our request fulfilled. This falls well within the scope of the saying: "Be careful what you pray for, because you just might get it!"

When we go to the market to purchase a box of cereal, there is a great deal more that goes into getting that box to the market and on the shelf for us to purchase than them simply placing it on the shelf. We don't give much thought as to how the cereal got there. We grab it and give them our money and then we're done. Simple!

But we fail to realize that oil had to be refined for the machinery in order for the crops to be planted and harvested. Steel and other metals had to be mined to make the vehicles that delivered it. Trees had to be cut and made into a paper and cardboard. And that cardboard had to be made into a box for the cereal. All of this, plus a nearly inconceivable amount of other activities had to take place before *you* could purchase that box of cereal at a reasonable price with such ease. Not to mention what is involved behind the scene when your purchase's financial transaction occurs. Can we shout out a hefty "Thank you!" to everyone who took part in processes that allow us this abundance!

Prayer is no different. In order for you to have your prayer answered, other things will have to give way. Our problem is that we often do not want those other things to go away and/or we often do not realize that they *need* to go away. We irrationally want the cereal fresh and in our bowl without having any of the activity occur that leads up to the cereal being on the shelf. When looking for this, over time, you will begin to see how often your prayers actually have been attempted to be answered, but you missed and rejected the answer because you did not understand that in order for those answers to properly occur, many other things needed to change too, some of which can be uncomfortable for you.

The blindness that we all have with regard to other things needing to give way in order for our prayers to be answered is very profound, and we end up with two problems: The first problem is that we actually fight that which we have prayed for. And the second problem follows, by us typically praying against the answer to our initial prayer. Sometimes this even occurs within the same prayers, which puts us in a very awkward position. Our bodies are not designed for this sort of mental irrationality and conflict. Our desire for instant gratification in the "I want it now!" feeling blinds us; and this blindness does not allow us to see that the prayer *has* been answered.

We see what we believe to be an unfavorable result in one part of our life, but we fail to understand that it is very possibly the answer to our prayer in what we think of as another part of our life. Because we cannot see this clearly, it causes us to become frustrated because our life appears to be out of control. We then proceed to make "corrections" in our life in order to try to stop the effects of the answers that just occurred as a result of our prayers. We do this because we are blind to the fact that— we do not understand that our prayer was actually answered.

When we blindly fight the answers to our prayers in this way it causes us even greater frustration. This is because we are not realizing the strength of our prayer and that our prayer has already been answered.

Remember this: When we have prayed for the wrong things for a long enough time, and received the best answers to our prayers but didn't recognize them, we then remain in frustration from our lack of recognizing the good and proper answers. Then we eventually break down and decide to pray about what we see as the new problem that is causing our frustration but which was actually a proper answer to our initial prayers. This puts us in a situation where we're praying against ourselves. Our problem is that we do not recognize the original answer for what it is, or we fail to see it altogether.

When we start praying against ourselves, we have trapped ourselves in having the circumstances reoccur again and again. The circumstances I am speaking of are the ones that caused us to make our first prayer to begin with. It is at this point that we get caught in a dangerous reciprocal trap. We cause a problem and then pray for solution and see the solution as a new problem, and then we fight that solution and pray against it. What result do you think that we should we expect from this sort of behavior?

We pray for the bandage, and if that prayer is answered we pray to get our job back, and then if that is answered we pray for a bandage again, and if that is answered we pray to get our job back... This needless oscillation happens due to our blindness because we fail to see that our initial prayer has already been answered.

To be able to overcome this we must get into the practice of always asking ourselves "What caused this?" And we must keep asking this question until we have gotten to the deepest root of the problem. It's the *base root* of the problem that we need to remove from life in order to have the painful end result of the problem go away. The end result is usually what we are praying to have removed. Treating a symptom does us no good. It is when we treat the source of the illness that it will prevent or stop the symptoms that we incorrectly put all of our thought into tending to.

When we pray against ourselves in this way, then asking ourselves "What caused this?" will help us to see if our prayer has already been answered. When we think "I need a bandage", then we must ask, "What caused this?" The answer will be "Something sharp at work caused this." Then ask again "What caused this?" and if the answer is "dangerous conditions", then are those dangerous conditions up to you to remove, or is it all up to another person who you have no control over? Which again, is another "What caused this?" If the "What caused this?" part is out of your command, then, as in our example here, leaving your job might be your best bet.

If you hear that you might lose your job and then you go on to pray that you don't lose your job, you are then praying to stay in a situation where there is a person who is **un**willing to correct the safety issues that are causing your injuries. This partly is the double-mindedness that the Christ spoke of in the Bible. In such cases, we are asking to have it both ways, we're asking it to be both light and dark, on and off, be in the water and not wet.

When we pray in this irrational manner, we are asking to be both at our job and not at our job. Our bodies, our brains, and our minds are designed for order; they are not designed for this kind of disorder. Wanting and praying for something to be both ways is disorderly. It's not that we need to lose a job, but rather, it is that we need to have a job we enjoy that will not be the root of our problems.

We can push this example further to a point where we are often living beyond our financial means, and therefore we believe that we "need" the particular job that is causing our injury. In this case it's our quest for status that becomes the problem. The answer to your prayer could be you being driven to a point of destitution until you decide that you are going to accept the truth about yourself and that you are living beyond your means. *Everything* is connected to your own self-created chain of events.

We feel confused because any time we try to see a clear picture of irrational thought we can only know that it is irrational. Beyond that it is technically impossible to make sense of an *irrational* thought or behavior.

When we function in a double-minded state, our minds and our bodies are functioning in a state of disorder. This contradictory behavior is not what we are designed for and it causes tremendous stress on our bodies.

We can easily and foolishly approach our example of being hurt at work from a perspective where we believe there is no Creator and still arrive at the same outcome for self-inflicted pain, injury, and misery. But to approach prayer in a creatorless mentality only increases our internal conflict. Through that internal conflict we increase our physical conflict, which puts our health at high risk of failure.

This section is not about a box of cereal, repairs to your car's engine, or your job. These analogies are only to illustrate how often we pray against ourselves using our double-minded rationale. We can see it easily in these analogies, but we entirely miss it in our own prayers.

Before we can even begin to know what to ask for in prayer, we need to remove our irrational double-mindedness from our behavior and from our thinking.

What to Ask for in Prayer

There has been a great assault on prayer by means of arrogance and mockery throughout the history of the world. Repeatedly, in the Old Testament, and in the New Testament, we're told to trust. But, because we do not understand the concept of trusting, we have adopted blind faith, which can be dangerous and foolish. This allows us to be misled by other people who are misled—it is "The blind leading the blind".

The Christ very clearly and vividly indicated that "Whatever you ask for in *prayer* and *believe* is already given to you." Here's the reason that we have problems with Christ's statement: In general, people entirely miss this statement when reading the Bible. The reason is because we do not understand the word "believe," we do not understand the word "prayer," and we do not understand what "faith" is.

Besides the fact that we don't understand the underlying concepts of the words *believe*, *prayer*, and *faith*, we are also blind to the root cause of our problems about which we are praying for solutions.

As we discussed in the previous section, we often pray against ourselves because we do not have the foresight to see the root cause of our problem. You will find it to be a wise action to utilize the "What caused this?" question before you start requesting any remedy for your problems when you pray. Our first prayer should be along the lines of "Help me to see the problem clearly."

If you don't ask "What caused this?" then there is a tremendous likelihood that you will be *praying against yourself.* In truth, those prayers are likely to be answered. It is the double-mindedness that we spoke of earlier that causes us to lose sight of what is truly occurring. More of our prayers are answered than we can ever imagine. But we will only see these answers when we look at our lives and ask "What caused this?" in total honesty, before we pray.

Once we have assessed our situation and have gotten into discovering the root cause of our problem, then we have to make decisions that are based on our assessments of those around us and of the physical capabilities of the world with which we interact.

In the analogy where you have a job at which you are being injured, you need to assess whether or not it is reasonable that the cause of injury can be removed by improvement. Also, assess whether the person in charge is willing to allow that improvement to be made. If they are not willing to make the needed changes and you choose to stay in that situation, then you will be fighting the prayer you made for the bandage. Praying for, and receiving, a bandage is the wrong circumstance in this case. A job that better suits your own talents and skills and where your boss or manager is a reasonable person is what is truly needed.

You might want the other person who refuses to correct the problem to get a different job. But while this could potentially solve your problem, the root problem is you being cut. If you get caught up in praying for the demise of a fellow worker or do anything in an attempt to get them fired, then you could be unjustly asking for harm to another person. Praying for harm to come to another person will not gain you favor with the Creator. You do not need to ask for them to be blessed, but you should at least ask that their eyes be opened.

All of Creation is built on an—order of *construction* basis; Creation is *not* at all based upon *destruction*. Whenever we ask for harm to come to others, we're asking the Creator to be a destroyer. Destroying is counter to the nature of a Creator. It is akin to asking a mother to intentionally end her baby's life upon the baby's birth, and that would be pure evil. The Creator will only destroy something to preserve what is being destroyed by that which the Creator will destroy.

In a situation, such as the getting cut at work analogy, there are two good possible prayers and they should be combined. The first prayer would be for the person who refuses to see the problem to come to an understanding that will cause them to correct the problem. A second prayer could be to have you find a new job at a better workplace, where you will be happier and in total harmony with the other workers while doing work that you excel at and enjoy doing the most!

Praying for the other person to see the light of the problem is similar to praying for a bandage, but, in the case of another person being involved, we must understand that each person has their own free will. It is likely that their problem and inability to see, runs far deeper than their simple refusal or inability to see the particular problems at work that caused you to get cut to begin with.

Only your example of *kindness, love,* and ***intolerance for injury to yourself*** without bitterness towards others will show the person, who is being stubborn, what true love is. In our example, intolerance would probably best be done through your willingness to seek employment elsewhere. It's important to note that at some point, even before you begin to pray, that you should have made an actual request to the person, in a kind and courteous manner, that the dangerous situation be remedied. And also, that *you* would do what you could to reasonably facilitate that remedy. It is then, after your clear and concise goal is in your mind, that you should ask in prayer for a remedy to be found. If we cannot, or if we are too lazy to properly and fully visualize in our minds what we truly want, then do we really deserve it?

Your ability to visualize your desires is critical to your success. When you fully visualize your desires then, it is clear in your mind what it is that you actually desire. If you are unable to visualize your desires, then you cannot realistically expect to be able to achieve those desires because you have no goal in view to actually achieve. Visualizing the details is very important; those details are your goal, and the overall picture is what you are praying for assistance with.

If the remedy to your situation cannot happen due to the stubbornness of the other person, then forcing them will only embitter them. It is at this point that it is probably wise to seek another place of employment. In our example, this would be done in a kind but firm manner where you are giving notice that you will no longer work in a place that is dangerous to you, and you inform them that you have found, or plan to find, employment elsewhere because of the situation. Handling the situation in this way takes care of your part of the duty, which is the physical action part or the "works" part of your responsibility. It is after it is reasonably clear in your mind that your requests should be made to the Creator for the best solution to be made ready for you.

In truth, there is little in our world that we really need to pray for. It is all before us as we speak. What we really need to be praying for is an open heart and an open mind with which to see the source of our errors, problems, and troubles. Then we need to pray to be courageous enough to utilize that skill in moving forward in our lives.

You'll find that when you set your heart right and *properly* analyze situations in your life, down to the root cause, then when you pray for the things to come your way, they will stand before you on a regular basis.

The problem we often have is that we get too busy trying to remove bad situations from our lives because we allow ourselves to be placed in situations where other people are bringing us down. For some unknown reason, we are afraid to confront people about the fact that their lack of dealing with a problem is causing us to be hurt or, as in the bandage analogy, cut. Our fear of confronting others, when it is proper to do so, traps us in a cycle of praying against ourselves.

When we are at the point where we have overcome the stubbornness of others by kindly and firmly stating our position, only then can we decide what to pray *for*, rather than what to pray *against*.

Praying for a bandage is praying *for* something, but then continuing with praying to not lose your job, that you dislike or is harming you, is praying *against* yourself.

You need to understand that one who Creates wants you to *be built up* rather than *destroyed*. This means that we need to be receptive, and always be aware and on the lookout for the good that comes our way. We pray for things, such as not losing our job, but what we should really be praying for is to find the perfect job. With a job that is perfect for each one of us, we can display our natural gifts and our best work! Our big problem in this regard is that we often cause ourselves a great deal of misery because of our unjustified quest for excessive riches. And so we take jobs that we hate and then complain to the Creator to remove the pains we experience in our lives, which are typically from the peripheral effects of doing this sort of thing.

If you have cleared the clutter from your heart and mind, and have begun to see what is true, then you will find that opportunities are regularly popping up all around you. These opportunities allow you to be the best that you can possibly be, allowing you to joyfully display what you were made for.

Sadly, our opportunities are often hidden in the darkness of our blindness, causing us to mistakenly believe that life is all about *money* and *prestige*. We end up fighting for money and prestige that are not rightfully ours—money and prestige that is far less than what we could have if we were to see what is true and best for each of us as we build up those around us while doing what we should be doing.

When we pray, we should not only be asking for bad things to go away, but rather for good things to occur for us. Because we focus on the bad things going away, we cannot see the good things that stand right before us every day. We certainly don't have to ignore addressing the bad things in our prayers, but when we address them we should be asking for insight, revelation, and guidance, rather than for the Creator to constantly bail us out of our persistently erred ways.

If you are working in a dangerous environment that does not suit you and you ask your boss to correct that situation, and your boss threatens to fire you, that is a good time to pray for a different job to come your way. Fighting with your boss only serves to cause your boss to give a bad recommendation about you to your next employer. However, praying for a job that allows you to display the gifts placed inside of you at your Creation will cause the best job to come your way when you pray for and have the courage to take the steps towards that goal. People often pray for this to happen, but then they lack the courage needed to take the steps and make the changes that are presented in the answer to their prayers. Being double-minded in this way only holds you back and is generally not what should be asked for in prayer.

Should We Pray for things like Weight Loss?

This book is about prayer, but since weight loss is an issue about which many people pray and fail, it is proper to address it here. Praying for weight loss is a very good example to use for explaining prayer that is typically misdirected. If you make a request in prayer to be thinner, but then regularly eat meals where each meal exceeds your entire daily calorie needs then you are fighting against yourself and your prayers.

There is only one way to lose weight. If losing weight is your goal and you continue eating too large of meals and you are also snacking between meals, then you have a misdirected sense of understanding of your situation. When you're overweight, it is not the *weight* that is your problem. When we gain weight to an unreasonable level, it is for one reason and one reason only. Our body is absorbing more calories or energy than it is using. It's as simple as that. So, to pray that you lose weight is to pray that your food supply is somehow interrupted, changed, or reduced, or maybe that your job is somehow changed to a more active position.

If we are overweight, it is because we have been eating too much, and in general, when this is the case, we don't take kindly to our food supply being interrupted, changed, or reduced. Our fight against a reduced food supply causes us to fight our own prayer to be thin.

This sort of contradictory futility is commonplace in our prayers, especially with regard to weight loss. At this point we come back to that same question of, "What caused this?" Often, we believe that our being overweight has to do with our genetics, but this questionable belief only keeps us overweight. Too much food is the cause of excessive weight on our bodies. What we must ask is not "What caused the weight gain?" but rather, we must ask ourselves "What causes us to eat too much?" We will always find that our desire to eat too much is habitual. Those habits were typically learned at an early age. (You can read more details about losing weight in the book *DreamThin-Learn to Lose Weight While Sleeping*.) Praying to lose weight is not what we should be praying for. Instead, we should pray for and work to understand why we have developed a habit of eating too much. And also, when praying, we should ask for the understanding and power to overcome the urge to eat unnecessary amounts of food, especially "junk" food.

It is the power of our mind that we are truly asking for control over in this particular situation. Once we have gained power over our thinking, the weight loss becomes automatic. It's not surprising that our culture has adapted so readily to becoming overweight, since we humans do not want to sacrifice our "I want it now!" desires.

Because of the Santa Claus Effect, we have learned to blind ourselves from things that we don't want to hear. It's the same thing that we do when trying to lose weight. In the Santa Claus Effect, we lie to our children and do everything we can in order to get them to believe the Santa Claus hoax. Then, when they begin to see through our lies, we often go further by presenting false documentation to them to perpetuate our hoax. Eventually, when children discover the hoax, they have lost an important ability to accept anything we tell them as *absolutely* true because we so deeply betrayed their trust. We have taught them to believe lies by attempting to gain the instant gratification we get through the Santa Claus Effect. In the case of weight loss, we do this to ourselves.

We want to be able to have our whole cake and eat *all of it* too, and *not* gain any weight. Closing our eyes to a weight problem by refusing to reduce the amount of food we eat or refusing to be more active sabotages what we are truly praying for. Choosing to believe that we are born genetically predisposed to being fat is the Santa Claus Effect in full swing, and it is dangerous to our health.

Always pray for a good remedy for the *source* of the problem. It's not important to know the remedy when praying, because that is what we are praying to have our eyes be opened to. If we don't want to get cut at work then we should pray for a different job. If we don't want to gain weight or if we want to lose weight, then we should pray for a desire for eating less and a desire for healthier foods to be in our mind, our heart, our prayers, and in our hands; or possibly discover our source of frustration that causes us to use food as our own release from life's stress. It is our thinking and habits that make our weight go away relatively quickly with little effort.

Part of the weight loss issues could also be partly due to our lack of activity. A prayer to bring something into our life that would help us lose weight may come in the form of an opportunity to do something that is not normal to our day-to-day habits. An opportunity could arise that would require us to be more physically active, and if you have prayed to lose weight, that opportunity could be the answer to your prayer. Rejecting such an opportunity will be a rejection of an answer to a prayer, and the rejection of a gift given to you from your Creator.

It is irrational to imagine in our minds that somehow the Creator will answer our prayer for weight loss while allowing us to continue in our unhealthy eating habits. Most prayers are answered in ways that utilize everything within the scope of what we refer to as the Laws of Physics. This means that the energy that you consume will be stored as fat, burned, or pass through your system. Imagining that any weight loss will occur outside of the fundamentals of body chemistry is choosing to be ignorant of reality. If the Creator Created all that is in the Universe with such a high degree of consistency, then do we dare to imagine than we can defy this pattern and lose weight while maintaining our poor eating habits? That's not likely to ever happen. And further, should the Creator defy the Created order of things just so that *we* can continue to eat badly but still lose weight just because we "prayed" about it? Of course this is a ridiculous thought and we all know it. It takes personal effort to overcome our own bad habits. What we need is to pray for the power to overcome our bad habits.

Praying for Healing

A few sections back we discussed praying for the wrong things. When praying for *healing*, it is especially important to realize we often pray for wrong things. The family disease lie is a good example of praying for the wrong things. What is the family disease lie you ask? The lie is when we believe we are predisposed to certain cancers, or weight gain, or diseases because our parents or grandparents had the disease. I am not saying that this is never a possibility, but I am saying that we often overlook the real cause of our problems. With the family disease lie, society and the medical establishment clearly indicate we have an increased chance of being afflicted by the same diseases as our parents and grandparents have or had. We are told that such diseases are genetically passed down to us. While this is a possibility, I would like you to consider that there are other more important underlying factors involved. In a later chapter we will get deeper into how our thinking affects our body, but for now, realize that the way we think and eat has tremendous impact on our well-being.

Our habits and our attitudes are so deeply imbedded in us that they *appear* to be genetic—but they typically are not. The way we think and eat is passed down to us from our parents, our family, and from our environment. Even though we might not fully realize that we have subtle unhealthy eating habits, those habits will still affect our health. The same is true for our thinking: if we are always uptight, it is certainly going to affect our health in a negative way. Much of the way we *think* has been learned during our early years with our childhood families.

If we do not understand that our thinking, actions, and behavior affects us, then when we pray for healing we cannot expect our prayers to be properly answered. To continue to partake in damaging behaviors and attitudes sabotages our prayers even if we don't realize we are doing it. You could think of it in terms of planting a flower garden, and praying that it grows healthy and strong. Then, just after you are done praying for a robust flower garden, you unknowingly sprinkle it with small amounts of poison that inhibit it from thriving. Every time you're done praying for your flowers to grow beautiful and strong, you go right back out and *unknowingly* water the flowers with poison-laced sprinkling water that pours forth out of the family spigot.

Is it reasonable for us to expect the Creator to choose to somehow ignore the blindness of our own actions by healing the flowers and making them grow *while* we sprinkle poison on them? The Creator wants us to see our errors and change so that we no longer poison the flowers. We wouldn't continuously allow our children to do wrong by always correcting their errors without somehow trying to teach them the proper way to do it along the way; otherwise they would not be able to ever come to understand that they are making an error when sprinkling poison on the flowers. In fact, if we did make their poison-laced flower garden grow, then they would believe that what they are doing is the answer to achieve a robust flower garden when it's actually not true. Doing so would cause considerable problems in their future lives. Sadly, far too many people do this, resulting in their children being spoiled. When we actually have enough belief in our hearts to a point that we actually begin to pray, we often do this same thing with our prayers when we pray for something like our own good health. Our prayer for a healthy garden, or healthy body, is not likely to be answered in the form of blossoming flowers or great health. Instead it is likely that our prayer will be answered in a personal revelation that *we* are killing our flowers with poison or that we are killing ourselves with the poison of wrong thinking and bad choices. But sadly when we do come upon our realization of our error we often suppress and ignore it.

If we ever manage to get over our self-inflicted ailments, we are often afraid to make an attempt to pray to be healed because we believe that the Creator is incapable of producing sudden spontaneous healing. Our lack of faith in this matter is in conflict with reality. Our belief is truly tested when it comes to the subject of healing—this is the belief that we often refer to as "faith". While it is true that this belief is our level of faith, the reality is that faith has only two levels. Those levels are **faith** and **no faith**—Faith is either **on** or **off**. Christ said if you had faith the size of a mustard seed you could move mountains. Later we will discuss faith and belief in greater detail because it is the central problem around which the failure of our prayers revolves.

There Is a Way

Our inability to understand what is true stops us from being able to find a way. Imagine that you are trapped in a room. This room has no doors or windows or any visible sign of escape. It is all white and you are there all alone. In effort to escape from this room you pound on the all of walls and on the floor. Much to your disappointment you find that the walls are made of solid concrete and you decide that escape is futile because you have no tools with which to chip through the concrete.

However, unknown to you and just above the highest level that you have already pounded on during your previous attempts to escape, there is a paper-thin covering that you can easily punch through. But you are not aware of this escape, so it is unlikely that you will ever find it because it is a passage that you cannot see which is just above where you can easily reach. Since it is above where you have already pounded, you do not know that it exists.

Because of the paper covering the walls, you are blind to the escape passage. You could quickly punch through the paper that covers the escape if you only knew that a way existed for you to escape. Our prayers for healing work in much the same way, and because we do not understand—we do not try.

If you're trapped in that room and someone told you that a paper-covered passage existed that was hidden behind the wallpaper, and that you can easily punch through it, then you would try to find it and would likely be quickly successful in doing so. But, if you have come to a belief in your own mind that no way existed, then when you exhaust your ability to hope any longer, you will give up because you incorrectly believe that there is no possibility of escape.

Knowing that a way exists is an important part of healing. When we realize that a way exists, then our next step is to see it.

As we discussed earlier, this is where understanding that—a Creator does exist—becomes very important for you to *know*. For instance, getting healed through prayer is best done when your faith is real and can survive outside of the testimony of the Bible. If someone takes your Bible from you and, because you now lack your Bible, your blind faith falters, then you have a problem with your "faith". When the Christ healed people he did not have the four gospels to use as his guide books. He healed people with his understanding.

The Bible is full of many words that are not understood properly by scholars, clergy, science, scientists, or people in general. The way we understand things is not necessarily the way things are. There are many statements in the Bible that lead people to believe that some of the accounts described in it are in conflict with other information in the Bible and in nature. Because of our own arrogance, we hold tightly to *our own* analysis of the words in the Bible. Our inflexibility of our own opinion makes it appear, to us, as if there is conflict in the words in the Bible. The conflict is actually in our understanding of those words. These alleged conflicts are thrown about in discussions and have caused many people to unnecessarily have doubt regarding the Bible and anything it discusses.

The reason that we are able to generate such doubt in our hearts is because, too often, we have been relying only on the Bible for our belief in the Creator. Adam, Noah, Abram, and Moses did not have the Bible. It's true that without the Bible it is difficult for most of us to come to certain conclusions on our own. The Bible might not be necessary in order to come to particular conclusions about a Creator, but the Bible does shortcut a great deal of thinking when we use it as our springboard. It has taken us thousands of years of toil, trouble, torment, and other experiences to assemble the words of the

Bible that help in verifying Creation and the Creator's promises to us.

Many of the doubts that we hold in our hearts are caused by the alleged conflicts in the Bible. Our doubt is like the paper on the walls in the example of the concrete room that we believe we are trapped in. Our paper-thin doubt hides our only way out. The evidence of Creation that too many of us have been ignoring for several hundred years, due to our doubt which has been perpetuated by naturalism and evolution, is because we have placed our faith in a book of paper with printing on it that is often misinterpreted, rather than in the Creator and the Creation that the book tells us about.

The obviousness of the fact that there is a Creator is equivalent to the obviousness of the escape-way once someone tells us that there is a way out behind the paper-thin doubt that hides what is really there. The Bible tells us where our way out is located, but because we fail to see Creation for what it truly is, we have nothing real to base our faith upon. Therefore, our faith is blind and we turn the map (the Bible) for our escape into nothing more than our paper-thin doubt. It is not bad or wrong to believe the Bible, until we believe our own, or someone else's, *inaccurate* interpretations of it. This causes us to believe that the Bible is filled with conflicting accounts of history, which is akin to wallpapering your home with hundred-dollar bills and then complaining that you have no money, all while not realizing your error. The people and their actions often conflicted, as recorded in the Bible, but the recording of those actions is generally *not* conflicted.

Some people have based their faith on nothing more than the Bible, and have subsequently chosen to turn away from the Bible because of these alleged "conflicts" in the text. Misunderstanding these "conflicts" is usually done by people, thus allowing others to lead them into believing that we have evolved from primordial soup. In doing so, we are allowing them to blind us with their theories made of paper-thin doubt.

We need to understand the fact that a way (or answer) is always there for us, but sometimes that road has bumps in it that we ourselves created. Look at Creation and the repetition with which it all exists, and at the order that is seen in all of it. Orderly repetition, in itself, should be evidence enough to know that the Creator exists. Once we realize that the Creator exists, then we can look to the accounts recorded in the Bible, not as something to base our faith upon, but rather as a map to show us how to properly accomplish that which we wish to accomplish. The Bible is mostly filled with warnings to us about humanity's foolish choices. The sooner we realize that those are warnings to advance our lives, then the sooner we can experience the joy we each seek.

It is very specifically stated in the Bible how we are to pray (to ask or request) for things to happen in our life. When we have chosen to doubt and not believe the validity of the Bible, then the Bible does us utterly no good. All those who have suffered and died before us trying to figure out all of what we have been discussing in this section, have suffered in vain when we doubt.

We will discuss more about healing, and prayers for healing, in a later chapter. But for now, we must understand that it is important for us to believe. If we do not believe, then we won't try to find the way out. Instead, we overlook our escape passage because of our paper-thin doubt and we give up.

We should continue to pray knowing that a Creator exists and knowing, that when we pray, the request has been received by that Creator. I am not asking you to blindly have faith without evidence. Rather, I am telling you that the evidence exists everywhere you look and sits before your very own eyes. But society has chosen to close its eyes to this endless evidence. Later we will also discuss, in more detail, the healing process and the subject of absolute faith.

When you pray, remember to ask yourself "What caused this?" before you pray. Not knowing what caused something and then praying about it is like saying you are going to hit the target, but then you aim at something else, believing it to be the actual target. We must at the very minimum consider our problems in an honest manner and ask for guidance or for something to be revealed to us about our actions that are causing our problems. Our prayers suffer and fail because we do not aim for the right part of the target and we don't believe in true things that are better than what we currently have. To top it all off, we don't believe or even realize that any of this is going on. Find out "What caused this?" first, and then pray for a revelation to a solution, while at the same time knowing that a way out *does* exist. Finding the way requires removing the doubt and then actually trying to find the way using prayer

Chapter 6

Give God Permission

When we pray we are authorizing full intervention in our lives; and by default, we are also authorizing intervention when we are not living in accordance with truth. If you are not in accordance with truth, it is certain that somewhere in your life you are in unjust violation of other people. When we unjustly violate another person, then our violations will eventually be corrected by intervention even though we typically think that we did not give the Creator permission to intervene in our lives. The Creator did not establish the order of things only to have it muddled up by a bunch of unsavory humans who refuse to embrace truth and then further insist upon violating each other.

Be assured that intervention will eventually occur and that your folly can then be used by the Creator as an intervention tool in order to correct you and the lives of others who are lesser violators in effort to get them in accordance with truth, all while you suffer the consequences of your own unwise actions.

The order of truth is full of irony in that way. If you have chosen to turn against the Creator, then bad or cruel people may be sent into your life as a form of correction in order to wake you up. The Bible has clear examples of how bad people with evil hearts were utilized to chasten those who turned their hearts against the Creator, all done in effort to put the willing back on their proper path.

When your life is in order, the prayer intervention that you authorized is not likely to come in the form of clouds descending from heaven with a treasure chest of riches for you. The intervention will likely be in the form of a friend lending you a hand. Miraculous intervention that stepped outside of the common day-to-day interaction with humans was rare throughout history—Think parting the sea, water coming out of rocks, and pillars of fire. The few unexplainable events that occurred are recorded for the very reason that they were unique and unexplainable. If these amazing interventions had not been amazing, then no one would have cared or thought to record them in writing.

Whether we misbehave and hurt others, or we pray and are kind to others, we are giving the Creator permission to intervene in our lives. Intervention will be done to the level that is needed in order to remedy a situation and to restore order. This is similar to the way parents are supposed to intervene in effort to teach their young children a good way in life. When we pray, we are making a request and an authorization of permission for specific actions to occur in our lives. If you are in need of a new car, and you desire that car, and pray for it to come to you, then it is **un**likely that the car will be delivered from the clouds of the sky. But, it is very likely that when that prayer is answered, circumstances will occur that will enable you to obtain the car. The car will likely come through a friend, an abundance of financial ability, a different better paying job, or in some other unforeseen ways so that you can obtain it. When our prayers are answered in this way, we have a tendency to give credit to dumb-luck instead of giving credit to our proper prayer efforts (and The Creator) that have been so eloquently answered. This is somewhat reverse thinking of what we discussed in our earlier bandage scenario. When praying for the wrong things, based upon what is in our mind, we are typically only giving the Creator permission for a bandage, when what we really are wanting is to have the wound healed and the cause of the wound removed. But when our prayer is properly answered, all too often we fight the answer.

In a mentally opposite, but similar manner, when we get a prayer answered in the way that we expected it to be answered for something good that we asked for, then we often attribute it to dumb-luck.

When we pray, we must give the Creator permission to examine the situation and go beyond what *we* believe needs to be done in order to remedy it if we ever hope to recognize it. Additionally, we should pray for our own single-mindedness, and for ourselves to better understand *all* of the actions that are required to accomplish our goals.

We want to be healed and no longer bleed, but we have only asked for a bandage. This is like you wrongly believing that you can't stop your car because the grips are worn off the brake pedal in your car, and then going to a mechanic and telling him that you need a new brake pedal because your car will no longer stop. When the mechanic debates with you on the cause of your brake troubles, you tell the mechanic to "shut up" and not argue with you and to just replace the brake pedal. You can be rest assured that the chances are about zero that replacing your brake pedal will make your car stop any better; much like a bandage won't stop you from getting cut.

When we fight against an answer to our prayers it is like saying to the mechanic, who insists that our *brake pads* need to be replaced, that we will not allow him to do it because we believe it is not the right solution. When we do this we have denied permission for him to proceed with the proper and needed repairs in order to make the car whole again. In cases where we actually gave the mechanic permission to do the repairs at his discretion and then he determined that new brake *pads* were required, we then go on to insist that he remove the new brakes and we refuse to pay the price that it takes to make the car stop properly. Then when we crash the car, because the brakes failed, we blame the trained mechanic for *our* problems. We do this because we wrongly assumed that the problem was caused by something other than what the mechanic determined. This is what we do when we fight our prayers and, to relate it to our other example, this is what happens when we only give permission for a bandage. This is why "What caused this?" is so very important for you to understand when praying. Without this understanding, two things will happen:

First: You will not give permission for the *right* things to be done.

Second: If the Creator steps beyond what you perceive as your permission, then you will likely fight, argue, and refuse to pay the price that it takes in order for the problem to be properly resolved; such as getting a different job, changing your eating habits, or in the example above, getting new brake pads.

Wise People **Welcome** Correction

In the Bible a proverb says "Do not correct a scorner, because he will hate you—Correct a wise man, and he will love you. Give instruction to a wise man, and he will become wiser: teach a just man, and he will increase in learning." All too often, we're insulted when someone tries to correct us. In fact, when correction comes in the form of life troubles, we usually complain about our situation and fight it. If troubles are in our life then we really need to ask, "What caused this?" When we don't ask this, we cause ourselves to be troubled and frustrated by the turmoil that subtly torments us. If we experience trouble in our lives, it is almost certainly because of *whom* we have allowed around us, or the troubles are from us trying to do things that are disorderly, such as overspending, or making decisions based solely upon money, rather than based upon our *true* and *pure* desires.

The troubles that we experience are corrective experiences in order to show us that we are doing something wrong. They are the warning lights on our dashboard. When we do things wrong or do wrong things, disorder *will* enter our lives in an effort to correct our bad choices that are the actual cause of the disorder we are experiencing. Disorder is the corrective nature of order.

Read this paragraph carefully and **remember it always:** Whatever is in disorder will either be destroyed and cease to be, or it will be *forced* to be corrected until full order is restored— Never forget that piece of information. It is your golden key of understanding! "Disorder is the corrective nature of order" means that when things are not going according to plan, you need to reexamine the situation and make sure that you are doing things rightly to begin with. If you are not doing things rightly, then you *will* have troubles. Troubles and disorder are signs for us to know that we must change our circumstances and our behavior in our lives.

> **Read this paragraph carefully and remember it always:**
>
> Whatever is in disorder will either be destroyed and cease to be, or it will be forced to be corrected until full order is restored—Never forget that piece of information. It is your golden key of understanding! "Disorder is the corrective nature of order" means that when things are not going according to plan, you need to reexamine the situation and make sure that you are doing things rightly to begin with. If you are not doing things rightly, then you will have troubles. Troubles and disorder are signs for us to know that we must change our circumstances and our behavior in our lives.

The whole point of everything that we experience in our lives is to grasp order and to abide by its nature. When we fail to grasp order, then at some point we are certain to have disorder in our lives. The only way to correct disorder is to bring order back into our lives. We cannot bring order into our lives when we continue to associate with disorderly people and be negatively influenced by them or when we choose disorderly paths in our lives. For instance, this can include having a job that is contrary to your born-in gifts and your Created nature.

Partaking in a job that is contrary to you or your beliefs is disorder. Being in disorder in this way is going to hold you back from *your* best potential. The sooner you choose to make the change to be in order in your heart, mind, body, and soul, then the sooner you will see the success and health that you desire begin to come into your life. But do not be deceived in "desires" because true desire will always be pure.

Allow correction into your life. We all need to understand that the troubles we experience are a notification and a form of discipline and correction. Troubles are a sign that something is not right in our lives. It could be a person, circumstances you have chosen, or the way you think. No matter what they are, troubles are a clear sign that something needs to change promptly in your life! When you are not realizing the source of your troubles or are not seeing how to make the needed changes, you are then allowing the wallpaper of doubt, spoken of earlier, to block you from seeing what is true.

Is God Superior?

The battles of whether or not there is a supreme Creator have been raging on since nearly the beginning of mankind. The *superiority* of the Creator was the first known mental battle that humans dealt with. The account of the fall of Man detailed in the Bible surrounds this very topic. The desire of mankind to elevate ourselves to be equal to, or above, the Creator was mankind's greatest error. Ironically, this was accomplished through our doubt, which put us in a position that was lower than we were initially Created as. While, in the Bible, it says that we are made "in the image of" the Creator, we cannot be equal to or above that which has caused us to be.

As humans, everything that we are is based upon the foundation of order that was laid down at the moment of, and during, our Creation. For us to somehow imagine that we can have command over—that which made us—is an absurd notion. We can, however, have command over some of the elements by which we are made into humans. When we use our Creative power and utilize our natural gifts, then we have command over the elements that we work with. We also have command over the elements that our bodies are made with, and we can greatly alter our well-being by how we behave and by how and what we eat. Acknowledging our Creator's superiority over us is a good place to start in order to get us to be humble and to be as we were Created. When we fail to do this, we are in violation of ourselves and of our Created design.

When we do things that speak against our origin, then our hearts and minds are in oscillation and cause us to be in a physically poor state of being. When we do so, our mind is contradicting what we see and experience as reality, even though we close our eyes to reality and deny it,

What we see and feel, is our physical Created presence— that is to say, our bodies. When we deny our origin we violate ourselves and inhibit the Creator from helping us in the way that *we want* as we pray. Additionally, we are physically harming our bodies while we are in a state of mental oscillation, meaning: we are being double-minded (discussed further later).

Our inability to grasp the nature of a *Superior Creator* causes us great difficulty and countless troubles. It's also difficult for us to acknowledge a superior Creator when we have chosen to believe any lies and inaccuracies that might come from the Church, or more commonly from science, rather than to see what is true based on the obviousness of the evidence that surrounds us. As typical humans, our problem is that we are lazy or slothful; if we were not, then we wouldn't simply accept what the Church says or what science says. Instead, we would demand proper evidence and accountability from both sides. We must realize that if they are unwilling to offer *full* accountability, *full* evidence, and *full* admission of error, then it is up to each one of us to research what is true and find the evidence and *properly* analyze it on our own by dissecting it and debating it. Once we have gathered our evidence, we should then go on and properly share that evidence with others and be open to discuss and debate our thoughts when needed.

We cannot simply say, "The Bible says so, and that is evidence enough!" Nor can we simply say that "The naturalist's evolution view is evidence enough!" We must require accountability—for *everything* that is claimed as absolute—from anyone who makes such claims.

When we choose to go down a path of denying the existence of the Creator, with all of the blatantly plain evidence surrounding us that demonstrates otherwise, it indicates that we have lost our objectivity. We will be bound by the blindness of our own lies until we choose to see. In recent years, the evidence is even more compelling with all that we are able to see using modern technology and scientific observation. This observation allows us to see the truth about how some of Creation works. The intricacy and accuracy that we observe shouts volumes about the superior design by which we are Created.

Acknowledging the superiority of the Creator does not mean that you must believe the Bible just because the Bible exists and says certain things are so. But it also does *not* mean that you should deny the accounts recorded in the Bible just because they do not appear to make sense in *your* eyes and mind. Instead, it would be better to remain objective and look at all of Creation, and then through that, understand the superiority of the Creator.

For most of us, our human mind lacks an ability and/or willingness to comprehend the infinite. A youthful mind, in a childlike state, will almost always set up a barrier to infinity. In other words, "If there's a Creator, then who Created the Creator?" This sort of thinking clearly shows our inability and/or unwillingness to conceive the infinite. Getting a grasp in our own hearts and minds about the superiority of the Creator will help get us back in synchronization with what we are, who we are, and where we belong.

How do We Get God to Answer Our Prayers?

"How do we get God to **listen** to our prayers" is how we typically think of the idea of "How do We Get God to **Answer** Our Prayers?" The importance of understanding the difference is critical to your prayer success. The Creator is always listening to us; it's just that we're a lot like children who are disrespectful to their parents. If your child asks for something with a disrespectful or arrogant attitude, then you are *not* likely to grant that request.

If we are going to admit to the existence of the Creator, that most of us are only aware of because of the Bible, then we should seek evidence of that Creator by looking around at the Bible's claimed Creation, rather than depending solely upon the Bible book itself as the evidence for a Creator.

Once we have come to the conclusion that the Creator spoken of in the Bible actually exists because we have witnessed that which is Created and the order by which it all is bound, then we can go back to the Bible to learn more. After all, the Bible is what led most of us to wonder in the first place. We can then check many other statements in the Biblical documents and test them too. In order to do so, we must read them on our own with an open mind and understanding while seeking only truth. If we do not seek in this way then we will likely never understand the truth behind the words in the Bible.

When you read the Biblical documents (the books of the Bible) you will clearly find that offerings and prayers made by people who are not in harmony with order and who violate others have been found to be "a stench in the nostrils" of the Creator. In the Bible, when the Creator says our prayers and offerings are "a stench in the nostrils", it is an acknowledgement that our prayers *have been heard*, but they *will not be answered* as we desired, due to our deliberate corruption.

In the Bible, it also says that "the prayers of the righteous avail much." This is a clear indication that we need to get our attitude and our actions correct *before* our prayers will be answered as we desire them to be. Sadly for us, our blindness causes us a great deal of trouble in this regard.

If we don't intend wrong or harm to others, but are still too blind to see that we are doing wrong to others, then our prayers might be answered, but we will also be too blind to notice those answers to our prayers. We must understand that, due to the fact that we are harming other people, our prayers might not be answered, or might include a bit of restitution for our own errors before we see the positive result. The only chance of truly having your prayers answered, as you imagine them to be, is to get it right.

"What caused this?" is going to be the key in your prayers. If you don't understand what the root of your problem is, then you are likely going to be tested in this until you figure it out. The quicker we figure out "What caused this?", then the more quickly we can end our pain by making corrections in our lives and praying rightly. The *What-caused-this* skill also holds true for things that are not specifically thought of as a problem, such as, wanting something good even when life is already pretty good for you, rather than only using the *What-caused-this* skill for removing troubles from your life. When we want something extra or good, we must still ask, "What's keeping us from getting it?" and "Why is it slow in coming?", so it's still a What-caused-this issue.

When you begin to understand how to use the What-caused-this method, you can quickly find many areas in your life that you will need to correct in your own behavior and decisions. When you have made the needed corrections in your life, then your prayers will proceed in a pure form to the Creator and will be heard *and answered.* But understand that the answer might not be exactly as you expect

We must stop asking for bandages and we must stop hurting other people. We must get our own hearts, minds, bodies, and lives in order so that we are in harmony with the Creation that we are Created within. After we have achieved harmony with Creation and our Creator, and after we have purified ourselves, it is only then that our prayers will be received with gladness and joy and will be clearly answered by the Creator.

When this is complete and our prayer has been answered, then we must additionally understand how prayers are answered. Without understanding *how* prayers are answered, we will likely miss the answer to our prayer when it sits right before our eyes. When our answer sits before us and we do not understand or recognize it, then we often perceive the answer as if it is a problem. If an alcoholic prays to be cured of their drinking problem, then the prayer answers might come through people trying to help, but if that help is rejected, then maybe the prayer will be answered through getting arrested and jailed for an alcohol-related offense.

Prayers are almost always answered through other people with whom we associate or who we know. As answers to our prayers, people are put in our path to offer us the opportunities that will build our lives and the specific future that we have been praying for, or it could be bad people put in our lives forcing us to change direction and make us aware of our errors that we are too blind or too stubborn to change. The rest of our prayers that are not answered through people, are usually hidden by our blindness and are typically answered by having things that caused us trouble to be removed from our lives. Often, the good things we requested in prayer sit right before us but we don't recognize them.

Do You Dangerously Deny?

A problem that is often seen in the realm of the naturalist's evolution beliefs is an outright denial of the possibility of the promises written in the Bible. By denying the Creator we revoke permission for the Creator to *effectively* answer our prayers the way that we want them to be answered. Denying invites correction into our lives. These corrections are typically not well-received by the person who is being corrected, similar to how children don't like to get spanked.

There are those who say with apparent and utter certainty in their hearts and minds that "there is no god". Yet, I never would want to deny the freewill right of that belief to anyone. The belief that there is no god is each our own choice and each of us may do as we wish with that right. However, it is important for you to realize that regardless of which position you choose, it will not alter the reality of whether or not the Creator exists.

Here is the problem with such a distinct level of mental certainty: If we have decided in our minds that there is absolutely no possibility that a god exists, then we will disregard any possible evidence that makes the possibility of a Creator evident to us. This means that we choose to close our eyes when we see something that we choose to not agree with, even though it is clearly true. Doing this makes us wrong, incorrect, ignorant, foolish, and downright stupid.

Having an absolute belief that something is only one way is a common practice and it is seen in both the Church and in the secular evolutionary science circles. This type of lack of objectivity is commonplace throughout our world. When we have so strongly chosen this absolute path, then we have shut ourselves off from considering true information that might be presented to us at some point in the future. In this way, most of us have barred ourselves from seeing truth and being correct. This leaves us with being in the uncomfortable situation of being incorrect, which is more commonly known as being *wrong*. The only absolute is truth and we must find that truth or we will be absolutely without truth.

When we approach life in an absolute manner that is void of truth, then it is already decided in our minds that only *particular* information that *we* want to hear is relevant to us, and thus, we voluntarily disregard all other relevant information. This is true for both information that opposes our views, and for information that agrees with our views. In other words, if someone is trying to propose a theory, and then solid evidence of opposition is presented to them, then the true evidence will be ignored so that the desired belief can remain intact within the mind of the person proposing the erred theory. This common behavior puts us in the oscillation that we spoke of earlier, where we are out of harmony with the order of Creation. Anytime we are out of synchronization with the order of Creation, *we* are violating our own bodies and our own right of free will.

Anytime we conclude anything in an absolute manner and reject evidence contrary to what we have seen and come to believe as true, we have shut ourselves off from actual truth and have likely chosen to believe lies. These could seem to be strong words since we have been talking about an *absolute* superiority of the Creator; however, nowhere in anything that has been written in this book have we discussed denying good evidence. In fact, it is quite the contrary. Someone who believes in what is true will never silence a critic, other than with truth, and they will typically *invite* opposing views as a test against their own ideas and views.

If a "critic" presents evidence, it must be examined and analyzed truthfully and it must be fully considered. If and when the evidence is found to be nonsense, it can be proven so and can be balanced with utter honesty and pure truth. If this is not done and their information is not considered, then *you* have chosen to be a liar and to believe lies because you are *unwilling* to consider alternate proposals. You have caused yourself voluntary blindness, and you will be incapable of seeing the truth when the truth sits before your very own eyes. *All* evidence must be considered! However, we must realize that just because someone presents their seemingly compelling evidence does not mean that the evidence has been truthfully presented.

Few people have a true ability to be honest enough to consider *all* of the evidence. This is because doing so forces us to have to admit to our own errors in thinking. Sadly, the more we practice denying what is true, then the more errors we will make; and the more errors we make, the more out of harmony with order we are, and the more we will practice denying what is true. Thus, we have deliberately trapped ourselves in an inescapable spiral of doom until we decide to embrace the light of Truth.

The more disorder we have in our lives, then the more strife we will have; and the more troubles and strife we have, the more pain we will have and the less healthy our bodies will be. When we're feeling low, our denial of truth is even greater because we have built our life upon what is not true.

Whether it is the superiority of the Creator or the simple facts that surround our lives, when we choose to deny anything that is true, we put ourselves in a state of mental oscillation that causes us health and life problems. We pray to have these problems corrected and then fight the solutions when those solutions are set in our path for us, and then we further go on to consider those solutions to be obstacles. If you pray to be saved from your torment and then the sea parts before you, but you are afraid and you decide that it is too dangerous to pass through the parted sea, then you have rejected the solution to your problem.

We must give the Creator permission to intervene in our lives in a positive manner by us first removing the sources of trouble from our lives. If we ask for good things to occur in our lives but we refuse to reject the sources of our troubles, then *we* are trying to stop the Creator's correction to our lives. The corrections are *required* in order for us to move on in life and have our prayers for good things answered. We give the Creator permission or reason to do *good* things for us, first by us removing the sources of our troubles from our lives, and then by asking for good things.

Chapter 7

Seeing Through the Fog of Science

We place things or idols, including religion, as the focal point of our lives rather than having the Creator be our focal point. We derive our focal points from various sources and then believe that we are "enlightened" through our focal points.

We feel that we need a focal point such as an abstract idol or statue for our spirituality. All too often these false focal points are needed because they are constant reminders to us of what we are supposed to think about. However, these focal points often become the *focus* of our admiration, rather than being the *reminder of* what they represented to begin with.

An area where focal points are predominantly used in effort to achieve peace of soul, is with certain physical or mental exercises, such as meditation and yoga. In that sort of meditation, we seek to empty our minds of everything and hold it blank, or free, while we meditate and are not seeking answers to the root of our troubles. Many people believe there is some sort of mystical power in these activities that will bring on deeper spirituality, when in truth they do not. Do not misunderstand this, it's good to get quiet and release all of the troubles we see or experience in our lives. But, to believe that these focal points are some secret passage to enlightenment or a mystical experience, steps over the bounds of what is true and rational.

It's not bad for a person to be alone and dedicate themselves to prayer or meditation briefly each day. But it's better to live your prayer actively and be at one with those around you, rather than being at one with yourself while alone and away from others all of the time. Our ability to communicate with others is a gift that we should utilize and celebrate!

If you take the time to take a brief look at the average lifespans of those who take part in solitary meditative activities you will quickly find that there is little if anything to be gained by godless meditation with regard to your life's longevity. Additionally, the health of a person who simply takes good care of themselves is at least as good as the health of those who take part in meditative practices, and maybe even better.

Saying that meditation does not extend life substantially, if at all, is not saying that you cannot or should not do these things. But rather, what we are trying to establish here is that we do not need to follow some obscure rituals for longevity and peace of heart and mind. Do these things if you wish, but do not expect your joy, peace, and healing to originate from those activities.

The activities done in the "spiritual energy" trends are not what make us healthy. We are designed for love, and those who have much joy in their lives and who have mastered their ability to live in truth and forgive others, typically outlive those who do not. People who have been alive and healthy for above-average lifespans often attribute their longevity to any number of their habits; when in truth it was their attitude that brought them long life. Our mental attitude is reflected in our eating habits and other habits that we have. This is why our habits (what we do) are often believed to be the cause of a long or short lifespan. Our habits certainly matter, but not as much as our mental attitude or the way that we think matters. Our thinking is the source of all of our actions, including what we eat. Our thinking also has tremendous effect on our biochemistry.

During my years in various engineering fields, nothing was more apparent to me than design and its purpose. Sure, someone can argue that things can be used for something other than what they have initially been designed for, but the item typically will not be as useful or efficient when used for things for which it was not designed. We are beings designed with intent. Our physical Creation has obvious intent, purpose, and design. When we set a focal point other than the Creator, those focal points become idols to us. Doing so violates our design.

When we violate our design, we degrade our health and shorten our lifespan. You will recognize this everywhere you look once you consider it and are sensitive to this possibility.

If we need to depend upon meditation and our vain focal points in order to relax, then we are missing the point. It's okay to do so, but to depend upon meditation or some other means of mental distraction is nothing more than that—a mental distraction.

What empty meditation does sometimes do is to get us out of our problems long enough so that we can see clearly enough to be able to detect the actual cause of our tension. This is where properly understanding prayer is of tremendous value to you. Prayer and meditation is a time where we simply need to clear and quiet our minds.

There is no need to practice empty meditation to detect our problems and purify our lives, because we can do this by simply repeatedly asking ourselves, "What caused this?" for each new level of cause we see, and we must keep doing so until we get to the root of it all, which is something that we seldom do. Doing so quiets the mind and focuses it on the *solutions* to your troubles.

Too often when we pray, we are praying and dwelling on our problems and we end up placing *all* of our focus on those problems as we pray. In doing this, our problems have become our focal point. When we focus on our problems, it only serves to give those problems more power over us and over our mind. Our focal point should not be nature or Creation, or some mental or physical idol, but rather, our only focal point should be the obvious endless nature of the Creator and Truth.

Always Looking for a Secret

Our false need for a concrete focal point is closely tied to *mystery*, and since mysteries and secrets are not specifically tangible concepts, we have a tendency to place mystery into objects such as statues or crystals. Mankind has a natural gravitation towards wondering about things and contemplating the awesome magnificence of the Heavens—We are intrigued with what we cannot easily explain, but we're typically not as interested in something once we think we know everything about it. We often use objects as our focal point, or as a point of reminder for us of what the focal point represents. When "mystery" is bound to an object in this way, then that object becomes an intriguing idol of our affection. When done properly, the focal point we choose can also be a technique of believing for us.

Our desire to seek answers to mystery is where the idolatry recorded in the Bible has stemmed from. Very early on in the accounts recorded in the Bible and other ancient writings, many people lacked the ability to think beyond the concrete, and they wanted a tangible connection and reminder to where they placed their admiration. Idolatry is nearly immediate relative to the entire history recorded in the Bible and other ancient writings, and it was a part of the reason for the Biblical flood of Noah. Within a few of hundred years after the flood, idolatry quickly became commonplace once again.

Eventually some of the idols were put aside and the people turned to nature after realizing that nature was closer to solving the mysteries they sought to know. The realization that—the idols that were shaped by the hand of man had no power—is recorded in the Bible and is said to have been realized by Abram (Abraham). Abram rejected the idea that the idols his father made and sold had any useful power. Abram also rejected the belief that *nature* was a god-like thing to be worshipped. While carved idols still persisted, once the realization came that serving idols was a foolish waste of time, then nature became the focal point for many would-be idol worshipers. The focus on nature was only slightly closer to understanding the mystery of our origins, but it still misses the point. An excessive focus on nature is still very prominent in these modern times. Later on in some recorded histories, allegedly starting with the era of the Greek thinkers and philosophers, "thought" became a predominant discussion of mystery. As each human blindness was revealed, our minds moved on to the next step towards understanding our true place in Creation.

We are always looking for a "secret" or some magical awakening. The magical awakening that we seek is truth *and* the ability to balance that truth. The reason that truth appears to be magical and is a difficult idea for most of us is because we have been lied to for so long that the utter simplicity of truth is radical and mysterious to us.

The dependability of truth is unlike the lies we all experience every day. The closer we get to what is proper, good, and true, then the more success we see in our lives. When we begin to grasp the idea, or concept, of truth, we then come upon the incomprehensible realization that a lifetime of inexhaustible intrigue and discovery stands before each one of us!

There has been a movement in the past several hundred years believing that if you think it, then it will come to you. Imagining that we can think something into our lives is closer to what is true than the past times of idolatry were, but it still terribly misses the mark.

There is no secret to any of this. It has been known for thousands of years. The only reason anything seems secret is because we have chosen to believe lies. Most of these relatively modern approaches are nothing more than hijacked Biblical information. If that is a part of the progression to get us all to understand, then so be it. But know this: None of these false ideas are needed, and the solution is free, fast, and simple! The solution that we are discussing throughout this book is also in perfect harmony with the Creator's words and the Christ's words in the Bible.

Natural "Sciences"

Naturalism or the natural sciences, including theories of evolution and the science of thought and the brain, are narrow and closed-minded approaches. All too often, in our feeble approaches to gain understanding, we refuse to evaluate all of the evidences that are laid out before us.

Evolution and the big bang have falsely laid claim to order. And the science of thought and the brain have laid claim to the functions of order in prayer. This hijacking of what is true has been a blind-spot for many people for a fair amount of generations. This will continue to build and will gain strength of blindness so long as we refuse to, or neglect to, teach what is true to our children. It will also continue to build when we ourselves refuse or neglect to embrace what is true.

How The Daughter of Evolution Affected You

This book is about understanding prayer and how to make it work. *Doubt* plays an enormous role in the success and failure of our prayers. Unless you are able to understand the part, which is best stated as the "What caused this?" part, you will continue to fail in your prayers. The "cause" part of "What caused this?", with regard to a supreme Creator, refers to our doubt.

Did the father of evolution have unending faith and belief in an infinite Creator? Based upon his own words, not likely. His inability to understand his own errors, and the errors of the world that surrounded him, caused him a great deal of doubt. He searched for evidence of origins and found very compelling information, but his doubt skewed his analysis of that information. His doubt has spread throughout much of the world and has now passed through several generations, and his words have affected us. When we couple this together with the Santa Claus Effect, we have destroyed much of the pure and innocent child-like faith of humanity.

When we read the written thoughts of those who initiated the evolution perspective, we can detect a great amount of bitterness. As always, the intently religious people fought vehemently against any proposal that challenged their own religious beliefs. Rather than embracing the challenge, and coming up with a good sound understanding of *all* evidence, those who did not agree with the new evolutionary proposals did nothing more than shout louder about how wrong they felt these new naturalist proposals were. This caused them to ignore interesting fossil finds and diminish many of the fossils as mere fairy tales. This only served to embitter the positions held by those who were making the new evolutionary proposals that were based on biased agenda-driven interpretation of the evidence that was found. This caused those who were proposing the evolutionary-natural-progression model to dig their heels in deeply and fight more vehemently than the recklessly stubborn religious types who fought against them and their new proposals.

Because the Church and its supporters could not offer sound understanding or explanation to the naturalists who found beauty and diversity in the patterns of nature, the naturalists had nothing to fall back on when problems occurred in their personal lives. The rigid unyielding irrational positions and lack of understanding held by some members of the Church caused heavy doubt in the evolutionists' minds.

When the daughter of Darwin the naturalist researcher had died, it only added to the frustration of the man. Sadly, the Church had no better answers for him than he could obtain from his blind observations of nature. The death of his daughter likely added to the bitterness he began to hold within himself towards the Church and its supporters. The death of this daughter may very well have been the breaking point that caused the man to take an unrelenting pursuit of impressing the godless conclusions of his research onto his peers, and subsequently onto the world. While his research was articulately done, his conclusions were flawed, thus causing increasing doubt to be cast over the world with regard to a supreme Creator. His observational research was accurate. However, his conclusions were speculative and have wrongly come to be accepted as "absolute fact".

Since those who were interested in this sort of research were from the scholarly factions of society, the naturalist origins became a race of superiority, and "religious" attitude was right in the mix with it all. For some reason, we humans have a strong desire to be above others. So, if we can show that somehow we are better than other people, then we typically seize the opportunity. This is exactly what happened with evolution.

It is important to note that the concept of evolution existed long before the middle of the nineteenth century. The difference was that in the nineteenth century someone had taken time to write down, in a book, what seemed to be a compelling argument by concisely listing what appeared to be sound points. This was done at a time when the minds of the people were ripe for the picking and automatic printing presses were becoming commonplace.

This was not a strategic ploy by this person, it just happened to line up in a particular way, at a particular time that was appealing to the arrogance of mankind. It was also at a time when printing and publishing was able to be done at a reasonable cost, quickly, and effectively. His information and speculations were spread abroad quickly, none of which speaks for the accuracy of his assumptions and conclusions. All of this caused an enormous amount of doubt in the minds of many as to whether or not a purposeful Creator exists. The importance of understanding the root origin of this particular version of humanity's doubt must *not* be ignored. The daughter of evolution may very well be the key that unlocked the abyss where this ugly beast of doubt was held captive. The evolution belief has become the focal point of many, especially those who have needlessly rejected the Creator.

The Elite

Once natural progression was introduced to the intellectual elite, they took these naturalist theories and ran with them as a point of elitist arrogance. They wanted to believe that their minds were further progressed or evolved than other people's minds were. These theories grouped people into racial categories, thus enabling the intellectual elite to take the position that their particular race was the more advanced and progressed race. These relatively new theories had no concrete human evidence at that time, causing a competition in a quest to find the proposed "missing links" to human evolution that, to their own minds, would prove their false evolutionary superiority.

Some of the examination of evidence was conducted in collaboration with universities during the nineteenth and twentieth centuries, and was done mostly from a naturalist perspective. Any university or person that could find evidence of evolutionary links that were geographically nearest to their location for their race of people, would, in their own minds, prove their evolved mental superiority to the world. This allowed them funding from government grants and from artifact sales to wealthy people or groups who in their own arrogance wanted to be able to prove themselves as superior over the other races of the world. They wanted to believe that the other races were not as evolved, meaning that the other races were inferior. Financial incentives to find the "missing link" were offered in the form of funding or financial reward from the sale of a prized artifact that might be found. This financial reward created hoaxes and misinformation that was presented for the purpose of financial gain and/or enhanced social status.

These superior/inferior beliefs still exist in modern times, but are cloaked by means of offering the "less-evolved inferior" peoples the right to say that civilization started in the "cradle of civilization" where they are from. If we are forthright and honest about this, it means that the promoters of evolution believe that the "less-evolved inferior" people are the "originals", and thus they are not as far evolved as the promoters of evolution are. These deceitful arrogant practices, that were financially and agenda driven, still exist today.

The "science" of evolution became far more about prestige and money than it ever was about finding what is true. Sadly, the greed people have for money and status is often the driving force behind their agenda and dishonesty. Some of these hoaxes still exist and are accepted as "factual" today. Some hoaxes are blindly referred to in textbooks and taught by those who support the theories but who have not adequately researched the topic themselves to filter out the hoaxes. If you are misled by these hoaxes and your faith waivers, then it very much will affect your prayers.

It's understandable that there are many who support these theories who would try to make accusation that these words you are reading here are biased and unfounded attacks against what they see as absolute and utter true evidence. But, while their finds are abundant, the progressive evolutionary *conclusions* that they suggest are sketchy at best. And the conclusions' theories are very blindly analyzed as well. All of the evidence is analyzed with a bias towards trying to prove that these theories are absolutely true. A bias also exists because they have fully invested their hearts, minds, lives, reputations, and money in their belief in evolution. If most of the people researching had to admit to their errors, their funding would quickly be gone and many of them would promptly lose their jobs.

It would be refreshing to have any evidence that is presented, be objectively examined so that we could realize the full and true accounts of the meaning of the intriguing evidence that has already been found and that will be found in the future.

People often wonder why I stress this point. It is because the elitist attitude that we have all been subject to is selfishly agenda-driven. Many of the people who promote these theories flaunt their ridiculous scholarly degrees to display their supposed knowledge and superiority, rather than being honest about the information that they have gathered. Then those of us who are more complacent tend to be drawn into the arrogance of their elitist mentality, causing us to believe in their flawed, biased, agenda-driven conclusions. This causes us to doubt the existence of an intentional Creator, and in turn, our doubt sabotages our prayers.

I do not suggest that anyone believe something just because someone said so. I firmly believe that we must test *all* reasonable proposals and conclusions whether they are Biblical or "Scientific".

Your Faith, Evolution, and the Realm of the Wealthy

We face a severe faith deficit in the world, much of which is perpetuated by contemporary science; your understanding of that point is critical to your future success. There's always a risk of corruption in life when money and arrogance are involved. It happened with the Church at various times over many centuries, and for the last few hundred years it has been happening in the world of science.

When the weight of the investment of life, heart, mind, money, and reputation in a scientific point of view is so heavy, then the humiliation that is felt from admission of error is also very great. The people who have spent their lives developing incorrect proposals do not want to lose face in this regard. If it were proven that some of these scientific "findings" are incorrect conclusions, and that some are even hoaxes, and many of the other findings are greatly misinterpreted, it would destroy the reputations of many people. People build their entire lives around these erred beliefs, and their entire life's work pertains only to their belief system. Any admission of error will destroy their fragile dominion. Their denial is much like when a very young child with chocolate on their face will deny having eaten the candy bar when they know they were not supposed to eat it. But with adults, the innocence of youth is no longer an excuse for the lies and inaccuracies.

Money plays a big role in this type of investment of life. Enormous amounts of funding from both government grants and private funds are granted to universities and researchers to further the investors' points of view. It's not necessarily that people are becoming rich from this, but so long as they are able to produce the supposed evidence, or at least reasonably promise to produce it to prove the theories, their livelihood will continue to be funded by wealthy sources. This is true whether those financial sources are government or private entities. There is nothing wrong with getting grants for research, provided that you are being honest.

Money itself is not corrupt, but the way we use it often is. If we use our money to hire someone to prove our point, it is likely we will believe that any evidence they find is what they claim it to be—even if it is wrong. Their claims will typically be what they are being hired and paid to search for and prove. In this way, we hire people to find what *we* want them to find. Sometimes we refuse to see their errors, and our refusal to see is mostly due to our financial, emotional, and social status investment. It is due to our arrogance.

Arrogant approaches that utilize money and prestige to further the agenda of being able to place one's self over other people and races, have brought about a whole new level of arrogance and utter contempt of Creation. The contempt shown towards the Creator occurs because we blindly believe in the evolutionary natural progression of mankind, even though it is clearly lacking a great deal of explanation. In other words, we are *knowingly* ignoring the massive oversights in the theories, while, at the same time, we are ignoring the obviousness of an intentionally Created existence.

Because the lies and inaccuracies perpetrated by some of the people from the churches did not bring comfort and love to people, it is easy to see why the people had turned away from the Church and the Creator, and then went on to embrace these newer theories of superiority. The superiority that is claimed through using these evolutionary theories is identical in nature to the superiority claimed by some of the Church leaders' arrogance that occurred at various times in the preceding centuries.

Any feelings of superiority that we have over anyone else are nothing more than our own arrogance. Money allows for people who are arrogant and happen to have much money, to build themselves up in their own minds to be of far more value than what they actually are, relative to others. When the opportunity arose for the investment of wealth to prove superiority, it was embraced with a level of fervor that is seldom seen in humanity. We essentially buy our *arrogance* and believe it to be *confidence*.

Even though, many years later, as some of the evolution "discoveries" were proven to be hoaxes, the lies and inaccuracies in those theories proposed in the past had already taken root throughout the world. It would be unbearable for those who embraced such inaccuracies if they had to admit to their errors.

Severe humiliation would be felt by them with regard to their financial and reputation status if the errors were broadly exposed.

Some of the original fraudulent findings paved the way for enormous amounts of money to be poured into the quest to find the "missing links" of the proposed natural progression of man; and it is likely that this is going to continue into the future. Also, those who have chosen to close their eyes to the inconsistencies within the inaccurate conclusions of these findings will *continue* to be duped by the inaccurate conclusions of the findings. Money and time *will* continue to be poured into the study of evolution, and with every dollar and every minute spent, the stakes become higher for those who are trying to prove this to be true and themselves to be correct. This will be done by them even if it takes being dishonest and defiling the truth to do so.

If you are wrong, nothing you do can make that wrong belief become correct. It can only *appear* to be correct in your own mind when truth is *hidden* and *ignored*. Much of what is found in archeological digs is real, but the *interpretations* of the findings are highly imaginative due to having the wrong focal point.

All of the arrogance and money involved in the naturalist theories have served to add to the doubt of mankind; doubt that has also been fed and nurtured through the arrogance that has resided within the Church for thousands of years. Humanity's naturalist arrogance has turned into an all-out assault on anyone who stands in position of the understanding that there is a Creator. All of the evolution-speculation being forced on humanity has caused tremendous doubt in the innocent hearts and minds of many people. Doubt and prayer *do not* mix!

The attitudes that arose from naturalist theories about the origins of man only served to fuel the uncertainty that so many people already had due to their pre-existing blindness. Much of the blindness was handed down from the religious factions of the world due to some of the Church leaders' unyielding denial of evidence that appeared contrary to their often erred interpretation of the Bible. This brought about much doubt and ushered in a new and deeper level of the denial of a Creator. This doubt was due to the fact that the things the Bible said *appeared* to not make sense and have come to be disregarded as if they are mere fairytales when compared to the supposed evolutionary "evidence" that was found either lying on top of, or shallowly buried in, the ground. In the minds of many, this made the Bible appear to be contrary to the evolutionary evidence which it was being compared against. To its credit, the newly found evolutionary attitude served to partially open up the tightly closed minds of those who were superstitiously religious, and helped them to realize that much of what we experience is of our own making, rather than a punishment of the Creator. But, for the most part, any of us who jump on the evolution bandwagon are doing the same thing with evolution that we did with religion; which is to say, we have similar blind-faith in what we believe, and we fail to demand full explanation of all evidence of the proposed conclusions. Instead we blindly follow whatever the "scholars" say.

Typically the naturalist point of view has been a creatorless view and has caused many people to doubt the existence of a Creator. Much of their doubt would likely not have happened if the Church had been truly honest and open over the years. But people were demanded to believe and do as they were told by Church leaders, rather than trying to understand more about what they were seeing. These two differing views do not reconcile. Because the Bible is incorrectly thought to be the only source for the Church's information, the text is frequently misinterpreted. Whenever the Bible was misinterpreted, the misinterpretation caused it to be discredited in the minds of many people as the naturalist's made their discoveries and then subsequently made those discoveries known to the public.

Sadly, we often lack the ability to see the truth through the fog of our own inaccurate beliefs and theories. We have left ourselves in the dark by thinking that we have seen the light when we actually have not. In this case we have set our focal point on naturalist evolution.

The Dawn of Enlightenment

While the concept of enlightenment and understanding was nothing new in the seventeenth and eighteenth centuries, that era did somewhat benefit people because it brought to the forefront of the minds of doubters that their ability to use their mind could greatly alter their own lives. There was a diverse group of people during this time that had come to a point where they no longer wanted to accept the abuses of certain arrogant community and Church leaders who sought to suppress them and their thoughts. In many ways, it was good for people to take a stand against the tyranny that was all too commonly found within some Church leaders over the years, as well as the tyranny that was found in the various government territories that the people lived in.

However, the enlightenment movement didn't stop at merely thinking that the Church and governments might be incorrect. It went far beyond and began a new movement of thinking, which is co-mingled with enlightenment and it was called the Age of Reason.

The Age of Reason

The Age of Reason was truly nothing new. It had been in existence for thousands of years. The difference was that during this particular period of the revival of freethinking, printing presses had become readily available to make a multitude of copies of the books written by those involved in the movement. This allowed the books to be seen by many people cost-effectively and very quickly. This is as opposed to the costly and tedious alternate task of manually transcribing text onto stone tablets and scrolls by hand, letter by letter, in order to make additional copies. This relatively new form of publishing greatly accelerated the free-flow distribution of people's thoughts, and allowed widespread sharing of the enlightenment philosophies.

People who indulged in this practice are commonly referred to as "Freethinkers." Everything we have been talking about in this chapter was happening somewhat simultaneously, and it was "freethinking" that helped to perpetuate the theory of human natural progression evolution.

Once the evolutionary natural progression theory took root in the freethinker circles, they began to "reason" through everything in their own minds in order to come to what they felt were logical conclusions. This brought about the term "science of the mind" or "science of thought" or "thought science"; and thus, to them all thinking turned into a scientific exercise. As the people of that time started to open their minds and reason through the evidence with their own minds, they failed to consider *all* of the information and were willing to readily dismiss information that did not seem to fit the puzzle that they were choosing to build in their own minds. Logical conclusions cannot truly be done while ignoring any facts—*all* available information *must* be considered and thoroughly analyzed.

When people use terms such as truth, reason, logic, freethinking, and enlightenment, we must be very certain that we do not become trapped in *their* determination of what these words mean—this is yet another reason to take definitions seriously and seek out the source information when in question. Look these things up for yourself if you are uncertain. *Logic* has the ability to come to incorrect conclusions, but *truth* does not.

Free thinking is nothing more than releasing your mind from believing something that is "common knowledge". But *true* enlightenment is when you actually understand it. For many of the people who became involved in this movement, much of what they were thinking "freely" about was not built upon truth. This is because their freethinking was often done only to defy conventional wisdom. Thus, they trapped themselves with *their* version of "freethinking". They would regard the way they saw things as "logical", and then they would reason through that and call it truth. At that point they felt that they were "enlightened". Their ability to break through their prior blindnesses allowed them to advance their thinking from where it had been, but not to *true* enlightenment. A true, open mind is a mind that seeks truth *regardless* of our own errors being exposed. Anything else is a closed mind.

When we "expand our mind" or "think freely" it is usually done by opposing conventional thinking, and typically only for that purpose. We should not oppose conventional thinking that is true and completely fits. But we should oppose conventional thinking and then exercise "open minds" when there are holes in a theory and/or the theory doesn't explain everything it claims to explain.

During the Age of Reason many people began to realize and understand that most of their problems were within their own power to correct. They also realized that they were not necessarily as wicked as what was proposed by some Church representatives and supporters. For the many people who were living guilt-ridden lives this was a very liberating realization. But sadly, rather than using their guilt as the warning signal that it is, in many cases they had done nothing more than jump from the frying pan into the fire. So absolute was their thinking, that no level of truth could break what they perceived as truth. They perverted truth through their acceptance of what they felt was "logic", and then reasoned that through and called it truth, which, subsequently redefined truth in their own minds. Often they referenced the Bible in a positive manner when they spoke, but in their arrogance they were bent on the belief that they had evolved and that their minds were superior, which conflicted with their Biblical references.

True enlightenment can only be found in the acceptance of truth, which is something that is written all throughout the Bible.

This can be easily found in the Bible when you realize that it is in the Bible, even though it is not referred to as "enlightenment". A focal point of "reason" without truth is futile.

Enlightenment is Not Magical Mystery

The meditation practices of the eastern religions are often thought of as "enlightenment". Many of us want to emulate the "peace" that the people who practice these forms of meditation appear to have. We want to emulate this because we want peace in our own lives. There is also an amount of "success" that is achieved by some who practice freethinking which has an appeal to the others who see the success experienced by some of these freethinkers. We all want to feel at peace and enlightened, and we often look to others, who *appear* to be at peace and enlightened, for our guidance.

Both of these forms of "enlightenment" are appealing to people who are struggling in life. When people who are struggling try to emulate the behavior of those who they see as "enlightened", it creates two very prominent problems. First, those who are supposedly "enlightened" may not be enlightened at all. Often they're hiding behind what they do to be enlightened, which appears successful to us. The second problem is if the person that is being observed actually *is* enlightened, then those who are seeing what the supposed enlightened ones are doing may be completely misinterpreting the situation. Often, actions are a result of a cause, but we see the actions as the cause that will bring about a result and therefore we miss the point entirely. This means that when someone appears to be relaxed and we see them doing some leisure activity, then we wrongly understand the scenario as the activity is giving them relaxation, when it typically is not. Instead, it is their ability to relax that allows them to enjoy the activity. How often have we ourselves gone on vacation or done some "leisure activity" but could not relax?

When we see people who *we* believe are enlightened, we all too often believe that their enlightenment comes from what they do. But if they actually *are* enlightened, then what they do is the result of being enlightened. What often happens is that a person sees someone who is actually enlightened, and then they imitate the behavior so that they appear to be enlightened too. Later they proceed to guide others to the enlightenment that they believe they have achieved. Again, this means that it is a case of "the blind leading the blind".

It's important to note that just because we think we're enlightened, does not mean that we are enlightened. "Enlightenment" is not some magical thing that is unattainable to the common man where we must meditate and hum for countless hours to achieve it. Enlightenment refers to being enlightened. To be enlightened is to have light. The light that is referred to in the "enlightenment" being sought by those who claim to be enlightened is the light that is referred to in the Bible. Some of the leaders in the enlightenment era likely had it correct, but many of the people following them did not properly understand the message. You can obtain this light while serving your fellow man at a restaurant, or driving a tractor in the field, or sitting at your desk while you're working, or any other time that you allow your mind to believe what is true. *Truth* is the light that we seek. Without it we can only pretend to be enlightened. No amount of study, arrogance, or meditation will produce an enlightened mind when the mind is void of truth.

Enlightenment is achieved when you have learned how to balance all available facts on a scale of truth without the biases and arrogance of trying to assertively force your point and your erred ways.

Relaxation and meditation are not the cause of enlightenment, but rather they are a result of enlightenment. This is because enlightenment causes you to be relaxed. When, of your own freewill, you have received the free gift of truth, then you will find the "light" in enlightenment. This is the light that so many people seek, but fail to achieve due to their attempts to start with the result and then achieve the cause by means of the result—a result that they improperly obtained to begin with.

Believing that you are "enlightened" when you actually are not, will only hold you back from your best and from the joy that you deserve. Saying you are enlightened does not make you enlightened, but being true does.

Know Me Better

The obstacle that blocks our ability to be truly enlightened is our arrogance and our believing lies. When we ignore the plain evidence that stands before us and we choose to gravitate towards what is *not* true, then these lies put us in a degraded state in our own hearts and minds. When we are degraded, we try by means of our arrogance to build ourselves up to be what we are not. Then we hide behind that arrogance—we hide behind money and prestige. It's not wrong to have money or prestige, but when we use it to hide our true selves then it is bad.

We must allow people to know who we are rather than hiding the best part of us. Our anger, frustration, strife, and depression all come from ourselves not knowing or showing who we truly are. This doesn't mean that we should dominate people and push them out of the way, but it does mean that we should take our stand and our rightful place in our own lives and be who we truly are. And then let our light shine to reveal the light of truth within us.

We don't have to make claims that we are "enlightened" when we have truth. Someone who shouts from the mountain tops how enlightened they are is obviously not enlightened. Enlightenment is not something you brag about. Rather, it is a state of being in truth and will be obvious to those around us. But be warned! Those who do not yet understand what truth really is will look at you as if you're trying to show them up and make them look bad when you have truth within you. If you are trying to make others look bad, then you're a despicable human being and you are not full of light, and thus, you are not "enlightened". If this is your case, then you promptly need to change that about yourself! But if you have the light of truth within you, then by natural comparison, your light of truth will make anyone who fails to embrace the truth, appear as less when compared to your acceptance of truth.

When we have truth, we need only to live by that truth, and then our light will become apparent in everything that we do. People will see the light in us and will want to emulate that light. This is why, in the Bible, the Christ was willing to allow his accusers to destroy his body through torture on a wood cross. It was an effort to show us the incalculable value of Truth. Sadly, most of us miss the beauty of this simple but painful lesson. And we also miss the richness of its teaching because we have bound ourselves with the blindness of lies and untrue things.

The focal points and "enlightenment" that society indulges in, come from many different sources; and while these are not necessarily in themselves wrong, they certainly are not how we achieve true enlightenment. We cannot achieve purity in prayer when we have incorrect beliefs and false focal points. If our focal points are not truth itself and the Creator, then can we really expect the Creator to accept our prayers as *pure* offerings? Can we really expect prayers that are built upon a false premise to be answered as we would hope? We cannot!

Chapter 8

The Path to Changing Your Attitude

We mentioned earlier about effects that our thinking and words can have on our bodies and minds. In this chapter, we are going to go more deeply into that. This chapter is critical with regard to prayer and its relationship to healing and answers to your prayers. Every aspect of your life will be affected when you understand the power of what we are discussing here. This is where your prayers will begin to shine and be received as a pleasing offering to the Creator.

One of the elements that arose in the "enlightenment age of reason" is what they called vibrations (the vibratory nature of our bodies). This is where the terms "bad vibes" and "good vibes" originate from. Our ability to change ourselves is often discussed in the Bible, but not in a technical or scientific manner as we would think of it today. All of the enlightenment movement's thought science is nothing new. It's just that in a relatively modern era we have been able to research the physical nature of things down to the molecular, atomic, and even sub-atomic levels.

We have been given the great advantage of microscopes, electron microscopes, electricity, and many other brilliant inventions with which to research and make evident our theories and proposals. Yet, even with all of this technology we still allow our own personal beliefs to blind us from what is true even when various known evidence indicates otherwise.

Consider the effects that our thinking and words can have on our bodies and minds. We often meditate to relax ourselves, but we fail to come up with any lasting results. If you want to meditate, then meditate on this: Contemplate the repetitive order of everything that you see around you, including people and our bodies. And then realize that just because we can explain something and how it works, does not mean that it was not Created.

The topic of us being Created is being heavily discussed in this book because if we are not Created, then we truly have no need to pray to anyone or for anything. There are many indicators and testimonial examples from people showing that prayer works very well when you understand it. To ignore all of these indicators about prayer is both ignorant and foolish. The fact that prayer works, becomes obvious when you understand it and know what to look for. If you imagine and insist that we are not Created, then you will have blind spots with regard to prayer and its effectiveness in your life. These blind spots will inhibit your life and your prayers. Even if you're only slightly in doubt that we are Created, you have, by doubting, put your prayers at serious risk of not being as effective as you desire them to be.

Always remember that the risk is not that your prayers won't be answered, but rather, it is that you will miss the answers occurring because you have rendered yourself blind through the doubt that you hold within you.

Making the assumption that we were not Created, and basing it upon the notion that we understand how our bodies work, is as ridiculous as taking apart a car to understand how it was put together, and then assuming that it evolved on its own because you believe you found a more primitive looking model in the scrapyard. Just because we can understand something does not mean that it is not Created by someone. And just because we found a fossil that we believe appears more primitive than the animals or people that we see today, does not mean that fossil is being interpreted accurately.

Once you've cleared your mind from all of the other clutter, and then thought about the vastness of the repetitions and consistencies within everything that we see that is Created, you will quickly begin to realize the nature of *intent* in all of Creation.

Understanding that *intent* exists is very important. If you cannot accept intention, then you will fail in many areas of life and suffer the consequence of you choosing to not grasp *intent*. Even young children get the raw concept of intent, but our doubt and skepticism as adults blinds us from seeing the intent that is inherent in everything around us. It's natural for us to understand intent. If we see a straight line or unusual geometric shapes in natural settings, we typically assume that it is *man-made*. Why is this? It's because we detect *design* and *intent*. If something is *man-made* then it has been *designed*.

While there appears to be a certain randomness to nature, there is always cause for what we see, and these causes do not necessarily show intent. This is because some things just occur because of the nature of their design. What we perceive as "randomness" is by design. If diversity was limited, then we would all look identical. But, complex things, like our bodies, have a repetitious and reproductive nature that shows intent, purpose, *and* design. The repetitious nature of Creation is seen in complex organisms, and has been occurring since before humans were Created.

The archeological findings that are unearthed are often misinterpreted. Even the random effects of nature testify to the power of order that we have been discussing. We look at things in nature that seem to have randomly occurred due to environmental effects, but even in this we see the repetitious nature of order. The repetitious nature of order that we are discussing here doesn't even begin to touch on the order that is also seen within the cosmos of space, nor has it touched on the smaller parts of Creation down to the atomic level and below.

The order and organization that we see cannot be denied by any sane human being. It is so overwhelmingly evident everywhere we look, and in everything we touch, and in everything we do, that to deny order is to be *deliberately* blind and ignorant. Considering the magnitude of order that surrounds us, including the order seen in our bodies, we would be remiss in our duties if we did not discuss the level of importance that this order has.

Are We Machines?

Machines are tools. We can make machines to play music by imitating or even creating new sounds, but in the end, this type of machine is just a tool to create sound. The same goes for computers. Computers do not have the same ability as humans do, but with all of the information that can be stored with them, computers become very useful tools for us to retain and retrieve information.

Our bodies are machines that are far more complex and sophisticated than anything that any human has ever been able to mechanically build or even imagine. Our bodies are chemical machines and they are made of chemicals that produce chemical reactions. It is these extremely well-ordered machines in which we each reside.

With regard to having your prayers answered and being able to be healed, it is very important for you to understanding the basics about the chemical order by which your body-machine functions.

To help prevent anyone from misinterpreting what is stated here, and then trying to use that misunderstanding outside of what we are discussing—about understanding that our bodies were Created with a tremendous amount of order by the Creator—know this: Your level of success in prayer will be greatly compromised because you will be out of harmony with order if you choose to deny any of the evidence that surrounds us all. Denying the surrounding evidence causes your prayer results to be left wanting and fall short of what your prayer results could have been. I can find no such evidence that denies the obviousness of the order of Creation without closing my eyes and knowingly choosing to believe things that are not true. The truths are obvious and are all around us. This is true without us even having to use the Bible as our evidence. To see this, all that we need to do is to look around. A tremendous amount of this evidence is found right in our very own chemical-machine bodies. Everything we do, experience, and think, affects the chemistry of our bodies.

When we're out of harmony with truth and order, we put our bodies at great risk by chemically degrading them through the chemical reactions that are a result of our poor thinking. Praying for healing while being in doubt and inner turmoil, is like trying to put out a house fire with gasoline—it just won't work.

Why Body Chemistry Matters to You

There is no question or debate in the Church or in the scientific community with regard to the chemical nature of our bodies. Since this consensus so overwhelmingly understands that we are chemical machines, we need to investigate the ramifications of our chemistry.

We are not going to get technical here. Instead, we will examine the obvious. These simple truths will give you a great boost in understanding how to get your prayers answered with regard to healing.

Since your body is a chemical machine, you must realize that the nature of chemistry is action, reaction, and chain reaction (That is to say cause and effect—Push something and it moves!) This is very important and extremely simple to understand. In chemistry, because when something happens, it causes other things to react.

Since our bodies are chemical machines, everything we do and feel is the chemical reaction of cause and effect. The unspoken evolutionary naturalist perspective is the following: Because we can explain things, it means that we were not created.

If we are Created, we must be made of something or we would not be here. The "something" that we are made of is, in human language, described as "chemicals". Our ability to study and discover this does not mean that we were not Created, rather it is clear evidence of the obviousness of the deliberate intention of our Creation.

The importance of understanding that our chemical bodies are Created is this simple: When someone says some words to you, then those words cause vibrations in the air. These vibrations travel to your ear through the air and cause movement in the solid component parts of your ear. These solid parts are made of chemicals. Then the movement of the parts creates chemical signals. And through a series of chain reactions these chemical signals are sent to your brain. Then your brain processes the received information causing you to think about the spoken words that you just heard. This in itself is amazing, and it is far from being fully understood by anyone.

Based upon the analysis done by your thoughts about the words spoken to you, your brain sends out chemical signal chain reactions. These chemical signals create all of the chemical chain reactions that cascade throughout your entire body resulting in various effects. These various effects include electromagnetic emissions, goose bumps, feelings of warmth or cold, intended physical reactions such as movement of body parts, and involuntary movement of body parts from reflexes, plus many other reactions.

It's true that one word can cause this cascade of events to course throughout your entire body, in turn causing your body to generate various chemicals. The chemicals that are generated can either be damaging to, or good for, your body. When damaging chemicals are generated in your body, they are generated in response to what you heard or experienced. Hearing is a form of receiving or sensing something.

All of our other senses affect our body's chemistry in a similar way that our hearing does. All of our senses as well as the chemical reactions that take place in our bodies are forms of communication.

Each of our senses: *touch, taste, feel, smell,* and *hearing,* receive information from other people and from the surrounding environment. These senses create a cascade of chain reactions that reach our brain, and then the chain reactions are analyzed by our thoughts. Our thoughts then create an outward cascade response that is electrical, chemical, and physical. These responses are all obvious observations that have reliably and repeatedly been done in science and medical laboratories, and are proved evident by the fact that the cascade of responses occurs, such as when we move our hand or blink our eye lids in response to something.

At this point you might be asking, "What does this have to do with my prayers?" There are two aspects to this: The *natural-physical* aspect and the *thought* or *mind* aspect. Both aspects are very important.

First, we will examine the physical reaction aspects. The physical part affects our chemistry when outside information or sensations, such as words, are received. I have not been able to find any proof or evidence as to whether or not the word, or other outside signal, causes any adverse effects due to chemical reactions that occur while the signal is *on its way to* your brain after being sent from your sensing-receivers (ears, eyes, etc...) However, there is a great amount of certainty that what our mind does with those received words or signals has a tremendous amount of effect on our bodies.

The second aspect is our mental reaction. Our mental reaction is what sparks the chemical chain reaction that cascades out of our brain. It is here that our prayers and understanding of what is true have a tremendous impact on our lives, on our health, and on our well-being.

There has been a lot of speculation over the years, that the way we think affects our biochemistry. Since we know, understand, and have proven repeatedly that our thinking affects our biochemistry, it should not take much light to be shed on the subject to realize the extreme importance of the effect that your thoughts have on your health. Few people are foolish enough to challenge these findings. In recent times, we have had the opportunity to witness this live, firsthand, by looking into the brains and bodies of people being studied while utilizing our specialized scientific equipment. This can be done *while we live and breathe*, with little or no risk or harm to our bodies.

This specialized scientific equipment allows researchers to monitor the changes in our bodies while we think and indulge in certain thoughts or emotions. Our various emotions cause corresponding chemicals to be produced by our brains and bodies. With specialized imaging equipment we can detect these physical changes when they occur as a response to our emotions. We can view the changes in our brain *while* those changes are occurring. This live observation allows researchers to monitor the brain while the person being observed thinks about or watches various kinds of information, most notably highly emotional information.

Can We Feel Good by Doing Good?

Serotonin is a chemical in the body that is said to be the "feel-good" chemical and is believed that it and other chemicals are produced when we experience sensations that give us pleasure. The experiences include thinking, seeing, touching, tasting, smelling, and hearing good or pleasing things.

Many studies conducted on people have indicated that when we are allowed to do an act of kindness, our own feel-good chemicals are released according to the level of the act of kindness, thus giving us a corresponding feeling of "joy". Additionally, when a person *observes* a good deed or an act of kindness occurring, then the observer's "feel-good" chemicals are released also giving them a corresponding level of euphoria. We can make a safe assumption that the person who is receiving the kindness, also has some level of feel-good chemicals released in their body. When you break down the body strictly in a scientifically chemical and mechanical manner it's easy to see that such effects are not only plausible, but are glaringly evident.

Some people believe themselves to be "dependent" on drugs, alcohol, or have some other obsession. They have become dependent on the feelings received from the rush of feel-good chemicals created by indulging in their obsession. With such dependency situations, the chemicals are produced when the body experiences the sensations produced by satisfying the obsession. There's an additional complication that happens with some chemicals. People build up certain dependencies on foreign chemicals that are taken into their bodies from external sources in place of the natural chemicals normally being produced internally as a response to the person's perception.

In situations of prescription drug dependency, when we artificially induce feel-good chemicals into our bodies, it causes a situation where the body no longer senses the need to produce the naturally occurring body chemicals. Artificial induction of substitute chemistry can cause a type of chemical-atrophy from which the person may not as easily be able to recover. Our mind gets lazy and subsequently our body fails to produce the needed chemistry, eventually causing us to degrade. To some extent this is likely true even for substances such as alcoholic beverages.

Drug Dependency

As we discuss this section, recall the importance of *order* that we addressed earlier.

Addictions are always thought to be a bad thing. However, let's consider that "addiction" is not bad, but instead understand that it is *what* we are addicted to that's bad. When we're addicted to something, it's really the feelings that we have while we partake in the addiction-behavior that we are addicted to. We want to feel good. Please note that this is referring to addictive behavior rather than obsession.

A desire to feel good is natural in us. What we are trying to do when we are addicted is to find or feel joy. But true joy cannot be found by any false means of stimulation. False stimulation is only a rough approximation and a very badly imitated version of joy.

When a person is in a state of true joy, then their feel-good chemicals are most certainly going to be released in fairly large quantities. When true joy is the root cause of the release of someone's feel-good chemicals, then we will notice that more good choices were made in the person's life than there are good choices in the case of the chemicals coming from an imitated source of finding joy.

Whether the addiction is a chemical addiction of drugs or alcohol, or if it is a physical addiction of money, status, or some other false sensory perception, the happiness we feel will be fleeting at best. When we don't change our thinking, then in the long run the negative addiction destroys the person who has chosen the particular addiction as their source of feeling good.

Pure chemical addictions from drugs and alcohol create a false dependency on those chemicals. However, those dependencies are easily shaken when we understand that the real dependency being sought is the true feel-good chemicals that are produced by our brains and bodies.

Drugs and alcohol numb the senses and the underlying emotions. In fact, the term "narcotic" means to *numb*. When our senses are numbed, the external negative things that happen in our lives are dulled down, thus hiding the pain that is masked by the drugs and alcohol. When our troubles are masked in this way, it allows us to have the feel-good chemicals released in our bodies, but it is more important to understand that in such cases there are less feel-bad chemicals released in us, allowing us to feel better about ourselves. A reduction in feel-bad chemicals allows us to perceive that we feel better relative to how we previously felt before the reduction of feel-bad chemicals took place.

Everyone deserves to have feel-good chemicals released in their bodies. But, it is important to understand that the chemicals being released are not actually what make you feel good. Feeling good is the result of *actually* thinking good. When we take drugs or alcohol we tend to free our thinking and allow our true feelings to be expressed. When we do this we are relieved of our pent-up emotions and feelings and therefore we feel good, or at least better. Thus, it is feeling good that feels good, rather than the drugs or alcohol making us feel good. We feel good because we free ourselves from our self-imposed emotional prisons.

When we are emotionally and mentally beaten down by our environment, we lose our joy. When we lose our joy, we lose our ability to produce the good chemicals that offer many benefits to our health. And in the same way that we are all trying to achieve the release of feel-good chemicals in our bodies, we must also realize that our bodies are capable of producing the negative, or feel-bad, chemicals.

Have You Thought about
the Power of Your Negative Thoughts?

As a testament to the typical nature of humanity, when studying our bodies and the effects that our actions have on our bodies, we often speak about the feel-good chemicals, but for some reason we tend to overlook the feel-bad chemicals. Feel-good chemicals are what we produce when we are feeling joy, love, and gratitude. These chemicals, in turn, tend to make us feel good even more so once the chemicals begin to affect our senses. Where, with feel-bad chemicals, our bodies produce them when we feel unloved, depressed, and rejected. The feel-bad chemicals have an opposite effect and they make us feel even more unloved, depressed, and rejected.

Feel-bad chemicals are produced when we are out of harmony with those around us and when we are out of harmony with order. As humans, we are either in harmony with, or we are out of harmony with, order. So, after all is accounted for in our lives, we either have joy or we do not have joy.

There really is no in-between with joy. If you are in-between joy and no joy, then you are probably dead because everybody is experiencing something to some extent. What we experience, and the way in which we respond to those experiences, directly corresponds to our willingness to accept what is true. When we are out of harmony with our environment and those around us, then we are out of order. And when we are out of order, we cannot have joy. When we do not have joy, we will not produce the desired feel-good chemicals, and instead we produce feel-bad chemicals that do our prayers no justice.

Feel-bad chemicals are harmful to our chemical bodies when those chemicals are constant. Some of these chemicals are emergency protective chemicals, but are dangerous to us when we dwell in them for too long. Some of these chemicals allow us safety and protection in emergency situations. Any emergency situation is a situation that is out of order. Some of those feel-bad chemicals are there for us to quickly bring things back into order in our lives. Abusing these natural chemical tools negatively affects our health. Since we are designed to be in order, it is wise to consider that we are best suited when we are mentally *and* emotionally in order.

While there are feel-bad chemicals, it is not so much that those feel-bad chemicals might be released in us when we're feeling down, as much as it is that we lack the feel-good chemicals along with the good feelings we desire. It is our lack of feel-good chemicals that causes our problems. This comes from dwelling on and then pushing aside and failing to properly deal with our real problems, thus causing our joy to spiral to extinction.

We do a great amount of damage to our bodies by dwelling on negative things and then following that with falling into a depressed state of mind. Dwelling on the negative will not serve us in any positive way, and doing so is a clear sign of disorder in our lives.

Depression is typically caused from our own personal *lack of willingness* to replace order in our lives and stand up to be who we truly are. Too many of us place our value in *things*. We must be ourselves regardless of the criticisms and condemnations of those around us who dare to try and hold us back.

The effects that negativity has on our bodies are so profound that it is apparent that this will be proved to be a leading cause of cancer and many other physical pains and ailments once we are willing to receive this information in our hearts and minds, and then thoughtfully investigate it. There are people studying these topics, but the research often is brushed aside by many medical professionals and pharmaceutical companies who have us and our problems as repeat customers. Because we are typically afraid to admit our own shortcomings, we accept what we are told by the pharmaceutical companies and the medical professionals who earn their living because of our problems. Our fear tells us to blame anything but ourselves.

A dangerous catch in our own attitude is that when we have chosen to be defiant of what is true and good, we then become agitated when someone tries to share truth with us. In our defiance we attack them and refuse their wise counsel, causing abundant amounts of feel-bad chemicals to be produced in our bodies, with virtually no feel-good chemicals being produced at all. Thus, we suffer at our own hand and at our own thoughts due to our stubborn and stiff-necked nature of rejecting—We violate ourselves.

Because we all seek joy, we foolishly attempt to feel joy through our terrible habit of ignoring our problems. When we hide our problems, we then believe that we have forgotten about them, but those problems still exist. Problems will remain in your life until you take a stand and remove the problems. We deal with our problems by hiding them so that we don't get trapped in focusing on the negative, but typically we then end up *never* actually dealing with the root of the problem. As mentioned a few paragraphs back, focusing on the negative typically leads to a depressed state of mind. How do we escape this trap?

Focusing on the negative and subsequently placing yourself in a depressed state of mind is difficult to escape when you have chosen to entertain any ideas of existence without a Creator. It is a trap!

The value of understanding the intention of our design is very important with regard to our joy or our lack of it. Hiding and ignoring problems is dangerous, and doing so contributes to depression, frustration, and health concerns.

It's understandable why we choose to hide and ignore our problems, but doing so cannot solve our problems. We feel that if we give our problems any attention, it will make us feel bad and down. If this is the case, your mind is not thinking rightly. Our ability to look at our problems is a gift of immeasurable value. To ignore your problems is to throw away this beautiful gift. Problems let us know something needs to promptly change.

Our problem with problems is not that we do or do not ignore them. Our problem is that we do not realize that—our ability to see our problems—has been Created in us for the purpose of bringing our lives back into order. You can't fix what you don't know is broken. Hiding and ignoring problems blinds us from seeing the solution, and thus, we cannot rectify problems because we have made ourselves blind to those problems.

Further, when we hide our problems, we still know, deep down inside, that they exist. The fact that we know our problems exist and that we are ignoring them amounts to lying to ourselves. This causes us to be out of harmony with what is true and good. Not only are we out of harmony because of our problems, but we are also out of harmony because we know that our problems exist and that we refuse to address them. Doing so only makes matters worse.

We are made for order, and anything that puts us out of order is *not* good for us. Our ability to see and learn is a gift. The more quickly we learn to use this gift, then the more quickly our lives will return to order. And the more our lives are in order, then the more joy we will experience!

Do You Appreciate Everything?

Once we come to the understanding that everything happening in our bodies is a chemical response to outside interaction and to our own thoughts, then we can understand the critical importance of learning how to appreciate everything in our own lives. This appreciation includes those miserable and unpleasant experiences that are either perpetrated on us by those around us, or are from our own poor decisions.

A few chapters back we discussed being out of order and having things go wrong in our lives. We also discussed the fact that the trouble we experience is a corrective nature of order. In other words: Disorder is the corrective nature of order.

When you notice something is not good, you notice it because you are hurt, frustrated, and angry. Your hurt, frustration, and anger are *signs* that something is wrong—signs that we all should appreciate and utilize!

We must quickly accept those signals so that we can change our disordered circumstances back into an orderly set of circumstances that are good for us and for those around us.

When preachers come along and tell us that we should "praise the Lord in everything", including bad situations, it speaks to what we have just said here. We do not have to rejoice in the fact that someone harmed us or that things went wrong. No, not at all. We must rejoice in the fact that we have our natural mental reflexes to detect disorder in our lives. In the same way that being overweight is a sign that we eat too much and that we eat poorly, so too, is the disorder in our lives a sign that something is wrong.

Our mental pain and frustration are no different than the pain we feel when we bump our body into the edge of something. When we bump into something, the pain we feel is a protective function to let us know that we should immediately stop that action. We figure this out quickly with physical injury, but, for some reason, with mental or emotional injury where someone is hurting us with their words or their actions, we have a tendency to repeatedly and deliberately ram our body against the corner that hurt us, resulting in only more and more pain.

Ignoring the fact that someone hurt you with their words and actions, and then staying in that environment and doing nothing to rectify the situation, is similar to going back and repeatedly ramming your body into the sharp edge that you previously bumped into and injured yourself on. It's obvious to us that we should not go back and repeat the same movements and bump our body into the sharp edge over and over again. It is also obvious to us that it is not a good idea to go up to that sharp edge and punch it repeatedly with our fist. We understand that this will only inflict more pain on us. Yet, when it comes to our thinking and the emotional part of our lives, we fail to see the protective nature of the pain that we feel. For some reason we choose to endure enormous amounts of needless torment from other people who are behaving badly towards us.

Hiding or masking our problems is like placing a thin cover over the sharp edge that you bumped yourself on so that you don't notice it, but the sharp edge will still be there. There are several ways to deal with the sharp edge. One way is to hide and ignore it. A second method is to remove the object entirely. Another way is to not *ever* go near it. The final method is to smooth the sharp edge so that it no longer inflicts pain on you when you pass by it.

Learn to appreciate everything in your life for what it is. Then when those bad experiences keep on coming, know that when they are done you'll be stronger and that you will have learned from those horrible experiences. Then you will be better able to avoid such trouble in your future.

Forcing yourself to appreciate bad experiences is not very comforting if you are facing a difficult time at this very moment, but it works in your favor in the long run *when* you allow it to. You must accept it as a learning experience. It may be a difficult and painful experience, but you will be a better person when it's done, provided you choose to learn from it and take action to make the proper and needed changes going forward. When you realize that your frustration and pain are signs of danger, then your frustration and pain can help you to more readily see and remove the source of the problem. This works just like when the pain from bumping into a corner or edge of something helps you to realize that you need to stay clear of or remove the corner.

Everything that is broken in your life is a sign of your need to take immediate action in your own life in effort to restore order to the situation—Praying for guidance and understanding is a good starting point. With *physical* items, like old worn out things, we either recycle them or throw them away so that they can once again become a part of, and in order with, the Earth. However, when it comes to our hearts and minds we typically miss the fact that we need to deal with our problems. Appreciate your ability to detect disorder in your life. This ability is a wonderful gift for you to use in order to restore joy to your life.

Showing Gratitude

Realizing that—the pain felt from the negative experiences in your life is there for a purpose—allows you not only to very quickly remedy the situation, but it also allows you to appreciate what you have learned. With this realization you can be thankful for having had the experience that allows you to become more proficient in learning how to restore order to your life going forward.

It would be nonsense to think that a human wants to welcome or invite hurt. We don't need to pretend that we somehow are okay with, or enjoy, the abuse done to us. But, when we take note of the hurt or pain as the *signal* that it is, then we can be grateful that the signal has occurred. Without that signal of pain we would continually accept abuse from people around us who violate us. When we don't realize that our pain is a signal, we are mostly unable to realize that order must be restored and changes are needed. Instead, we wrongly focus on the problem and miss the underlying cause.

There is a rare condition where people cannot feel physical pain. If a person cannot feel pain, then they must be very cautious to not injure themselves. They have to pay close attention to everything that they do and must stay clear of harm. People who feel no pain would rejoice to be able to feel pain because they could know then that injury was happening to them. A person who cannot feel pain could break a bone and not realize it, or they could get a deadly cut and not notice that it happened until it's too late. So realize that all pain is a good thing because pain is a sign that something is wrong. The term "pain" that we are using here includes your emotional pain. Pain is a gift! But this does not mean that we must seek pain.

It might interest you to know that the word "pain" has its origin roots in the idea of *revenge, punishment,* or *payment.* The word "pay" has its origin roots in the word *peace.* When something is out of order in your life you will *pay* the price for the *disorder* until you bring it into *order.* When things are in order in your life you will have *peace!*

We discussed the fact that prayer means to *request* or *ask,* and mentioned a bit about praise. *Gratitude* is *grace* and *grace* is *praise* and *praise* is to *show esteem, respect,* or to *make an offer in appreciation.* Showing gratitude to the Creator for everything in your life is good to do, and it is a good way to show appreciation and respect. However, if we misunderstand and only *pretend* to appreciate the negative things in our life (like pain), then we are lying and we are out of synchronization with harmony, and we are also out of harmony with order.

It does us no good to miss or hide the fact that pain is a gift. You must understand that this gift informs us when something is wrong. Pain is a warning bell; it is our smoke alarm. Always asking "What caused this?" is our best approach to get to the very bottom of the root of the troubles that cause pain in our lives. It is when we ask "What caused that?" that we begin to realize that the pain we feel is an indicator and a wonderful gift that we have been given in order to recognize the disorder occurring in our lives and the need to correct that disorder.

When we offer praise to the Creator it's best that we do it accurately and understand what we are saying and what our true intentions are. Our true intentions cannot be hidden even if we ourselves do not realize that we are blind to our actual intentions. The Creator knows our true intentions even when we do not.

It's hard to be grateful when bad things are always happening to us; but often bad things happen to us because we are not grateful. When we allow lies, bad things, and bad people into our lives, we will always feel violated and dissatisfied with our lives. When we are unhappy and dissatisfied we feel that we have nothing to be grateful for and forget about what we should be grateful for, thus causing us to be even more discontented and ungrateful. Having an attitude of gratitude is of great value to us.

We can certainly be grateful for simple things like air and light and jobs and food. But to really feel grateful, most of us need to have things in our lives be pleasant enough to feel grateful for them. The way to do this is to separate ourselves from bad things, bad people, and from lies. Then truth and good things can fill their place, leaving us feeling grateful!

What is the Real Power of Your Words?

Because our attitude affects our words and because our words are heard by other people, and those words affect their body chemistry, we must realize that their *thoughts* and *beliefs* are affected by those words as well. If their body acts on their beliefs that they incorrectly adjusted because of *our* erred words, then when *our* words are wrong we have caused their body to be in conflict. Through this conflict, our words inhibit their ability to be healed due to too much feel-bad chemicals and too little feel-good chemicals being output in their bodies. Depending upon who you talk to regarding "feel-good" chemicals, they might include the chemistry produced from lustful activities such as eating too much or contemplating illicit intimate relations in the "feel-good" chemistry. But this differs from the chemistry produced when offering authentic *kindness* and *true love*, and experiencing *true joy*.

The first thing to realize when praying for healing is that you are thinking negatively when you believe words that are contrary to what is in order and true. You inhibit your own ability to be healed because you are allowing your body to react negatively with its chemistry. This negativity feeds more disorder into your body. You must come to an understanding to speak truth and to accept only truth. Without doing so, there is little hope of being healed when you pray. You must accept truth with childlike faith (a very important point that will be discussed later).

Lifespan of Tibetan Monks

As mentioned earlier, people who practice meditation do not really live any longer than people who are joyful throughout the majority of their lives. In fact, it is the joyful people who take good care of their bodies that we see living long robust lives typically surpassing the average lifespan of those who remain in solitary meditation for the majority of their lives. This is not to say that meditation is a bad thing to do, but let's be honest with this and come to the realization that the primary cause of human longevity is joy, and stop blaming our condition on anything and everything other than our own thinking.

If meditation and prayer were the answer to long life then priests, nuns, and Tibetan monks would be living very, very long lives, yet, this is not so. They tend to live close to an average lifespan. We cannot attribute a long lifespan only to living a life filled with joy, because there are other factors such as health and lifestyle choices that affect our lifespans. When we eat poorly, excessively eat, drink harmful beverages, smoke, etc. it is an obvious contradiction that puts our body in a state of excessive chaos and disorder. Most people who live long, want to and plan to live long. They have lived joyful lives and have taken reasonably good care of their bodies.

Prayer is a part of a healthy body, and prayer abides by the nature of order. If we are praying for something that we feel is not quite what we want, or for something we know we should not have, then that prayer is out of order and it puts us in dangerous oscillation. This is true even if we ourselves have not come to the realization that we are praying for the wrong things. When our prayers are out of order, our thoughts are also out of order. This is because our thoughts are where our prayers originate. If our thoughts are out of order, then our bodies will produce feel-bad chemicals and will *lack* the production of feel-good chemicals. Generally speaking, this is more damaging to our bodies than poor eating habits are.

On average, people who have spent a great deal of their lifespan in solemn meditation, live only a couple of years longer than the rest of the population. Since such statistics are based upon averages (and do not account for deeper details) much of their couple extra years is more accurately attributed to the fact that they are less likely to die in traffic accidents, wars, or similar tragic events.

Our attitude originates in our thinking and our thinking becomes affected by our attitude. Our thinking and our attitude feed upon each other, and in this case, the result of this self-feeding circular trap causes the production of the feel-bad chemicals. When our body is out of sync with truth and order, our lifespan will be shortened, our health will decline, we will constantly be frustrated, and our joy will be fleeting if experienced at all.

Learn to show proper gratitude with your new attitude in everything. Hold this gratitude in your entire being and keep your heart, mind, and soul in a grateful state of joy. Doing this is far more powerful than any medication or meditation that ever was or ever will be! The value of a proper attitude of gratitude to your prayers is incalculable.

Chapter 9

Science, Infinity, The Unknown, and Faith

Our level of doubt about a Creator, and therefore about our prayers being able to be answered by that Creator, has been greatly altered by the information that scientists and scholars demand is "factual". Quite often these "facts" are only mere speculations of the scientists and scholars. Because we place our trust in people, rather than placing our trust in Truth, we miss a great deal of the basic true information that anyone who chooses to can plainly see with their own eyes and reason through with their own mind. This information is missed by us because we don't bother to look. And we don't bother to look because of what we are told is true based upon the so-called "facts" presented by the people we wrongly placed our trust in. There are many simple evidences that any one of us can clearly see that indicate a great deal of conflict in many of these so called "facts". There are aspects of the Creator and of science that we somehow imagine are not connected. But I propose that all aspects of science and the Creator *cannot* be separated.

An aspect of the Creator that we really did not get into yet is the *infinite* nature of the Creator. The blindness of our humanness causes us to believe that something always has to come first. This is problematic for us because once we find out what is first, then we try to make something else first by insisting that something put the first thing there. This is an infinity issue within us. We typically do this each time we mentally settle on a first, and then once the first is finally accepted we reason it through and decide that something had to be before that. We continue to do this and invent ideas like cyclical creation theories, such as the big bang. But even cyclical creation fails to address how everything initially came to be. Explaining this by imagining that something such as "singularity" actually exists, takes a great deal more blind-faith to believe in than deliberate Creation does. "Singularity" is a somewhat recent and weak scientific theory and belief that everything, in all of the cosmos, was once packed into a space so tiny that you would not be able to see it with your eyes or any instruments. Then, defying every scientific rule and law of physics, this infinitely small point in space suddenly exploded and made everything we see, including ourselves.

If we accept that there is a Creator then we can realize that the Creator was first and no thing, and no one, came before. We can also better understand that the Creator Created everything that can be seen or detected. But this presents a problem to many of us in our minds because we have a difficult time not placing something first. And we also have a difficult time understanding that something can exist that is not tangible and therefore cannot be touched or seen. A doubtful mind that lacks understanding will proceed to question: "Who created the Creator?" This is a fair question, but if you answer it saying that some other means created the Creator, then this way of thinking testifies to your inability to be able to conceive the infinite. It is possible that the Creator didn't always exist, but this depends upon what the Creator is. With our tendency to gravitate toward only believing things that we can see and touch, we fail to comprehend that not everything is detectable with our current scientific equipment.

All Matter is Nothing

To begin to understand how everything came to be we need to understand that "matter" exists. Everything is made of, what we humans refer to as, *matter*. But "matter" is an arbitrary term that really has no specific meaning. It was not all that long ago that it was believed that there was something in space called "æther". The notion of æther was debated and eventually was replaced with other far reaching concepts such as dark matter. However, the replacement for æther is not certain because regardless of each person's speculation about the topic, it is all nothing more than utter speculation. If these theoretical terms were more than just pure speculation, then we would know much more than what we do about the Universe in which we live.

We really don't know what æther or dark matter are so we invent ideas and words so that we can discuss our thoughts about what we do not understand, yet these theories are discussed as if they are truths. Terms such as *æther*, *matter*, and *dark matter* are our attempt to describe and understand what we can, to some extent, see, detect, or sense, but are unable to explain.

For instance, the scientific community has a difficult time explaining how light travels via waves, yet those waves are seemingly created of nothing. Using water as an illustration, it is the water itself that is the carrier of the wave seen in the water. Within the empty voids of space, at this point, we cannot detect anything that might carry a "wave", so we invented ideas such as æther, which is now considered an outdated term and theory

Some scientists are unwilling to admit that everything is Created from nothing. Everything that *is*—is Created. If it is Created it is thought that it must be made from something, but this is not true. The "something" part had to be Created at some point, which is where our problem comes in with regard to the cosmos, infinity, and a Creator, because if everything was already there, then were did it come from? A logical mind understands that at some point everything had to have come from nothing, but since nothing and no person was there to make everything, then how could it have come to be?

It doesn't matter what you choose to believe about the beginning of Creation, because at some point there is a choice that you will have to make or have already made, though you *can* change your mind at any time. If you want to believe that the elements were always there, then I ask you, how did they get there? Just saying that the elements were always there comes up short of any sort of explanation at all.

In the twentieth century, people were told by science to believe that everything we see in space, all of the planets, stars, and all of the debris, was at one time in an infinitely small single point—singularity. Then through tremendous force it spontaneously exploded with a big bang and brought about everything we see. People were further told that, at some time in the very distant future, it will once again collapse into a single point and repeat the explosion, or maybe it will keep expanding. In other words, they truly didn't know and still do not know. It is all speculation, and there are many versions of such speculation. These speculations are based on mathematical formulas that cannot be proven to be able to be *accurately* applied to the extent that they have been used. In other words, just because we can mathematically calculate the Universe into singularity, does not mean that it can be brought into singularity in reality, or that it ever was in singularity, or that it ever will be in singularity.

There is no consensus in these theories because they are theories, and we are still trying to figure everything out. By many scientists, this is considered to be "rational" thinking that we are to accept just because someone said so. There is no specific evidence of a single point big bang origin anywhere. To learn more about Creation, the big bang, and science, the books *Bending The Ruler* and the book series *The Science of God* go into more detail about Creation and the big bang. The stellar bodies in space that we see are reported to be so distant from us that it is not within our current realm of possibility for us to ever be able to go to one of those distant galaxies or even to the nearest star.

There are some bodies in space that are said to be coming towards us, but most celestial bodies are said to be going away from us. There is no consistency in these reports with regard to the expansion of a single spontaneous big bang explosion having occurred. This big bang is pure fiction and has not been able to be proven. To assume that a big bang is how it all happened and that no other option exists is a grievous error on humanity's part. We do not need to be astrophysicists to see these errors. And when we follow error, our only result is doubt.

Light, all vibrations, and all other things are Created. Often, people want to believe that the Creator is *light* or *vibrations*, but those are Created things. The Enlightenment movement, during the Age of Reason, worshiped the light and vibrations as if those Created things were their god; this method of thinking still exists in various forms today. However, the Created things are not the Creator, they are only Created things. Believing those things are a god or gods from which we get our diverse sustenance is as ridiculous as worshiping the Sun, Moon, nature, plants, animals, or any other Created thing.

Plants may nourish us, and the Sun may warm us and give us light by which to see, but those things are gifts of the Creation that are put here, by the Creator, and we are able to enjoy and discover them.

Because we have such a difficult time conceiving the infinite, we fail to recognize the non-created, which is the realm of conscious. All thought is *not* tangibly "Created" and thought does not abide by the physical constraints that are placed on our bodies. Thought can likely travel faster than anything physical no matter where you are in the Universe. Your thoughts are instant and everywhere. Since we can communicate with the Creator through thought, distance is of no concern. We are bound to the Creator through our thoughts, and the Creator is everywhere. While the physical-Created realm must abide by the vast constrains of Creation, our minds do not have to abide by those same constraints. We are free to destroy ourselves.

When we accept true things, we gain the ability to imagine infinity. Without this ability we will always imagine that the Creator is something which has been created. When our minds can think beyond the blinding lies and inaccuracies that we have been taught for so long, then the true facts of any situation become undeniably evident.

The further in-depth that science is able to get with regard to understanding the *subatomic particles* and *matter*, the more we can see it is all made of nothing. Based upon this, one could say that the Creator does not exist since everything is made from nothing. If you're looking for a concrete Creator that you can touch and feel, then you have shown your inability to grasp the infinite.

The Creator Created Creation. This means that everything that we see, feel, smell, touch, and taste is Created! It also means that everything that we use to sense these things with are also Created. If it is tangible and can be seen or touched by us, then it has been Created, including light.

In reference to the physical realm of "scientific" existence, our thoughts do not exist and neither does the Creator or Heaven. The narrow-minded view that the Creator must be a part of Creation needs to be realized as an absurd notion. We will be unable to attain the needed level of understanding of the infinite unless we learn how to embrace what is true. We are here to try to *understand* the Creator, not *dissect* the Creator. So while the *Creator, thought,* and *Heaven* do not *"scientifically"* exist (because they are not scientifically detectable), it does not mean that they are not a reality or that they do not exist outside of detectable science.

Does Reading More Books Make you Better?

Many people believe that if they have more books on their shelf or if they read more books they will be better or smarter, this is especially prominent in the science fields. In our quest to obtain understanding, we often seek to read many books. It's not wrong to do so, but to believe that by reading *more* books, or that having more books on our shelves makes us any better and smarter, is not true or accurate in any imaginable way. It is not how much you read, but rather it is *what you read* and *what you choose believe about what you read* that matters.

Much of what we read is the splitting of hairs of unimportant information, information which is largely unnecessary once we have learned how to accept truth and weigh everything on the scale of truth. There are many books written that have good information in them, but many of these books are repetitious of previously written material and other contemporary material that reference each other as their source of information. This cross-referential nature of these books binds them together to depend upon one another. This means that some books that are written can only be as reliable as the earlier books that they reference and are dependent upon unless they are debating against those books. Additionally, each of the books can only be as reliable as the author's interpretation of the books that he or she referenced.

Cross-referencing and quoting other books in these books does not make these books wrong, but when a previous book is the source of reference for most of the content of someone else's subsequent book, then we wind up in the same situation that we had with some Church leaders in regard to the Bible in past years. Basing our foundation of understanding of the Creator solely upon the Bible does the same thing as basing book upon book. It is placing a premise on premise, which is very dangerous indeed. This is not because a book is wrong, but rather, it is because some of our interpretations of the book are often in error. Thus, if we reinterpret someone else's information, we will possibly explain it inaccurately with our own words as we pass the information along to others.

When we think that the more books we read, the smarter and wiser we will become, then we open ourselves up to the dangers of building premise on a premise. It is simply not true that reading more books will make us better or smarter. It's not bad to read books, but thinking that reading *more* makes us better, is simply wrong. It's not how much we read, but rather, what we read *and* if we understand it properly that matters. *Properly* understanding things assists in enlightening us.

When we choose to embrace what is true, we cannot get smarter or better because we have become perfected in truth and realize that our own personal improvement is a never-ending task. The more we know in truth, then the more we realize that we know very little. Whether through reading, or actual interaction, we gain experience and collect trivia through research and observation. However, if we fail to embrace truth, we will be led astray by reading, and subsequently believing, bad information, or by us misinterpreting information. In that case, the more we read, the more we will be led astray. Our incorrect beliefs become more and more cemented in our erred minds with every book we read that builds and feeds our error. There is no end to the amount of errors that we can make in this regard. Reading and then believing books, or just simply believing wrong information about anything, keeps us in the dark about what we think we "know" from our reading.

Why Do Bad Things Happen?

Would bad things happen if we truly served God? We often attribute bad things as being a punishment from God and then say things like, "How could a loving God do such cruel things?" But why is it that we never question this as a form of protection? What will happen, will happen, and we will be harmed when disasters occur. But what if we could be protected from those disasters **only if** we carefully followed the instructions of the Creator? Ignore the Creator and go it alone, or embrace the Creator and be protected! We could think of this like a father protecting his children, where if one of the children decides to reject their father and leaves the father, then the father can no longer easily protect them because they chose to leave his protective care.

In an earlier chapter we spoke of praying against ourselves when we pray for a bandage, and then having that prayer possibly answered by a push in an unexpected direction to pursue a different job. We view this same effect as—bad things happening—when it actually is not necessarily bad.

Another reason bad things happen is because we are often warned about the potential troubles that are caused by our own actions, but we choose to proceed in our stubborn ways regardless. In the Bible it talks about cities being destroyed with fire and brimstone, or peoples being overthrown by invading armies. And in these cases, warnings to get out of the city or to change their ways were not heeded by the people who were warned. The people who are referred to in the Bible were warned of impending doom, and told that if they would change their ways then the doom could be averted. Yet they refused to follow the form of order that was handed to them by various messengers. Because of their refusal to change they suffered the consequences of their own choices. It's easy to forget the importance of *order* and be drawn back into the debate about why bad things happen.

Bad things happen because we get into disorder. Since order is the normal way in which all things properly function, it is logical to imagine that the Creator would want to rectify the situation. It's ridiculous for us to imagine that this would not be the case. The Creator Created with a magnitude of order that is unparalleled, and anything that violates order must and will eventually perish!

The same consequence model of order can be used with regard to health problems, and potentially even in children with birth defects. Some people may want to attack the statement and assume that they are being blamed, but this simply is not the case. If we are out of harmony with order, then we are often unaware of disharmony. While we may have some fleeting feelings of joy, often those feelings are nothing more than forced or unintentional happiness. Happiness is random. "*Happiness*" comes from the word "*happen*" or "*hap*" which means by *chance*.

We try to force joy with our money, status, or things, and believe that we will be happy with that, but we will not be happy because we lack joy. Joy is a deliberate reaction of accepting what is true. If our bodies are out of synchronization with what is true, then our bodies are out of order.

Since everything in our bodies down to the sperm cells and ovum are composed of chemical elements, it is reasonable to entertain the possibility that our lack of accepting truth affects the physical well-being of our offspring. And that is in addition to the environmental lack of order that might occur shortly before and during fetal development, including the foods we eat. In thinking about this, consider what was discussed in a previous chapter about our body's chemical production and how it affects us.

From the Dead, The Raging Argument

Will we live infinitely? For many years people have questioned the existence of a single and supreme Creator. Along with this common debate is the debate about a life after death. This has been a point of contention between the Church leaders of various religious sects, and it also has been a contentious point between philosophers.

The debate of whether or not there is an afterlife has been raging on for thousands of years. This is one key point of contention that the Sadducees and Pharisees who are mentioned in the Bible debated about, and it was the primary difference between their beliefs. From a New Testament Biblical perspective, the Christ rose from the dead. And there are eye witness accounts of this recorded in ancient and in Biblical documents. It was further testified by these eyewitnesses that the Christ was taken up from Earth into the clouds. On our own, we must each choose whether or not we believe those accounts are accurate. The question is, how do we do that? How do we decide if these accounts are accurate, or if they are lies?

This debate of whether or not there is life after death has been going on for a long time, but only those who have died know for certain whether or not this is so. You need not look far to hear accounts of people who have been revived from the dead who tell their stories about their glimpse of an afterlife. There is a multitude of information available about these death experiences for those who care to study them.

Efforts have even been made to duplicate some of the reported effects experienced when "dying". Some of these experiments have been successful in duplicating what was experienced in some of the reports from people who have reportedly "died" and then been brought back to life. There is no conclusive evidence about what people experience, other than it is a common phenomenon that they relate to others about what they experienced at the point of death and shortly after being brought back to life.

It is up to you to decide what you will believe in this regard. If you look for it you will find consistency in many of the reports. If you choose to allow all of these reports to be explained away by "scientific explanation", then that's up to you. However, while those explanations might be "scientific", it does not mean that the people did not truly experience something that goes beyond this tangible and physical Creation that we all see, feel, touch, smell, and hear. Further, the experiments attempting to duplicate the "death" sensation may have brought the subjects in the experiments closer to death than they realized. So they could have actually experienced something real and near to death.

There are stories with very explicit claims that we must weigh in each our own hearts and minds. In recent times, a man who was one of many eastern spiritual leaders was said to have died and then later came back to life; he reported seeing his dead family and friends in a tormenting fire. He also related seeing other spiritual leader counterparts who died before him that he had previously worked with. He claimed that they said to him that "their godless way of believing is wrong and that it is not the way". What we choose to believe about these types of stories is up to each one of us.

Just because some people do not believe death-experience stories does not mean they are not true. Nor does it mean that just because we choose to believe them that they are true. We will find the truth to these accounts at some point, but in the meantime it is wise to consider not jumping to conclusions and thus disregard the possibility that these accounts might be true.

In the Bible there are reports of people rising from the dead with similar experiences as those noted above. There are also other writings of antiquity, besides the Bible, that have recorded similar accounts. Apparently this has been occurring for thousands of years and has been disbelieved by some people during those years. Often we see things of this nature, and then we decide that we need to be more "realistic" so we discount the information, then when another instance is presented to us we say that there is no past evidence. We sometimes put people in prison, for life, based on loose testimony of a single witness, yet we cannot find our way clear to at least consider the death experiences that countless people have detailed to us over the centuries. We always seem to find a way to explain those accounts away.

We have become more willing to believe that everything spontaneously exploded from a single infinitely small point randomly floating in space, and, by defying *all* "laws of physics" and rules of science, that everything we now see exists because of that explosion. And that mankind progressed through long periods of time from a single primitive cell to become what we are today. Some people are even more willing to believe that we were put here from some other life form from a faraway alien place. We are more willing to entertain these highly imaginative origin stories than we are willing to entertain the possibility of a joyous life after this Earthly life, or the potential long-term torment because of our poor personal choices we made here on Earth.

Believing in the big bang or believing we were placed here by other life forms is a blind spot that cannot be backed up by order or by truth or by science. This is now and has always been, the folly of mankind since the beginning. If we cannot back something up with the order of truth, then we best not believe it. We can keep things like the big bang or believing we were placed here by other life forms in the back of our minds as possibilities, but to accept them as *true* without proper evidence is to doom ourselves to error.

Reasoning that everything and all matter was always there is somewhat short-sighted and unrealistic. To begin to grasp Creation we must allow our minds to imagine infinity and realize that everything had to have somehow started from nothing. If you are unable to grasp the concept of infinity, then you will struggle with the idea of a Creator. Struggling with the idea of a Creator will cause you to doubt, and your doubt will compromise your prayers.

Chapter 10

Being Single-Minded Versus Double-Minded

Being single-minded means to be focused and to not waver in what you want to do or in what you desire. When you are single-minded you will be more concerned about why and how you got injured than you will be about the bandage to patch the wound.

We all must understand what is required of us to be in harmony with *order* and *truth*; if we are outside of these two most basic aspects of Creation, then it is ridiculous for us to hope for joyful success in our lives or to expect to achieve it. We will unavoidably be double-minded, rather than single minded, when we are without order and truth.

When we lose our single-minded focus we become double minded. There are several ways to be double-minded. We touched on being double-minded earlier when we discussed someone praying for a bandage when they want to stop bleeding, but then complain and fight the solution when it comes along. Another area where we are double-minded is in our prayer requests. Too often we lack the ability to request anything in a concise and well thought-out manner because our desires do not properly match our requests. Because we stray from being single-minded we become double-minded and we try to believe but we doubt at the same time.

We want to be happy and content, and we know that we must do certain things in order for that to occur, but we are afraid of what will result if we take the proper actions required to achieve the happiness or joy that we desire. The aspect of wanting to be happy and content that makes us double-minded is that we waver in our minds. When we pray, we typically don't have the concise focus of mind that is a technical requirement needed to accomplish perfect prayer. We need to be single-minded and thus not waver as we do when we fall into double-mindedness.

Being double-minded is like wanting to turn the lights off but then being afraid to be in the dark. To be single-minded is nothing more than to stop double-minded thought by means of being focused on what you think or pray for in a concise, decisive, and clear thought-action. Know exactly what you desire and do not be inconsistent! Every decision we make has consequences. If we pray for something but are not willing to accept the requirements needed for the prayer to be answered, then we are being double-minded. Most of us cannot manage to free our minds from our negativity and our limited prayers. Our inability to clear our minds limits our requests and casts doubt on the full potential of the Creator. Doubting the full potential of the Creator, in turn, causes us to limit our requests. If you need money and ask me where you can get some, and I tell you the location of a treasure chest full of riches that you can have if you go and get it and that it will solve all of your financial problems, then I have answered your prayer. But if you're too lazy or too afraid to go and get the treasure, then *you* have voided your own prayer.

Are You Hedging?

When we're double-minded we're trying to play both sides and hedge our lives. Hedging our lives is bad. Hedging is lukewarm at best! A phrase in the Bible states, "Because you are neither hot nor cold, and because you are lukewarm, I will spew you out." That statement was speaking of our complacency and of the fear that we have in actually making a decision. If you're the type who wants to sit on the fence and not make a choice because you're afraid to make the wrong choice, then you're being double-minded.

A person who is wrong but is passionate, at least has the courage to speak his or her mind. If they are not too arrogant to hear what is true, then they will change their mind and adjust their thinking to agree with truth at some point. Then that person will likely be as passionate for the truth as they were for the lie they had formerly believed and embraced. This is why the Christ said he would rather have you *hot* or *cold*.

We don't want to turn the light *off* because we are afraid of the dark, and we don't want the light *on* because we don't want people to see our errors. Hedging in this double-minded manner separates us from being able to see truth. It puts us in a lukewarm state of mind and makes us utterly useless to ourselves, to the rest of humanity, and also to the Creator.

Are You Confused About Success?

A part of being double-minded is our inability to see through the veils of arrogance that people often put up for show. When we believe things improperly, we are then double-minded about our improper perception.

There was a woman who was confused about "success" while growing up. She truly disliked when people would steal the stage and attention from others who actually deserved recognition, which is often called "grandstanding". In youth, she never quite understood why she felt this way. It wasn't until she was older that she realized why she didn't like it. She began to question her own reaction and distaste towards people's *grandstanding*. Later on in life, as she thought through this, it became clear to her that the reason people grandstand is due to their jealousy. Jealousy raged all around her while she was growing up, but she never realized this because jealousy surrounded her from birth on. Those around her covetously despised anyone else's success and would mock the success that they saw others achieve through talent, skill, and diligent effort, while at the same time during mocking, they were always indirectly saying, "Look at me, look at me", but never actually did anything worthy of being looked at.

They pretended success without performing the actions needed to achieve success. They wanted to receive good credit for poor behavior. Sadly, they had the false impression that everyone around them thought that they were great because their grandstanding gained them attention from others. This happened in two ways: First, they demanded the attention through—to put it kindly—prominent behavior. And second, they gained attention through mockery at the expense of innocent people and other peoples' fear of being unjustly attacked. Mocking causes weak and fearful people to rally support around the mockers, ultimately ending with them all losing—a common scourge of social media.

The all too common behavior of grandstanding *steals* attention rather than *earning* attention. It's not the grandstanding part that we culturally dislike. Rather, what irritates us is the grandstand *stealing*, which is the arrogant result of their jealousy. We can see the contradictions that dwell in someone who is grandstand stealing, but often we don't understand these things when we're young. And we typically don't understand when we're older either. This is because we generally don't question our feelings about grandstanding. Many of us don't question our feelings because this is what we grew up with and it is all we know. Having undeserving people demand our attention is "normal" to us, and therefore we do not easily recognize it as improper. This is like the *Hot Water* effect that we experience when stepping into the shower and eventually become accustomed to the water temperature, where after a while it no longer feels extreme to us.

We often condemn the skill of others who succeed, such as singers, actors, famous personalities, or even successful people near us. The condemnation being done attracts attention for a person who is doing the condemning, and at the same time the condemnation sends out a message that the value of the beautiful talent that other person offered to humanity is worthless. Condemnation and mockery do not make any sense in these cases because, typically, when someone is mocking a person, the person being mocked has worked very hard to earn their place in life and the person is typically very talented. Condemnation and mockery are irrational behaviors and are counterproductive. We are held captive when we fall prey to taking part in unjust condemning or mocking, or when we are happy to watch others do so.

Mockers sit in their living rooms mocking talented people that they see on television, or they lurk in the shadows mocking anyone whom they see as a target of their vain, arrogant, and foolish mockery. They will remain in their covetous-jealousy hiding their own insecurities as long as they choose to believe the lie that they themselves are worthless or of little value compared to the person that they are mocking. They continue in their mockery, making themselves feel lower with each cutting remark that they make against others who have the type of success that the mockers are too afraid to achieve for themselves due to their own fear of personal failure.

A mocker's double-minded way of thinking, that they are both great and a failure at the same time, is hidden beneath their veil of self-doubting mockery. We can only be single-minded when we embrace truth and shed our double-minded ways.

When someone chooses to be the type of person that mocks, they are also often the type to *steal* the grandstand whenever they can manage to do so. When we cut others down and grandstand ourselves, we feel higher and wrongly believe it to be success, but it is *not* success. The only true success is to follow the order of truth. Cutting others down for their talents only brings a mocker lower than before and more fully exposes the mocker's abundant insecurities to others.

Clarifying Your Needs

When you do not have a clear vision of your own needs then you inevitably will be in a double-minded state. Too often when we pray, we struggle in our minds because we have confused what *wants* and *needs* are. We *want* money, but we *need* air. "Want" simply means that we are short of our desires, where as a "need" is a requirement for continuation of something vital. This takes us back to our bandage example. In the bandage example there are *needs* and *wants*: If we are cut, then we *need* to stop the bleeding. If we *want* to stop bleeding, then it typically is more important to stop getting cut than it is to find a bandage. If we *want* to stop getting cut, then we *need* to remove the source of the cutting. If we *want* to get rid of the source of the cutting, we may *need* to get rid of where the cutting occurs, or the circumstances that bring it about.

You can break the idea of *need* down into two basic categories. One kind of need is what helps to sustain life and the other kind of need is the need to take action to get your desire. Regardless of how you break "need" down, it is still going to come back to getting things in order in your heart, mind, and life. If we don't eat for an extended period of time, our bodies will fall into disorder and begin to rapidly degrade. If our life is in disorder, then our joy will rapidly degrade. The situations may differ somewhat, but the function will always be the same: order is needed if we wish to sustain anything anywhere at any time. Without order, anything good cannot be sustained. Always remember the phrase, "What caused this?" This is where your need will reside, and where your problem will be solved.

"Prayer" serves two purposes. One is the need for you to create clarity of your desires within your own mind. And the other purpose is a request for better things that you want to come your way.

Clarifying Wants

Our *wants* are our desires. These are the things that give us motivation. Consider this thought: If you won't choose to desire good things, then trouble *will* come your way, and you *will* be forced to desire to be free from your torment—which in the end, is to desire a good thing!

We *choose* what we *want* to desire. The corrective nature of order forces us to desire *something*. This means that if we choose to believe things that are not true, then our lives will eventually come into disorder and we will be forced to have the desire for disorder to no longer be in our lives and to have order restored.

Human desire is one of the most important aspects of humanity. When we fail to have desire then we have given up and we are certain to lose our mental faculties and our ability to mentally and physically function effectively as we age. The corrective nature of order will torment us with our self-inflicted disorder until we concede and make a conscious decision to embrace order. If we fail to embrace order, we will be tormented by the corrective nature of order until we die! When we die we are forced back into order.

There is a danger of being caught in the trap of disorder when it comes to prayer. This is because, when we allow disorder in our thinking and in our lives, our mind focuses on the disorder, which brings on more disorder. Disorder is a voluntary distraction that is always the result of a lie or inaccuracy or injustice. When we grasp this and embrace true things, then we begin to see our needs through the fog of our wants. Our needs will always be dealing with the cause of any disorder in our lives, including the need felt by our *lack of order in the preparation* of achieving the good goals or desires that we want.

Whether we confuse our needs versus our wants, or if we confuse someone's arrogance for their confidence, or if we are hedging, it is all our part of our being double-minded. Even though we don't intend for this to be so, it still causes problems for us in our prayers. We see that something is not quite right, but then continue in our inaccurate perceptions regardless. These perceptions affect what we think, do, and want. If we do not see this in ourselves, then we will have much difficulty delivering a prayer that is not double–minded, nor will we be able to properly focus our mind on seeing the answer to the prayer when it arrives.

Chapter 11

Learning How to Pray

We cannot legitimately expect to have our prayers answered when we're unwilling to get the needed things in order in our own lives in effort to have those prayer answers able to occur without trouble and pain to ourselves.

Be Focused

Imagine for a moment that you need an entirely new wardrobe of clothing because all of your clothes are worn thin. Now, imagine you are praying for a new wardrobe of clothing: If you do not prepare your mind and life for the possibility of new clothing, then can you really expect for it to occur?

In our attempts to pray properly, our first *need* will always be to see it in our mind first, as in, "I want a new wardrobe". Then we need to realize in our minds that it can happen in *any* imaginable way. Or in the case of most of us, due to our lack of imagination, it is in any **un**imaginable way.

The first thing you must do is to prepare your mind for the possibility that your new wardrobe could come from an unexpected provider. If you do not prepare your thoughts, then your mind is not in order with your desires and you are at great risk of being double-minded.

The next thing that we need to do is to prepare the way for our prayer's answer to occur in a more tangible way—while still realizing that it could come from an unexpected provider. In the meantime, you will need to save money or get a job in order to earn the money for the wardrobe. But this does not mean that you should *only* expect it to come from working and earning the money to buy it. The fact that you are making a diligent effort shows that you are willing to do your part, but the wardrobe can come from somewhere other than your earned money. Also, it's a good idea to let others know that you desire a new wardrobe because they or someone they know might be the answer to your prayer.

Beyond those few actions, there's not much more that you can do to make your prayer fulfilled. You have created order in everything possible in your life with regard to your desire for a new wardrobe. The only thing left for you to do is to understand that if you remain steadfast in what is true, your prayers will be heard and answered according to what is good for your life. If you do not understand this, then you are not in order for truth, therefore, your prayers are not in purity and will not be acknowledged as *you* desire them to be.

An additional point to keep in consideration is, in order to have prayers be pure you must have order in *all* areas of your life. If your life is in disarray everywhere else, but you get your mind in order for a specific thing, such as a new wardrobe, you may have that part in order, but the rest of your life might be in utter chaos. Having discord and strife in the rest of your life is going to put your mind and thoughts in a double-minded state. Imagining that this is not so is like thinking that you can consume deadly poison and have it only affect and kill off one specific spot on your body, such as an unwanted mole or even cancer. I assure you that this will *not* occur in that way because the poison will go throughout your entire body affecting and destroying the vital functions needed for you to live. In the same way, discord in one area of your life will affect all other areas to some extent. Ignoring this fact is choosing to be blind to what is true, and doing so will inhibit your life and your prayers.

Get Things In Order

It is vital that we get our entire lives in order. When we do this, and our lives are distinct and well-ordered, then our prayers can be pure. This is not only about the physical things we have in our lives. It also thoroughly, completely, and most prominently includes our mind and thoughts.

Getting your life in order is very important. But what is more important is—actually understanding that your life lacks order and for you to proceed with a complete and legitimate effort to get order properly in place within your life— understanding this is a key step. You can have things be placed improperly in your life and still have order as long as you know that the problem exists and you admit it and you are actually planning the solution and removal of the problem. Order does not exist in your life because you are organized. Order exists in your life because you have truth. When you understand what is wrong and are actively working to correct those errors, then you have order. But, if you lie to yourself by hiding and masking your problems, then you do not have the order of truth within you.

Answers to our prayers are sometimes a difficult thing for us to detect. This is because we have become accustomed to reading or following the wrong information with regard to an answered prayer.

If I pray for air so that I can breathe, then is my prayer answered? I suppose we could say that it is, but why would we ask for what has already been so graciously given to us? We should certainly offer our gratitude and praise, but to pray for what we already have is a waste of our existence and a waste of the Creator's infinite existence. Air is certainly something that we should offer our gratitude and praise for, but a true answer to a prayer can be the smallest and most petty little thing, or it can be about some major experience in our lives. Regardless of whether the answer is small or large, it will share the common element of being uncommon and unexpected outside of being an answer to a prayer. It is important to note that once you have come to understand prayer properly, then proper answers to your prayers will become common in your life.

What to Pray For

After we receive what we have prayed for, we often attribute the result of the answered prayer to luck, chance, or happenstance. To an extent this makes sense, because most of us rarely have our prayers answered as specifically as we believed we desired them to be answered. Because of the rarely noticed and unusual nature of the real and serious answer to our prayers being recognized by us as the result of our prayer requests, the answers seem sporadic, random, and seldom. So when prayers actually are noticeably answered it appears to us as a random event, and we often attribute it to luck.

If we have been blinded by our lack of understanding, and thus attribute answered prayers to chance or happenstance, then we are blocking ourselves from being able to detect and differentiate successful prayers from unsuccessful prayers. When we are blind and have blocked ourselves in this way, then we no longer know what to pray for because we are confused about what works and what does not work with regard to our prayers.

For most of us, we are more likely to believe that praying for air and then being able to breathe the next morning is an answer to a prayer. And we are less likely to believe that someone offering us some money in a time of need is an answer to our prayer even though we had prayed for a financial boost. In fact, many of us won't hesitate to take money from the Government by making illegitimate claims for government hand-outs or by cheating on our taxes, but we would be insulted if someone offered us money to help us out, even though we have prayed for a financial boost.

Knowing what to pray for takes open eyes. Earlier we spoke of asking "What caused this?", which is one aspect of knowing what to pray for. But this is often an area of blindness that resides within us when it comes to *receiving* answers to our prayers.

If we accept an impassionate and doubtful approach to prayer by praying for things such as air that are a given in our lives every day, then we are praying for the wrong things! Praying for things that are already granted, such as praying for air to breathe or something to stand on when your feet leave your bed in the morning (as opposed to falling into the abyss), falls short—very short—of understanding what is true, and falls short of being in harmony with order.

There is an interesting situation that has occurred in many of our minds, having to do with testing the Creator. The Bible is incorrectly said to have contradictory information in regard to testing the Creator, where in one place we are told to "test the Creator in this", but in another place we are told "not to tempt the Creator". The second situation is telling us not to defy or ask for proof because of doubt, but the first situation where we are told to "*test* the Creator in this", means that we are supposed to get our lives in order and ask for wonderful circumstances and things in our lives while following a few basic guidelines for good conduct.

In truth, the "test" is not us testing the Creator, it is us testing our own belief of truth. We are instructed to ask for things which are *not* given like the way air is given. By asking for things that are not obvious and given, *we* test *ourselves*. The test is a test of our ability to *not* doubt. The Creator is not being tested—we are!

We can "test" the Creator, but that is a ridiculous notion because the Creator Created all things. We must have an open mind, both, to be able to ask, and to be able to see the answer when it comes.

Think of a scientist doing a test in the laboratory. Is the testing changing what will be? Is the order of physics and chemistry going to change because of his testing? No, most certainly not. What is being tested is the scientist's ability to understand what can be done with physics, chemistry, and with the materials with which he or she is working.

Our test of faith—or truth in believing that our prayers will be answered when we are in harmony with truth—is dependent upon our own test results. It's up to each one of us to open up our eyes to this simple understanding. If we misunderstand, then we will imagine and believe something that is not true about prayer. Misunderstanding greatly inhibits the effectiveness of our prayers. Test the Creator in this by asking for good things to come rather than asking for bad things to go away.

Do You Ask Questions Wrong?

People often ask questions *improperly*. How do we know they asked improperly? Because typically, we know the answer that someone wants when they ask a question even when they ask it improperly. In these cases, if we return the answer exact to the words of someone's question, then often, they tend to get frustrated and feel as if they are being mocked, even though they are not. Asking questions improperly is a very common error that many of us make. Sadly, this is even more common in prayer. There are many things that we are considering or thinking as we speak, and we typically do not consider or even realize this fact. When we believe things that have little to do with our actual request, then we make certain assessments and conclusions and subsequently have desires and make our requests based on that filtered information.

For instance, someone might ask us where we put something, so we respond that "It's in the drawer." But they may have looked in the drawer already but did not see the item. In this case they are likely to become frustrated with our answer because it's not making sense to them. They need to know specifically that it is underneath something in that drawer, hidden from plain view and from easy access.

It's common for people to ask questions improperly because it is our habit to ask for things in a vague way, such as, "Where is the scissors?" Replying in great detail to a person who asks this sort of vague question often frustrates them if they do not need the high level of detail that you're offering to them, and so it comes across as insulting to them. If it's in plain view in the drawer, then simply stating that it is in the drawer is enough information for them to readily find it. However, it may insult them if you give them its exact location in the drawer when it is obvious upon opening the drawer. Since they are the person making the request, it is up to them to make their request in a manner that is specific enough so that they will receive the proper answer they seek. The problem we have in this regard is that we're lazy and we do not want to say all of the words or think all the thoughts that it takes in order to accurately convey our message or question to the person who has the information that we desire. For instance, the person seeking the item should say something to the order of, "I looked in the drawer for the scissors and didn't see it. Do you know exactly where it is?"

The Creator does not want your filtered and lazy prayers—you need to offer it *all* up! If we're too lazy to take the time to think it through and define our own specific needs within our own minds, then do we really deserve to have our prayers answered at all? That would be like walking into your local bank and saying, "Give me some cash!" You will be promptly rejected if you do not offer more information to the teller, such as, your name, bank account number, the amount, and even the size bills desired. If you fail to do so and they do not recognize you then they might assume that you are trying to rob them. Or if you ask for a loan without well-laid plan, the loan will be rejected. Do we imagine that the Creator would not require a similar accounting of your request? The accounting of your desires is for you and is required of you. Make sure to be adequately specific in your requests, especially in your prayer requests.

How to Figure the Right Things to Pray For

What can we do to get through our own blindness so that we are able to figure out what the right things to pray for are within our own lives? As mentioned earlier, you need to ask the very important question, "What caused this?", and then think it through exhaustively and be very specific as you answer the question.

Get down to what your question or request really is. If you have already looked in the drawer for an item, then do not ask the person where the item is. You need to tell them that you have looked in the drawer and cannot find the item, and that you would like more detail as to where to be able to find the item. We must do these same mental actions when we pray. This is not for the person answering our request; it is so that *we* ourselves better understand what we want.

Very few people truly take the time to understand the detailed nature of what we are actually requesting in our prayers. We typically only state in our prayers that we need the item, but then we fail to even begin to understand the rough questions of *where* or *how*. Generally, we never even come close to understanding or defining the finer details of our prayers. As mentioned in an earlier chapter, often we are requesting *air* when we pray, which is similar to how we ask someone where something is. Our lack of being specific is a very big part of our problem in prayer. When we're trying to figure out what to pray for we need to get specific in our own minds about "What caused this?" before we even make an attempt to request anything in prayer.

Being specific in prayer is not for the Creator—it is for you! Once you have become proficient at accepting what is true by getting down to the real problems in your life, then you will see how often your prayers were actually answered in the past but you missed your opportunities to receive those answers, thus, causing you to suffer the consequences of that blindness. Most parents can attest to the fact that allowing a child to get away with asking for something in a poor and lackluster manner, and then giving it to the child without correction, will cause the child to become lazy in that regard. Do we imagine this to be any different for us with regard to our prayers and the Creator? How will we ever learn if we are given things that we are not specific about? Will it teach us a good way to live? No, it will not. If we ask in prayer without understanding our own details, we will be blind to the answer when it sits before our very own eyes due to the fact that, typically, we cannot recognize it as the answer because we have not become familiar with it through our own asking (our prayers).

You will find in life that *asking* creates clarity. When we have a question formed in our mind it is easy to see the answer when it comes. But that same answer could stand before you and you will not see it if you have not previously formed the question in your mind.

Do You Make Your Own Future?

Opportunities are all around us every day, but we fail to see them because those opportunities are like air to us. There is nothing mystical or special about them, they are just there— always! It is up to us to utilize these ever present air opportunities by having enough courage to act upon them. "Air opportunities" are opportunities that are always there for us.

Simply acting upon an opportunity, in itself, will take many people from a point of feeling like failures, to feeling very successful. However, these air opportunities have little to do with actual answers to our prayers. You may want to pray that your eyes become open to all of the air opportunities that surround you, but the air opportunities are *always* there for you to utilize regardless.

Opportunities that arise as a result of prayer are often going to be profoundly out of the ordinary and very wonderful. However, if we have not figured out the right things to pray for, then even if the opportunity that resulted from our prayer comes to us, we cannot recognize it because we did not specifically ask for it. In general, it will not register in our minds because we have not thought about it, and therefore, we cannot recognize it as the thing we desired.

Consider the following: There is a type of blindness that we experience every moment of everyday of our lives, and this blindness is very important for us to understand: I call it "red car blindness" or "The Red Car Effect". When you drive down the street, in your car, you see cars everywhere but you don't really notice them, this is red car blindness. According to The Red Car Effect, after you buy a new bright-red car, then the likelihood is very high that you are going to notice other bright-red cars everywhere you look. Nothing changed in the amount of red cars on the road, with the exception of yours. But your thinking has changed because now you are sensitive to red cars and you notice that they seem to be everywhere you look!

Answers to prayers work much the same way as Red Car Blindness does. When you have not become sensitive to the answer of a prayer, you will not see or recognize it when it passes you on the street.

Being very specific and detailed in your prayers is not for the Creator, it is for you in order for you to become sensitive to what you need so that when the answer comes along you will recognize it. Thinking through detailed thoughts to the end of the process is like you buying the red car and becoming sensitive to the other red cars on the road. If you ask for a bandage, then you'll be walking down the street looking for bandages. However, if you realize that you need a bandage because of the wound that you received at work, then you'll be walking down the street looking for a bandage *and* a job because you're then aware of your true needs and desires. We need to learn to think more broadly when waiting for the prayer's answer to be bestowed upon us, because the prayer typically requires changes to occur in our lives that we fail to realize and then recognize. That is why being specific in your prayer request is so important; it forces you to think about all of the aspects of your life that affect your situation about which you are praying.

This has often been referred to as the "law of attraction". The law of attraction has been tripping people up for a couple of centuries by having them believe that by thinking it, it will bring what they want into their life. This is not at all true! It is not the thinking about something that brings it into your life. It is the ability to notice or recognize it that allows you to embrace what is already in your life and all around you waiting you for to utilize it.

Just understanding the specific details of what you truly want allows you to recognize the desired things or circumstances and receive those into your life. This alone will bring much success to your life. This is the secret that many have been utilizing without actually understanding what it is that they are doing. This is not some mysterious prayer, it is air.

Air is already there for the taking, we just need to be sensitive to our needs so that we can pick the fruit off the tree that always stands before us—a tree of abundance which we previously did not notice. Imagining this to be some secretive law of attraction will only dupe you into believing it to be a magical effect, thus hindering your ability to progress your life to a truly joyfully abundant state. Having the ability to recognize the opportunities that already surround you on a daily basis will aid you in deliberately making your own future better, but this is neither prayer nor the answer to your prayer unless your prayer was to become aware of opportunity. Prayer goes beyond these secret air opportunities that are always around us. The only reason that people believe air opportunities to be mysteriously secret is that they have been blind for so long, that finally being able to see anything at all appears to them to be a virtual miracle.

When our prayers are answered, things that normally would not be available to us are presented to us in unusual places, at unusual times, and in unusual ways. But, if we have not specifically asked for these things in detail, then we will be unable to recognize them when they come our way.

Our inability to recognize real prayer answers is increased because real answers to prayers usually come in a manner that we do not anticipate, making it even more difficult for us to detect and see them. Getting a red car will allow you to notice many other red cars, but realizing that you have a specific year, make, and model with certain options will make you sensitive to that extra detail. Being sensitive to the extra detail not only allows you to notice all of the red cars, it also allows you to notice other cars of the same year, make, and model as the one you just bought.

Getting your thoughts down to the root of what you really want by asking "What caused this?" or "What could create this for me?", will begin to get your mind closer to where it needs to be in order to recognize the real and true answered prayer opportunities when they come your way.

Getting to the root of what you really want opens up your ability to be receptive to the answer to a prayer. It's not bad to ask only for a bandage in order to stop the bleeding, but it is very shortsighted and it will inhibit your ability to see a perfect and wonderful job opportunity when it comes your way.

What about Apparent Success of Others?

Sometimes we see people who we believe to be very dedicated to God, and they appear be "doing great things for the Lord", but then suddenly we see their worlds crumble. True success varies in people because of what is in their hearts. On the outside it appears that someone is doing all of the right things for the Creator, but internally they might be arrogant. Someone who does great things could have their heart in the wrong place, and because of this they are taken down from their high place of internal status. (That is to say, the way they see themselves.) If we see someone who appears to be doing "Godly" things who gets taken down a few notches, then we can be pretty sure that a correction is taking place in the person's life and/or that they are being purged, or tested, or prepared.

Sometimes an almost reverse scenario can occur when someone is not going towards where they belong and they are fighting the call to do *their* thing. If we're going to claim to believe in the Creator, then we must be honest enough with ourselves to realize that the Creator is not going to use us in a manner we think feels positive when we are arrogant and need to be corrected. Further, if we claim to be dedicated, but refuse to advance to where we are being called to, then also—we need to be corrected.

Our lofty thoughts are of no appeal to the Creator, but our purity of heart is. When your heart is set only towards the truth of the Creator, your path will be made clear and no one will be able to stop your progress. But if we ever lose that purity we can be certain that our misguided path will lead to anywhere but truth. And when we lack truth we can expect correction to enter our lives. The more blind to the truth that we allow ourselves to be, then the more pain we will feel during the correction process.

When you are pure and you let the Creator guide your steps, then joy and success will be within your grasp. Now is the time for you to decide if you believe in truth, or if you do not believe in truth. If you do believe in truth, then be true. If not, then suffer the consequences of your own decisions and choices. These are decisions and choices that *no one else* can make for *you.* Others can only inform you of the truth, the rest is solely in your own hands—you control your future in this regard. When you are pure and you let the Creator guide your steps, then joy and success will be yours!

Chapter 12

Why Do We Have Problems?

We have problems in our lives because we ask for the wrong things, such as in the bandage example we have been using. When we pray in this way, we fall short of requesting what we are actually wanting. We also fall short of realizing what may be required in order for our prayer to be best answered. This is why we usually are disappointed with the outcome of our prayers and our lives.

In general, people do not handle disappointment very well. This is understandable since disappointment is the releasing of hope. Our *hope* is our *ability to desire*. Without hope there would be no advancing in our lives, and we would live boring, lackluster, uneventful, and even miserable lives.

A real prayer is a display of hope. When we give up, we feel crushed because we are letting go of a belief that we held deep within us. Our hopeful beliefs help to produce, within us, some of those "feel-good" chemicals mentioned in a previous chapter. Our hope becomes our desire and our joy *when* we release our hope to our understanding of what is true.

Do You Hold On Too Tight to Your Hope?

We must transition from hope to truth at some point. Our hope is our ability to desire something that has not yet come to be. At a certain point we must convert our *hope* into *trust*.

We ask the Creator to release us from a situation, and yet, we hold on tightly to our current situation because we are afraid to lose the little that we feel we have. As a matter of technicality, hope is our ability to be able to, in our minds, create desire of something which previously was not imagined by us. Once this has been done, then desire takes over.

It is possible for us to have unrealistic hopes. Unrealistic hopes are hopes that cause harm or damage to others whether directly or indirectly. It's difficult for us to see far enough in advance to understand that what we want is sometimes not a good thing for those around us and may eventually destroy them or us. When this is the case, then can we really expect our prayer to be answered the way we imagined it?

Additionally, we must convert our desire into trust. If we do not convert it into trust, then it becomes an anchor around our necks that will drag us into the abyss of blindness.

Our hope is our ability to think ahead far enough in order to be able to properly ask something and make our request or prayer to the Creator. It is at the point when the request has been made that we need to transfer that hope and desire into *trust*. We need to trust, meaning that we need to understand that if we are in harmony and are pure, then our request *will* be answered provided that it serves good people in a constructive manner and does no harm.

If we do not understand that our request will be answered when we are in harmony, then, in many cases, when the answer comes in an unexpected manner, we will experience a very rough ride. We end up holding on tightly to our current circumstances so that we don't lose what we currently have. Often this is not the right thing to do because it fights the beautiful and robust answer to our prayer. We keep *hoping* for relief, but then we refuse to release the cause of our problem because we will not release our hope to trust.

Recognizing Answered Prayers

Red Car Blindness is a very problematic part of our ability to receive the gift of an answered prayer. We simply do not recognize the answers to our prayers when they are standing right before our eyes. Don't confuse this with what we referred to as "air opportunities", which are always present much the way air is always present.

Answers to prayers are usually peculiar or out of the ordinary, where air opportunities are everywhere all the time. It is important for you to be able to make the distinction in this regard so that you don't make the mistake of assuming an air opportunity is an answer to a prayer. But this does not mean we should not appreciate and be grateful for the air opportunities. We can certainly offer thanks and praise to the Creator for the air opportunities, but to mistake them for answers to a prayer is very shortsighted on our part, and it is inhibiting to our imagination and creative abilities. It shows our own doubt of the Creator's infinite abilities.

Your ability to realize the difference between real answers to prayers and air opportunities is the beginning of you being able to recognize a truly answered prayer. Truly answered prayers come in ways that are not expected, such as, cancer spontaneously going away, or some unattainable thing that you have been needing ends up in your path multiple times. It is these peculiar occurrences that we often miss that are actually the answers to our prayers.

We miss real prayer answers for two major reasons even when we're actively looking for the answers. The first reason we miss answers is that we actually believe air opportunities are answers to our lackluster prayers because *our expectations* of prayer are limited, doubtful, and, typically, very low. The second reason is that when we actually do have higher expectations and we pray for more specific things that are not normally around us, we still miss the opportunity that the answer provided because we do not expect the unusual way in which it was presented to us. Because we do not expect the unusual answer, we're not ready for it and did not recognize it due to the peculiar nature of the answer. All of this is due to our doubt, unbelief, low expectations, and lack of mental preparation. It is the Red Car Effect not realized.

An Answer to a Prayer is Not a Reward, It is a Result

An answer to a prayer is not a reward. We have this notion that just because we finally decided to take the time and ask for something from our Creator, that somehow we should expect a reward, as if there's a sign posted somewhere that says a "$25,000 reward for praying!" We believe that if we actually take the time to pray that somehow we are serving God, but praying has little to do with serving a God. In most cases we are serving ourselves when we pray.

Even in our prayer requests for others we are typically praying for those around us who *we* want to be successful and have good things. We are looking for a pat on the back from the Creator for praying, with an accompanying "good job praying" compliment. This ridiculous motivation has been taught to us from society as a whole. We are always seeking bonuses and rewards, as is demonstrated in people when they hold out in a job they don't like, just to get that bonus for being with the company for 10 or 20 years. This is more plainly recognized in our desire to win a money gambling game. A job bonus may be a bit different, but either of them is sort of waiting for that extra thank-you bonus or reward for which we have not specifically worked. The only work we need to do is truth, and then everything else will be easy!

Our problem in this is not that this bonus or reward is there. Sadly, our problem is that the bonus is often the basic reason that we do something to begin with. The reward becomes our purpose for doing things. An answer to a prayer is a result, it's not a bonus or a reward.

The answer to a prayer is a result, not of the prayer itself, but of our ability to come into harmony with—the order of things that was laid down at Creation. We are always asking for everything to be done for us; "Make my problems go away", "Give me a better job", "I want more money", and other such demanding requests.

Prayer is not for you to get what you want without you doing your part of *order*. When we get our lives in order and are in harmony with truth, it becomes very easy to see what we must do ourselves and the way in which we must think in order to accomplish our goals.

When we have accomplished harmony and truth, and we pray to be advanced in what we are built to do, it is at this point that the true opportunities will present themselves in unique and peculiar ways—some might call it miraculous ways! These unique completions of the answers to our prayers are not *rewards*, they are the *results*!

Rituals in religion give some people the impression that if we do certain things, then at some point there will be a reward. For instance, if we pray enough or attend church enough then our prayers will be answered. So if your child shows up for supper with the family every night and asks to use the car but is *not* trustworthy with the car, are you going to allow them free use of the car whenever they ask to use it just because they came to supper every night? Not likely.

While we can look at an answer to a prayer as a reward of our actions, it is more accurate to realize that a concise unique answer to a prayer is a *result* of our choices, of our mental attitude, and of our effort to think the request through thoroughly and then properly ask for it in prayer.

Repetitious Prayer

This is not an attack on repeating "The Lord's Prayer" or even on repeating the "Hail Mary"; rather, it is to make you aware that we were told to *not* pray in vain repetition. While you will likely not feel the fiery pits of hell for repeating your prayers, we are told that it is useless to do so. "The Lord's Prayer" was given to us as a *model* of **how** we are supposed to pray rather than as what we were supposed to say. We were told to "pray in this manner". The point that was being made is that there are several elements to prayer that you should include, but to recognize those elements you need to figure it out on your own.

It is very important regarding prayer that your intentions are pure and authentic. Read the "Our Father" prayer for yourself and dissect each phrase and get to the underlying intention of each phrase. Then make your own prayer following that same general pattern together with the understanding that you're getting from this book.

Repeating a prayer over and over does little good for you when you do not understand what you are actually saying. In truth, you are not saying the words that you think you are saying. You are actually professing the underlying intentions, and since you have not understood them, those underlying intentions in your prayers are void; meaning that you were sending *empty* prayer request envelopes to the Creator when you prayed. You were not requesting much of anything because your prayers were empty and have little meaning because you don't know the meaning.

Me telling you what the elements of "The Lord's Prayer" are, or you lazily looking it up somewhere, will not ever be able to have the same profound effect that is obtained when you actually read the text and think it through on your own to figure it out.

Once you have figured it out, then you can go on to check your findings and analysis compared to other people's conclusions to confirm your own understanding.

Asking for Protection

In truth, we would rarely even need to pray for or request things if our minds were focused, but since we allow ourselves to become distracted by all that surrounds us, we lose our ability to know that more good and order will come to us when we are in harmony with that good and order.

Because we are not clear minded, we need to pray and make these requests for our own good. Making clear-minded requests allows us to understand what it is that we need or want. And through that, we can then see what we should be expecting as an answer to our prayer.

We pray because we, or those around us, are in turmoil and are desirous of having things better in our lives. When we pray, we are placing an index in our own mind as a sort of reminder that there was something that we wanted, causing us to wait upon the anticipated result. In this way, we will recognize it—it is the Red Car Effect in full effect!

When we ask for protection from our enemies, or from illnesses, or from hard times, we often fail to understand that if we kept our lives in order and in harmony with truth, we wouldn't even need to ask for any sort of protection. Protection would simply come automatically with perfect harmony. Often, it is because we fall out of harmony with what is true that causes bad or evil things befall us. There is a big difference between asking to not be harmed versus asking for safety.

The Christ said: "aren't two sparrows sold for a penny? Yet not one will fall to the ground apart from the father. And even the hairs of your head are counted. So don't be afraid, because you are of more value than many sparrows." So long as we are in order and harmony with truth, we must understand that we are protected and cannot be destroyed. This does not mean that others, who have embraced bitterness and have fallen out of favor of truth, will not make attempts to try to bring us low like they themselves have become low. But, it *does* mean that you'll understand that when you are in truth, they can do you little harm so long as you stay in perfect harmony with what is true.

Do You Accept Lies?

In our quest for truth, "the age of enlightenment" came to be. But in our arrogance, we perverted the meaning of truth in the minds of many who wanted to be "enlightened".

Learning how to be true is very simple and fundamental, but if we have chosen to believe what is *not* true, then being true is a daunting task. The arrogance of "the age of reason" or "the age of enlightenment" brought about a perverted sense of logic that seeded the minds of many people with noxious weeds like mentioned in the Bible. It built "premise upon premise. Do this, do that. A rule for this, a rule for that. Here a little, there a little".

All of our misinterpretations of truth have built up a house of cards of unbelief which has no foundation. It seems that, due to our human arrogance, the closer we get to knowing the Creator, then the further we get from being able to accept the endless vastness of the Creator.

The fully imagined theory of evolution has succeeded to the extent it has because we cannot seem to bring ourselves to believe that something we cannot detect actually exists. We might say otherwise when asked, but the way we live our lives and our explanations of our origins indicate our excessive level of belief in the erred theory of evolution. Typically our human view is, if we cannot detect it with our instruments, then it does not exist. The danger of building premise upon a premise in this way causes us to take many good pieces of information, and then improperly assemble and interconnect all of them. In this way, we stand them each upon another lie.

Some Church leaders did, and still do, the same thing with the Bible. They took all these wonderful books and the information in them, and then interpret the books in the Bible in the way that *they* felt the books should be interpreted. This is our only choice, but our troubles begin when we *refuse* to consider alternate viable interpretations. Additionally, they only shared it with the congregation as those leaders saw fit. This is exactly what has happened with the theory of evolution during the nineteenth, twentieth, and into the twenty-first century; people share the findings the way they *want* them to be, rather than the way it was found. The words of the Bible say what they say, but some Church leaders and preachers often add to the text when relaying the information in effort to describe it the way *they* imagine it or understand it, rather than trying to read and understand the text from a perspective that is not their own. Even scientists who refuse to believe that the Creator exists interpret the Bible incorrectly in vain-effort to discredit it.

To not accept lies is to be in harmony with truth. When we have achieved the ability to banish lies and what is not true from our lives, then our prayer is pure and will be promptly answered in accordance with our level of readiness for our next place in our own lives and in Creation. Then our problems begin to diminish.

The Four Cornerstones of Life

Life has four important cornerstones that we all must set down in our own lives in order to achieve lasting joy throughout our lives. These four cornerstones are *yourself, your relationships, your family,* and *your prayers.*

You can get three of these correct and have some success in finding joy, but your joy will be fleeting and even confusing if you are missing even one of them. This is because each of these cornerstones bleeds in to the others and they depend upon one another.

There are four corresponding books that may be of interest to you dealing with each one of these four cornerstones. The book *Hot Water* deals with you. *Red Hot Marriage* exposes the hidden problems in marriages and relationships, and how to eliminate those problems. *Strong Family* digs deep and gets to the core of why families struggle and how to correct the problems we suffer with. And *Understanding Prayer*, which you are now reading, tackles the reasons our prayers fail and how to get them to work as promised by our Creator.

It is not required that someone read all of these books to obtain joy throughout their life, but each of these books exposes the many errors in our lives and thinking, which almost all of us are unaware of in each cornerstone area of life.

It is my intention that your life is joy filled throughout, and that it is *deliberately* done by you and your family. If you are not living life deliberately, then you can only have joy because you are getting lucky, and you cannot repeat it on demand when you do not fully understand what you are doing right versus what you are doing wrong.

If we are unable to cause true joy on demand, then we are truly in a trap and we have no control over our own lives—this must end today. These cornerstones are your right, and understanding them is your own responsibility. You and your family need to reclaim your cornerstones from the world and build your life of joy upon them—you deserve it!

Chapter 13

Out of Our Minds and Regaining Order

Earlier we spoke of being trapped in a cement walled room with wallpaper covering a hidden escape-way. We also touched on understanding the fact that if we are unaware of something, such as a way out, then we are unlikely to ever find it. Here you need to consider the Red Car Effect *before* you bought the red car.

We might question whether or not there's a solution to our current problems when we're trapped in a situation, but all too often, we give up too quickly and put it out of our minds.

If we believe, in our own heart and mind, that something cannot be done, then we will not be able to do it. We make choices *to do* or *not to do.*

Our choices *to do* or *not to do* are black and white choices. Any clouding or graying that we have in our minds with regard to our choices is from our own blindnesses, biases, and is of our own making. If we choose to stop looking for an escape in our wallpapered room, then we will *not* find the escape. But, if we choose to continue believing that there is a way, then it is likely that a way will appear to us in an unexpected manner.

We expect a doorway in a room and that door-*way* is like air to us. But we generally don't expect a secret passageway hidden from plain sight to exist. This is partly because we do not believe, but is mostly because that possibility never even comes to our minds. Someone anticipated people being trapped and created a way for them to escape from the trap. The biggest reason that these possibilities never come to mind is due to the fact that we do not believe that something is possible. Because we do not believe, we have become accustomed to not even trying to imagine it. We have caused ourselves to have no hope! Our society perpetuates such myths of non-belief by culturally discrediting the possibility that there are ways to escape.

Always seek to find the passage that is hidden which you are blind to. When, as our own choice, we choose to believe that something cannot be done, we then have barred ourselves from being able to accomplish our desired goal. We can change this through the joy of knowing that "thy will be done" if we choose to embrace this idea.

Do You Need More, More, More?

Our culture has led us to believe that we all "need" more, but we really don't *need* more, we **want** more. It's not the fact that we want to increase the level of abundance in our life that is problematic for us, rather, the problem is that increasing our abundance is our *primary* focus. When we want more, the implication in our hearts and minds is that we don't have enough.

Two people could both be striving to have more than what they currently have and for one it could be a failure, while for the other it will be a success. The reason this seemingly unfair situation occurs is because of where the two people's minds are with regard to what they each want.

We can want more because we see abundance and good, or we can want more because we feel that we don't have enough— A very important distinction to be aware of.

If you believe you do not have enough, then you have trapped yourself in a mentality of poverty, want, and need. Your focus becomes your shortage, and your desires are then built upon your feelings of that shortage. You end up believing that you do not have enough, thus causing all of your actions to be based upon not having enough. Then your quest becomes an effort to fulfill the lack that you believe you have in your life. When this is the case, it is *lack* that you will be focusing on, and lack is what will be answered in your life; and in doing so the result for you will be lack. This results in negative feelings in your heart and mind. Technically, it means that you have believed a lie, and in so doing, you have trapped yourself in blindness and negativity. This is why even "bad" people can be financially successful, and "good" people often fail—it is because of where their minds are focused.

Are You Suffering From Creativity Lows?

The nature of the order of *our **mind*** and *our **focus***, allow us to understand that *it **can** be*. When we forfeit our "it can be" focus, then we have forfeited everything! Order is the only thing that truly matters to us.

It's said that many people's creativity in many developed countries has been reaching new lows for a good amount of time. This is somewhat predictable when we understand that if we choose to accept lies and place premise upon premise we will lose our ability to think and desire in an abundant manner. Our desires turn from beautiful, robust, and imaginative actions, into doubtful and selfish lies. This is nothing new. Culturally this has been repeated too many times through the thousands of years of recorded history. Arrogance always destroys itself because the corrective nature of order is a part of the order of what is true. As long as we defy truth, society will rebuild itself and then eventually always be overcome by selfish arrogance only to be rebuilt and then self-destroyed again and again.

People will argue about what they believe, but no amount of debate or argument will change the simple fact that when we stray from what is true, we eventually lose our ability to create anything lasting.

We stop short of doing wonderful and great things and making lasting and useful discoveries when we have chosen to stop looking. The theory of evolution is one such perverted premise. Evolution, as well as the big bang theory, have many strong robust points, but the overzealous and arrogant attitudes of some of the followers of those beliefs have taken beautiful truths and built them upon lies to create the perverted theories that are being perpetuated onto society in effort to deter blind sheep from understanding the awesome nature of the Creator. This of course, is often denied, but for the diligent amongst humanity who decide to take a small amount of time to look into this, you will quickly find the elimination of a "God" to be an obvious agenda of naturalists. These doubts cast into your heart are not helpful to your prayers. To avoid the negativity we ignore the doubts, when what we should really be doing is to truthfully investigate it all ourselves.

You need not look very deep in to this to see those who believe in human evolution have an agenda to stomp out any thought of a Creator. Sadly, this is needed because many people, and some Church leaders, have, for too long, used only the Bible to prove the existence of their God. Regardless, the evolution agenda rejects any sound information that does not promote the evolution agenda. For many who have chosen this perspective, the possibility of a Creator is out of the equation and will not be considered even if the Creator was to become known. If you doubt this, then consider that many have chosen the godless evolution belief system but still foolishly reject the fact that a certain man existed, whom we refer to as the Christ. In making that statement I am only referring to the man, and not the possible status or position or purpose of the man. Despite the evidence and the non-Biblical writings throughout the world, they still discount Jesus of Nazareth as a fictitious figure. Rejecting the possibility that there is a Creator blocks us from seeing truth because we have rejected a possibility that has no refutable evidence. Rejecting possibility without just cause is to choose to be deliberately ignorant. We must ask ourselves, what evidence did those who *wrote* the books of the Bible have for the existence of the Creator?

What has been happening in the science world over the past few centuries is exactly the same thing that happened with the Church prior to that. It is a deep rooted and arrogant blind-spot that cannot see its way clear to turn the Lights of Truth on. Creativity lows abound and fewer people are being creative because these attitudes have filtered down to the youth of the world, and now doubt prevails in the hearts of many youth. Arrogant people desire all of the credit and are willing to make things up that are not true in order to get their desired fame, all at the expense of others. They do not want to work for what they have, so instead they believe and invent lies.

Much of the information that we receive on a day to day basis cares nothing of Truth or order. It is only concerned about sensationalizing headlines to warp and increase people's curiosity in order to sell more advertising space and/or receive more grant money in effort to shore up their own job security. This abused and agenda-driven model works for them, and it has served to bring humanity to its knees in stupidity and blindness once again. This cycle of self-serving arrogance has been repeating itself from the moment humanity was born.

Are You Ashamed or Guilty?

Shame and *guilt* play a big role in our prayers. Within our blindness, guilt is on behalf of the liar, and shame is on behalf of the believer of the lie. Both shame and guilt are terribly painful places to be and are clear signs that we need to make corrections in our thinking, in our hearts, and in our actions.

When we do something with the intent of obtaining something that is not rightfully ours, we are guilty of coveting. Coveting is seeking that which does not belong to us. Seeking credit that does not belong to us can only be done through being deceitful by, to some extent, presenting lies to other people. We also go through life in the self-delusion that life is about *things*. Anytime we lie, we are doing something to deceive those around us, or we are doing it to deceive ourselves. It doesn't matter what we want to believe we are doing when we lie, because the underlying motive of a lie is always to deceive.

It's possible for someone who is innocent to believe a lie, such as the child being told that there is a Santa Claus, Easter Bunny, or a Tooth Fairy. Lying to an innocent child about something like that, places *us* in a state of guilt for trying to get someone, in their innocence, to believe something that is not true.

Assuming you are the parent, for the child, they trusted you with their whole heart since you are where they are from. Upon finding out that they believed a lie, the child will potentially feel shame because, depending upon their age, they will likely be mocked by their peers when their peers tell them the truth. Then they will be brought low for something they did not deserve. Young children get put in this position because no one warned them otherwise. The shame that they feel is not their knowing whether or not something was a lie. The shame that they feel is that they believed that the lie was true.

With regard to believing lies, if you are the other person who is hearing the lies, and you choose to believe those lies, then you have deliberately taken on a state of *shame*, or better stated, an absence of an abundance of truth. Depending upon your motives for doing so, if you have chosen to believe lies, then you are also guilty of arrogance and bear both shame and guilt.

Believing a lie is our ultimate shame and doing so traps us and bars us from praying effectively.

People Who Want to Hurt You

Liars typically shame people for believing things that are true. An example of this is the Adam and Eve story, where Eve was lied to by the serpent, and the serpent said "Surely you will not die." Eve, in her doubt and arrogance, thought that she could be more than what she was Created as, and through that she believed the lie.

While to an extent, Eve was innocent, she was still guilty of wanting to be more than she was Created as. She believed the lie that *she* wasn't good enough *as she was!* Eve was humiliated from her guilt of trying to be more than what she was Created as. She was ashamed from believing a lie.

Evil, in the form of the serpent, was jealous and covetous of the Creator's attention to the newly Created Adam and Eve. Evil sought to bring them low so that the Creator would hold them in lower regard than the evil one who came as a serpent.

When people are jealous and want to hurt you, you are best served to walk away rather than to be hurt by them. However, once your heart is properly strengthened in things that are true, then you can offer kindness and truth to those jealous-covetous people while not being negatively influenced by them because they can no longer harm you in that way due to your adherence to truth. Eve would have been better served to just walk away.

The Christ could have avoided the doom of the Cross. But because the Christ's purpose was to fulfill a promise, the Pharisees were provoked to covetous-jealousy, by the Christ's brief true words and actions, through the evil that resided in their hearts. The Pharisees' arrogance caused them to harden their hearts and request the destruction of truth. However, *order*, in its simplicity and beauty, defeated them and the darkness and evil that they followed, and thus, restored order and harmony in Creation. Let us all regain our order and harmony by removing our shame and guilt by rejecting lies and by embracing truth.

Chapter 14

Do You Know Where You are Going?

We typically think that we are made up of the sum total of our experiences. There is some truth in this because everything that we have seen, felt, heard, smelled, and tasted has altered the way we perceive ourselves and life. Our perception of life and of ourselves dictates our lives through the decisions that we make based upon this perception. This is often the determining factor of whether we will succeed in our future, or experience failure and turmoil.

When we allow a skewed perception of ourselves within the world, it's like walking around in the dark in your home but someone rearranged your furniture without you knowing it. We end up tripping over things in our life because they are not where we expect them to be. This slows us down and holds us back from excelling in what we are best suited for.

We often skew our perception of ourselves because we spend too much time looking over our shoulders to compare ourselves to others so as to see how we rank. Comparing ourselves is not necessarily a bad thing to do unless we are trying to live the life of other people. When we listen to others who demand that we live our lives *their* way, or when we monitor the way others live and then try to copy them, it skews our perception of life and of ourselves. It's like the example of the furniture after it's been rearranged that we tripped over while in the dark. The darkness or blindness that we experience, shields our eyes from being able to see, in both where we have been, and in where we are going. Our own realization that we have been walking around in the dark allows us to know where we have been—and that realization is very important. But, knowing where you are going is far more important.

We typically believe that we know where we are. If asked, a common answer would likely be, "I am right here!" But right "here" is an arbitrary term. Most of us are lost and have no map with regard to truth. Nor do we understand where we are with regard to our own life's map.

Do You Know Where You Have Been?

Our perception of ourselves and our perception of the world around us are seldom what is good and true. Our perception is typically very skewed because it's based upon the feedback that we received from those around us. This feedback is often highly inaccurate. And when we believe this inaccurate information to be true, then we have chosen to believe what is not true—or more directly, we have chosen to believe lies. Our beliefs are a choice that we each make, but most of us do not realize this or even think of beliefs as a choice.

Believing lies about ourselves places us in a type of darkness that we will stumble through until we come upon the realization that we are immersed in deep darkness. When we come upon the realization that we were functioning in darkness, it's like turning on the lights. When our personal lights are turned on, then we become capable of looking back and can see everywhere we have been, both good *and* bad. It is at this point that we become able to admit to ourselves which things from our past were *good* and which things from our past were *bad*. This helps us to know who we are and from where we have come.

It is not the dwelling upon our past errors, but rather, it is the recognition of those errors that allows us to progress in life. Only when we can admit error are we able to look back at life and compare those past errors against our successes to determine how corrupted or distorted our path has been throughout our past.

Do You Know Where You Are?

Everything in our lives is a system of measurement and comparison. Usually we make the unfortunate error of comparing ourselves against others and against things that do not matter—we compare ourselves to *lies*.

We look around and see successful people, not truly understanding the origins of their success. We look at their *things* and the *money* that accompanies all of their success and feel that we fell short because we lack what they have. However, in most cases, when we strip away all of the whitewash of money and status, we find that other people are the same as us whether or not they are using money or status as a cover. Of course, in this case "the same as us" is relative to the amount of truth each person has within them.

Even if someone's money and status are a result of their true understanding and of their desire of what is true, *we* typically see it incorrectly and believe their money and status to be the goal or reward, rather than the result that it actually is.

When we use money and status levels as measures of our own lives, then we bind ourselves in yet another lie and have a skewed perception of where we really are in life.

Knowing where you have been in life is an index to knowing where you currently are in life. And knowing where you currently are in life is your index to knowing where you are going in life.

If we have allowed others to be our personal index of our own self, then we are walking in the dark and we will not be able to accurately see where we have been, nor will we be able to see with any accuracy where we currently are.

We are **not** other people. We are our own selves. And only our own actions matter as to where we have been and where we currently are. Other people may flaunt their status or wealth in order to build themselves up over us, but it is only when we believe that this matters, that it holds us hostage in the darkness of our own doubt.

When we overcome the lies about money and status and we focus on ourselves, we then become better each day by trying to make each day better than the last. As we work to make each day better, we look back and see our path becoming more orderly with each passing day. The straighter our path becomes, the more readily we can see how crooked our previous paths truly were.

It is only when we turn on the light of truth that we will see where we have been and where we truly are at any current moment. It is the combination of these—*our past* and *our present*—that allows us to utilize the key to understand where we are going.

Do You Know Where You are Going?

We needlessly struggle in life because we make our comparisons in utter darkness. We don't know where we have been, and we do not know where we currently are. Therefore, we cannot know where we are going.

If we're planning a trip to the tropics, but we're using our neighbor's map of northern Siberia with which to navigate, we will not get to our destination. We must choose to stop using the wrong comparisons and, in turn, learn to have truth be our guide. We cannot do this when we use other people's personal maps.

Don't be afraid to look back at your own life and see your past errors. Those errors have created your own roadmap to your future—and it's a far better future than you have ever imagined when you live for Truth! Your errors are a gift of understanding of what *not to do* in the future. So use them as a guide of what *not to do*, or perish for ignoring them.

Knowing where we are on our own map is a wonderful gift that we have been given. Without understanding where we are on our own map, we cannot choose to go where we will be our best and most successful in our future. Without this understanding we end up on a cold dark continent because we lost our way due to the fact that we are using other people's maps.

Once we grasp that only our own map matters for each one of us, we can then see the truth of where we have been and the mistakes that we have made. When we realize and admit our errors, only then can we correct our course and make for ourselves a new and far better way in life.

It's not what you did yesterday that matters. What matters is the fact that what you do today affects your tomorrows. ***Each day is a new day for you to restart and re-adjust*** your course to your destination!

When the astronauts traveled to the Moon or when navigators of old sailed the seas, they would frequently re-index themselves to get a new fix and an orientation on where they currently were located. They didn't just quickly look at a map and take off on their voyage without rechecking. No past voyages would have had any amount of success if they had failed to regularly reposition and reorient themselves.

Contemporary technologies reorient or re-index location even more so. The electronic Global Positioning System (GPS) mapping systems made available to society during the late twentieth century updated every few moments so that anytime the navigator takes note of their location on the map, they are instantly informed of their exact location and orientation within a few yards. This allows for safe, accurate, and timely arrival to each future destination.

Yet, as always, today we repeatedly fail to look at our own personal map to reorient ourselves and see where we are on our map. Our past does not matter with regard to where we are going, but if we analyze our past, it is useful in avoiding making those same mistakes again and again. Our present matters, but it is not our destination. Our destination will always be tomorrow, and our today is the trip to get there! We should always enjoy the ride to our destination each and every day, and occasionally take a *brief* look back at our past to make sure that we are not repeating past mistakes and then look to see that we are on the right course for our tomorrow.

What we do today *will* affect our tomorrow. If we take a wrong turn on the trip because we failed to look at our map, then we will end up in some unintended place tomorrow. What we did yesterday does not matter for tomorrow, but what we do today does matter very much! However, it is what we *decide* to do tomorrow that will always have the biggest impact on where we are going in the future—our **plans** for our future will always have the biggest impact!

It is where we're going that is most important to us. If we choose the go to a cold and dark part of a continent, then we can expect a cold rough voyage through a desolate and lonely wasteland. There is no changing course until we turn on the lights and look at our own map in an honest light. But to do this is a choice that each of us must make on our own.

Do You Understand Free Will?

Our choice of turning on our Light of Truth gives us the freedom to go where we want to go and to do what we want to do. But if we have chosen darkness and we follow other peoples' maps then we will go to the wrong place and will be bound by and limited to what we follow. We can change course on our map at any time we choose. It is a choice without limits that is inherent in each of us at our Creation—it is free will!

It's a peculiar experience to listen to people's perspectives as to what "free will" actually is. We frequently hear people make the bold statement that they "don't care what anyone thinks", and that they're "going to do whatever they want to do", but then out of those same lips comes, "How could such a loving god let such a horrible thing happen?" This contradictory way of thinking is, in itself, the explanation of their not understanding what "free will" truly is.

Anytime we have chosen to believe something that is not true, we have robbed our own selves of our own free will. Only with the order of truth can our free will exist!

We cannot be free when we have chosen to believe something that is not true. Choosing to believe something that is not true is the single most heinous crime that we perpetrate onto ourselves. And humanity has not yet been able to overcome it.

Depending upon your religious views or beliefs—or your understanding that the Christ came to us and died to overcome this very problem—it is believed by many that the Creator, or at least the very essence of the Creator, was embodied in this "Christ". The whole point of the exercise of the promise of the crucifixion was to restore our free-will by opening our eyes to the darkness that we each live within.

Overcoming your situation through proper understanding frees you and makes you far more capable in your future. If we understood the Bible for what it is, then we would all be far more successful today. Sadly, our dangerous blind-faithed approach is harming each one of us. We must end this approach.

Too many of us have spent our entire lives and all of our *being* investing in the "Santa Claus Effect" belief system—a system which is easily dismantled by anyone with the ambition to do so.

Whether Christian, evolutionist, or anyone else, if you are arrogant, then you are blind. A good amount of Christian doctrine is taken from the Bible. I have found the Bible to be a very accurate set of historical documents. When interpreted properly as it is written, these documents align with the truth by which we should strive to abide. My personal beliefs are not based upon what the Church leaders say, or for that matter, even what they interpreted the Bible as saying. We should only subscribe to what is true. Every "conflicting" piece of information claimed to be in the Bible, as proposed by those who doubt it, is easily rectified once we take off the blinders of all religion—including the religions of evolution and big bang. There is plenty of evidence of Creation without even referencing the Bible. I encourage everyone to consider that point or look into it for yourself.

When we have free will, we greet people's doubt with enthusiasm and as an opportunity to be able to share what is true with them. But if we believe we are going to convert people because of the Bible and what *we think* it says, then we are without sense. This is how too many people behaved in days long gone while killing and plundering in the name of the Bible or the Quran. There is a better way, and that way is the way of truth. It does not necessarily require teaching with the Bible, but it can.

When we use a blind-faith approach in any part of our lives, we are held in bondage by our blindness and unwillingness to consider other ideas. Historically, we attempt to force our will on others saying "Believe what I believe or die!" This is contrary to everything that it says in the Torah, the Bible, and the Quran. It is humanity's own hatred and doubt that causes us to not be able to understand the true messages within these ancient, yet amazingly modern, texts.

The very sad truth is that a vast majority of those who have in the past, and are now in the present, willing to kill or hate for their particular held beliefs, have never actually read any one of the three major holy texts in its entirety. And for the few who actually have read any parts of any of these books, for most of them, it was often done in their younger years as a forced part of some curriculum. Further, people often read the books selectively by focusing on a questionable interpretation of a particular version or translation that *they feel* justifies their lies and inaccuracies. But they either ignore or refuse to read and consider the rest, all of which conflicts with their questionable interpretation of a single verse upon which they build their entire false doctrine. Additionally, you will find that if you ask someone if they have ever read the Bible the answer will be "Yes", but if you ask if they read it **cover to cover** then the answer is "No." Far too few people have actually read it all and done so without prejudicial agenda.

Of our own free will, we have chosen to blind ourselves and we have stripped ourselves of the very same free will that we have used to bind ourselves in darkness. This single act of ignorance and arrogance has shut off the Light of Truth within us, and has disabled our ability to readily turn the Light of Truth back on within our own hearts and minds.

It is possible for us to instantly regain truth once possessed, but truth becomes a painful double edge sword for us when we have chosen darkness through so much of our own past history. Truth convicts us of our past darkness the moment we choose Truth. The problem we have is that most of us foolishly run from truth's wonderful conviction. Running from this is like we spoke of earlier with regard to repeatedly banging ourselves into an edge of something.

Hiding truth will only cause you to continually repeat the unwise actions that have caused you so much pain throughout your years. This continuous repetition of error will continue to occur until truth is received by *you*. Our prayers cannot be pure and will not be readily received by the Creator while we are in a state of doubt. Amongst the first actions we need to take to get our prayers to become effective, is that we have to understand that we must believe only things that are true and always seek to achieve that. Falling prey to the lies of a blind-faithed religion of any kind will cast doubt in your heart and mind because you have likely chosen to believe some things that are not true. When we do this we notice it, but we typically do not understand the discrepancies that surround us, thus causing us to doubt more and more.

When we limit our belief in the Creator and of the Creator's ability to deliver, we fail to understand that the Creator can deliver more blessings than we could ever imagine are possible and more than we could even handle in an infinite amount of our lifetimes. It is our *doubt* that destroys our joy and stops us from being able to accurately use *our own* map to clearly see our true destination.

Chapter 15

Religion
Are You a "Religious" Person?

People struggle with the term "religion" because the word's true meaning is different than what it has come to culturally mean in our hearts and minds.

In its original context, "religion" means to *rejoin* or to *bind together*. When we say Catholic, Muslim, Christian, or Jew, we immediately think "religion" and about the set of beliefs that corresponds with each religion's label. Religion, as we understand it today, is far more widespread than those few labels just mentioned.

Many understand religion as a set of beliefs that we have chosen to follow simply because we chose to follow those beliefs—it is blind-faith—and for no other reason than it is what we were familiar with or it is what we like. Typically, our religion was taught directly to us during our youth as members of a church, as students in school, through mere social interaction, or from family.

Evolution is no less of a religion than Christianity or Islam are. Each of these mentioned labels uses its own interpretations of each of their foundational information sets. Just because each of these religions believes their interpretation of their information to be accurate, does not mean that their interpretation is accurate.

If one of the patriarchs of any one religion had it wrong, then that patriarch's error is deeply embedded within the belief system that they founded. Without the patriarch's original errors, or at least our erred interpretation of the patriarch's beliefs, each of the erred religions, *as we know them*, would crumble.

Those who subscribe to the errors upon which many religions are built, have chosen to believe things that are not true. This is not to say that everything within the religion is wrong. In fact, even the patriarch of evolution gathered a multitude of useful information that helped to remove a particular type of blindness from many church-going people. Yet, in his zeal to prove a point, the father of evolution overstepped his authority and made a mockery of himself as well as a mockery of all of those who have chosen to believe the entire doctrine that was built upon his foundation. The error in evolution functions identically to any error that might be embedded in any other religion that has ever existed.

Again, religion, as we typically understand it, is a set of beliefs that we have chosen to believe regardless of the evidence contrary to our beliefs.

When we choose to believe with blind-faith, then we are "religious" people. Christians, Jews, and Muslims all have a respect for the documents we call the Old Testament of the Bible, but few of us have actually read the text, or sought to understand it *if* we actually took the time to read it at all. Yet, we fight for our often erred beliefs with petty arguments, both within our own sect, and without—even unto death.

Somehow we feel that if we are willing to die for our own lies, which we have *chosen to* follow, that those lies will be justified. I assure you that our *false* beliefs will not be justified— ever! And neither will we when we hold such false beliefs to be true in our own hearts.

We must learn to stay far from those who have chosen blind-faith as a religion. If the tie that binds a religion is a lie, then that is not a place that we, who believe in and love what is true, belong. We must stay far from the lies in any religion because those who have chosen this type of religion will tap and drain us of our positive energy and of our love of truth, which will rob us of the love of our fellow man.

Do You Try to Control Others?

Anyone who has chosen the darkness of lies and untruth will typically try to control you in some way, because anyone who has chosen this has chosen it because they believe a lie. This is a circular problem, meaning that we chose the lie because we chose the lie. It builds on itself and it will continue to build upon itself. The more it builds on itself, the lower we feel, and, subsequently, the more we feel the need to control or manipulate those around us to keep them from becoming greater than we are. Anytime we have chosen this path we are instantly making everyone around us better than we are. And we do this of our own free will. The only way we can again become equal with everyone else is to embrace what is true. We cannot be elevated above being true. Truth is the highest level of existence.

If we are encountering others who are trying to control us, and we make an effort to stop their interference, then their response will typically be vicious and full of malice. You will typically be accused of "judging" them, or perhaps be accused that you are trying to tell them what to do or how they should be living their lives. However, telling someone to leave you alone and let you go about your business is not judging them, nor is it trying to control them in any way. It is simply telling them that you will no longer put up with their unreasonable demands or behavior.

You currently have free will and you always have had free will! Free will is always accessible to you. The only time that it is not is when you have denied truth. We can speak against anything we want and it is of little consequence and is easy to recover from, but once you have chosen to deny truth, then you have become eternally bound in your lies unless and until you reject those lies and decide to choose truth. Lies have you bound in chains until **you** choose to reject lies. Nothing can or ever will be able to unbind you from lies, except your own willingness to dispose of the lies and arrogance and then only seek things that are true

The dangerous double-edged sword of truth, called free will, is the most precious gift we have ever received. But when we wield that sword recklessly, we often injure ourselves to a nearly irreparable state. In our quest for healing, we shout out for a bandage, forever trying to patch the hemorrhages that we have caused with our own free will.

You Cannot Please the Unpleasable

We become unpleasable or insatiable, never being satisfied with anyone or anything around us. And always demanding more and more, ever increasingly failing to be able to stop the profuse bleeding of our own self-inflicted wounds. When we do this, or when we encounter others doing so, we become frustrated and angry.

Trying to please an unpleasable person is a futile effort, and it is technically impossible to do since they are **un**pleasable.

We frequently become trapped in trying to please these people because we all want to be loved and trusted. But when someone continually makes us try to prove ourselves when we already are living by what is true, then there is nothing more that we can do to properly please them. Attempting to alter truth, just to please someone, is a lie and places us within their lie. Doing so is a very foolish decision that puts *you* as *their* servant (Recall Eve in the Garden of Eden.)

Being correct in truth is the ultimate in perfection and purity. Doing anything other than truth will foul you. Sometimes we are able to briefly please an unpleasable person by following their lying and cheating ways. They may even appear chaste and upright on the surface, but their underlying ways are founded on the doubt that they have chosen to abide by. If we choose to follow their lead and submit to their will, we have then bound ourselves to them as their servant. Submitting to their lead places them in control of us, and thus allows them to expose our lie and accuse us of ill deeds, even further binding us in our fear of exposure and shame.

Trying to please an unpleasable person with anything other than pure truth will frustrate us and cause us to end up praying to rectify a position that neither ourselves nor the Creator can control due to the free will of the person who is frustrating us, to whom, of our own free will, we handed our own authority. It is a recipe for prayer failure. If we fail to please the unpleasable with what is true, then we have truly won the battle and they hold nothing over us—their guilt rests upon their own shoulders! But when we alter truth in us, we turn the information into a lie and cast truth aside, causing our guilt to rest upon *our own* shoulders.

They Will Dispose of You

When an unpleasable person accomplishes the task of getting us to bend from what we know is good and proper, we will typically be disposed of by them. This is the sort of thing we frequently see in politics and depicted in movies. While movies sensationalize everything for entertainment value, many of these movie plots or representations are not random or without merit. This form of art is a reflection of the poor condition of human nature, and these ideas are often written by people who have experienced and then embellished the circumstances, and then, further, wrote their embellished circumstances into movie scripts for entertainment value.

The most precious thing that any one of us has is our free will to embrace things that are true. So long as we abide by this simple application of order we will always be useful and needed, making us invaluable to the world around us and most everyone we know.

While there may be threats against us and attempts to make us feel wrong or incorrect, or to discredit us due to our choice of the beauty of truth, nothing presented can ever shame us or lay guilt upon us when we know what is true and choose to abide by it.

Are You Selfish?

It is in our nature to want to please people, and this in itself can be selfish. Our quest for acceptance often causes us to make concessions with regard to our truth, and doing so requires a heavy price. When we try to bargain with someone who is out of synchronization with the order of truth, we then forfeit our power to whomever we have bargained with and made concessions to. This destructive form of selfishness does us no good in the long run—Again, think Eve in the Garden.

People who are trying to please others practice another form of selfishness that is destructive to themselves, but it is also destructive to the others who surround them. When we concede to the demands of the unpleasable, we then have entangled ourselves in a selfish circle of destruction between ourselves and the unpleasable person. This is selfishness built upon selfishness, all in order to please ourselves. Once we have fallen into our selfish self-made trap, regardless of which position we are in within it, there is a tendency to look around us and misunderstand what selfishness really is. There's a feeling that if we help someone accomplish their task, that we then are not being selfish. But, if the task that we are helping them with is not pure, and we know it, then we must question our own motives.

It's not selfish to walk away from this sort of behavior. It is selfish to take part in this sort of behavior. Do not fear if a selfish person wants to discard you, because their discarding of you is a blessing to you and will keep you pure, just as you were Created to be!

Any person who embraces truth does not have the ability to be selfish so long as they hold tightly to truth. Truth is your life! It will keep you afloat when you are adrift in the abyss. It will pick you up and carry you when you have fallen. It will set you on the right path when you've lost your way. It will purify you and perfect you for the Creator.

The Seed of Betrayal

Our adoption of blind-faith and our interpretation of it have presented us with a dilemma that is difficult to escape from. Just as a child places their entire trust in their parents by expecting that these people, who brought them into this world, would not *ever* do anything ill to them or mislead them in any way, so too, the people believed that some Church leaders would not ever mislead them or tell them anything that was not true.

We expect that the Church will be a place of support where we know that we can go for good and true guidance because that is what it is supposed to be. We *trust* the preachers, priests, and teachers because they claim they are teaching from the Bible. There is an inherent sense of accuracy in the Bible that we feel when we hear the words, but because these words are often misinterpreted, due to our choices of what and who we choose to believe, the interpretations can be highly misleading. This then becomes "The blind leading the blind".

When our lives come into disarray, the Church often gets blamed, and rightfully so, because often some of the Church's representatives betrayed our trust via their inaccuracy in interpreting the text. The same thing is about to happen to evolution and its patriarchs, pharisees, priests, and teachers, because it, too, has betrayed the trust of its followers. Consider not go too far in turning against any religion, but rather embrace each religion's truths to better know what **Is**. And I further suggest considering disregarding each religion's lies. It is a foolish mistake to disregard a religion in its entirety without just cause. The Church has done very much good over the centuries, far more good than bad. And the bad was usually a result of a select few unsavory people.

Allowing the seed of betrayal to become bitterness within us serves neither the Creator, nor the Creator's science that we use to better know our Creator with.

Our common response to betrayal is to lash out and attack. This usually results in an approach that steps outside of its bounds, ending by causing us to attack with a vicious effort to destroy that which we feel betrayed us. This approach is of little use to either the betrayer or the betrayed. It only serves to provoke an unneeded and unproductive battle.

We all have *expectations*, and it is these expectations within us that are betrayed or violated. When we place our trust in someone and they give us incorrect information, they have violated *our expectations* of trust in them.

The Dangers of Sharing your Dreams with Negative People

When someone holds erred beliefs they will generally give bad advice and have a negative outlook. We must change our expectations in accordance with what we understand about the world around us. If we've chosen to believe things that are not true, we will then also place our trust in those who should not be trusted. Trusting those who have chosen to be untrustworthy will result in the betrayals just spoken of in the last section.

When we confide in someone, we are also placing our trust in them. "**Confide**" means *with-fidelity* or *with trust*. Just as we place our trust in those who lead us, we also place our trust in those with whom we share it. We share with people because we want to have them be a part of what we are and of what we are doing. Through this, they are, therefore, a part of us. Our *expectation* of confiding in them is that they would support our goals.

A common result of sharing our desires, goals, or dreams with those who we confide in is that it brings about betrayal and/or negativity against us and our dreams. Our dreams are often dashed to pieces by negative, covetously jealous people who doubt that anything real and substantial can actually occur or who do not want us to have anything good or anything perceived as better than what *they* have. Beware of this and remove yourself from these relationships! Strengthen yourself with truth and abide by it before you ever return to these people.

When people who are negative and/or doubtful about your ideas finally achieve an understanding that cuts through their own doubt and negativity, and their newfound understanding shows them that something good can actually happen, then they will often attempt to hijack your dreams and discard you. It is unproductive and painful to place our trust in negative people who are willing to cut us down with sarcasm and disdain, and then steal our good efforts.

Our goal as human beings is to create more order in this world and to make it a better and more beautiful place by teaching those around us to be kind, loving, and creative; and also to say and do things that increase mankind. Allowing anyone to crush our dreams with their negativity is not a wise choice! However, this should not be confused with other people correcting us.

If you share your dreams with someone, and they come to you with some ideas of correction, then do not mistake their correction for negativity. Even though you might not like to hear that there may be flaws in the way you propose to achieve your dream, you must still welcome considering these corrections that are offered to you from those whom you have discussed your dreams with. We must mentally process and consider their corrections before we move on so that we don't err again.

If what someone offers you, in the form of advice or correction, can straighten and smooth your path to achieve your dream, then you should welcome that with open arms and embrace it! It is when their advice discourages you from obtaining your dream that you must question their negativity. If you're discouraged because their good advice means that you will need to do more work, then you're just lazy. And if you are unwilling to do the work properly, then you do not deserve to accomplish your dreams.

If someone tells you that your dream is dishonest, you best consider processing their analysis of the goal that you shared with them. This should be done in order to assure yourself that you are in harmony with what is true.

Steer clear of those who will not depart from their negativity because it will do you no good to be with them. It will not do your family any good to be around negative people. Negativity drags you down into their lie of disbelief, and causes you to be unable to rise up and do great things. Be pure in what you do, and stay true, and then you will be successful and no one will be able to stop you! A person of truth will often be wrongly considered a negative person by those who actually are negative because truth shows errors and errors are negative. It is not negative to correct things.

Also, do not share the dreams that you have with those who will *only always agree* with you. Nor should you only share your dreams with those who are always negative. Rather, share your dreams with those who, with truth and love, will build you up and correct you and set you on a straighter and better path to achieving your dreams and desires!

When we have wrong associations with people, it inhibits our prayer-effectiveness because we are cast into a state of doubt about things that are actually true. Live in truth and be positive and be honest with yourself and then you will be better able to detect and remove negative people from your life.

Chapter 16

Focusing on Others

Negativity and *correction* are often confused in our minds. It is important for us to *not* confuse *negativity* with *correction*. When we choose the way of negativity for our lives, and then someone corrects us, we see this correction from them as being negative. This occurs because we know that what they are telling us is that we should not be doing bad or wrong things. Whenever we avoid doing something that is negative, it is a good thing for us! When we do negative or bad things, we should be, and we need to be, corrected. Correction tells us not to do *bad* or *wrong* things.

Negativity that is not a form of correction is a disease that must be eradicated from all of our lives. The further we get from negativity, the more successful, productive, and joyful we all become!

When we place our focus on others in this negative way, rather than perfecting ourselves, we condemn them and hold ourselves hostage in the process. It's like we spoke of earlier with regard to using other people in place of our own personal map to navigate our own lives with—It distracts us from our work and puts us on the wrong path.

Negativity is doubt, and it is unproductive. Even the world of science has embraced *doubt* and crowned it as king. In the science world, it is often said that "We must doubt everything!" The only things we must ever doubt are doubt itself and lies!

When we place our focus on others by using *their* personal map, then we are trying to be *them*. This does us little good in trying to improve ourselves. We must have courage to rise up and be ourselves and *not* allow others to dictate our lives with their sarcasm, negativity, and doubt.

The attitudes of sarcasm, negativity, and doubt have a very strong draw that holds many people hostage. Any people who practice this sort of negativity generally are good people when they are not filled with the sarcasm, negativity, and the doubt that they foolishly spew out to, and at, others and themselves. This behavior has caused many good people to fail throughout their lives—and sometimes even unto their deaths. There is no need for us to falter like this, because we only need to focus on our own desire, on our own kindness, and on truth itself!

Praying With Negativity
Why Don't My Prayers Work?

We fail at prayer because of our negativity. Earlier, we spoke of the situation about requesting a bandage when praying to solve problems, but praying with negativity is a bit different. Many of us doubt that our prayer will be answered, but even that is not what I am referring to when I say "praying with negativity." Earlier, when we spoke of asking in a wrong way, we did not specifically discuss the negativity aspects and how it affects our prayers.

Far too often, there is one particular sort of negativity in which many of us partake, which is: we want bad things to go away in our lives.

Another type of negativity is thinking in a limited manner. When we want *more*, we are usually focusing on the *shortage* that we feel rather than on the *abundance* that we claim we desire. Focusing on the shortage that we feel, dooms us and our prayers.

The perspective with which we approach our prayers is a prominent problem with regard to the success versus the failure of our prayers. The reason that we focus on shortage is because we feel inadequate in our results even though our results may be quite successful. Most of our feelings of being inadequate are there because we are in an area in which we do not belong, or in which we no longer belong. We can never feel fulfilled when we're out of harmony with where we are Created to be. This is because it is not technically possible to feel adequately fulfilled when you are out of harmony. And you cannot be in harmony when you are not where you are designed to be.

When we are not where we belong, doing the things that we each are built to do, then we will always feel that we are falling short. Thus, we will always be desirous of getting more in an effort to feel fulfilled—we have put ourselves in a mentality of *shortage*.

Most things that we do in life are temporary, and as we grow in understanding and clarity, we graduate and are promoted to our next place in life.

Because we set our focus on the wrong things and the wrong people, we miss when it is our time to graduate on to our next place in life. After we have prayed for improvements to our life, due to our misapplied focus we typically miss the opportunities that are the answers to our prayers.

Think of this like deciding that you want to add another level onto your home. You'll call a carpenter to come and do the work, and when the carpenter gets there, he informs you that in order to achieve your dream home, you have to remove the old foundation and replace it with a new stronger foundation in order to support the new improved and larger dream-home.

If you hang onto your old foundation, then you will not be prepared to move on to your new improved two-story life. What you build on top of the old foundation is as weak as the old foundation is. If the old foundation begins to crumble under the weight of your new improved two-story life, then your new life will also crumble, and it will be destroyed along with the old foundation when the old foundation gives way to the weight of your new life.

Negative People are Mistaken for Discerning People

It is wise to go to other people and ask them to scrutinize your plans. This is so that you can have clear and unbiased opinion on your plan. But, we must be careful in who we choose to go to for this sort of consultation.

There are several types of people and friends who we commonly encounter when reaching out to consult with someone about our plans. One type is a person who is negative and will criticize and try to destroy anything that you have presented to get their opinion about. They will have no suggestions on how to appropriately approach your actual plan.

Another type person is the traditional, and useless, "yes man" who will agree with you no matter how ridiculous or impractical your plans are. Due to their fear of rejection, this type of person only seeks validation from you. They have discovered that when they agree for the sake of being agreeable then they are accepted because it strokes and feeds their master's ego—In the long run, they are very dangerous to you and they are very dishonest.

Another non-helpful type of person is one who will not give you any feedback, has no ideas, and generally is full of doubt. Wasting your time sharing your dreams with this type of personality is of no avail to you.

Finally, the last type of person is a *true* and *valued* friend! They are the type of person who will offer good and sound opinion and thoughtful observation of your end goal. This type person is kind but honest, and they will be sincere and will offer alternate thoughts that allow you to better achieve your goal. This last type is a true friend indeed!

Negative people are commonly mistaken for *discerning* people who are true friends. *True* friends are always very considerate and honest with regard to your hopes and dreams. Negative people are usually eager to offer their negative, and often mean and/or sarcastic opinions on your situation. If you're a person who likes to do things correctly, then you could be somewhat more subject to the errors of negatively critical people because your desire is to receive correction so that you can do the task right. In other words, you are willing to hear someone out and then correct your thinking if their proposal appears to you as good. This is especially true when the negative person speaks with such arrogance that it makes them appear as confident. The world has an urgent need to be able to recognize negative people, and then avoid their foolish counsel.

Listening to a person, who arrogantly professes a negative opinion as if it has any value, traps you in their chains of negativity. It is their arrogance that confuses us and lures us into believing that they have the confidence of a true confidant. They promote their arrogant lies with a brazen attitude that makes them appear confident, when in reality, they are actually *wrong*.

A *true* confidant will always support your good end goal and help you to achieve that good goal. If there is an error in your end goal, they will help you to correct the error(s) and adjust your goal to better make the goal possible.

A true confidant will never crush your goal unless it is required for your well-being. But, a negative person will crush your goals and leave you sitting in the ruins. Steer clear of their negativity and you will soon be back on the road to success!

Leading With Negativity

A very big problem for us with regard negativity from others is when one person spreads bad feelings to others about someone or someone's thoughts or ideas. Many people have been turned away from truth and from good people because of an outspoken foolish person that only speaks negatively about the people or subject. This is what occurs with the Creator and the blind-faith that people typically have.

When someone speaks against your blind-faith you are best suited to investigate for yourself to see if their claims are true. If you know the person, or topic, or about the subject being discredited, then search your thoughts and your heart and decide for yourself if you are being *unjustly* influenced by the person who is being critical.

There are many people who allow such unjust information to influence their thoughts about other people and about the Creator and Creation. This causes us to doubt and lose faith because we are too lazy to properly verify the information, and in doing so we lose our faith.

Getting Rich with Prayer?

We often pray for good fortune and things we truly do not need. But "now it's time to learn how to get rich with prayer! Let's use it to our advantage and make lots of money!" Right?

If the preceding statements I once heard excited you, then it is certain that you are likely to fall prey to *anyone* promoting any system that allows you to succeed by following a few simple rules or steps. Protect yourself from this selfish attitude. If your goal is to use prayer to become rich, you have come to the wrong place because this book is not about *false* wealth. *Real* and *true* wealth has little to do with money.

Abundance of money is a typical *result* of *real* and *true* wealth. When you have true wealth, you will not worry about money—ever! Money comes to you as is needed to serve you as you fulfill your design; with, of course, the realization that you must do your part of the work.

Be wary of those who require large sums from you in order for you to achieve success. I am not referring to business investments, but rather, I am referring to instructional programs that, for substantial fees, teach you how to be better.

Advice for "getting rich" that is true and is proper, will always be free or have a small fee such as the cost of a typical book or the nominal price you pay to see a program. But, much beyond that, a program is suspect if you must pay a great deal of money for it in order to learn how to "get rich". There are brief educational programs that can teach you skills of a particular trade. These often have a hefty price tag and are sometimes worth the fee for people who have a true interest in what the programs are teaching. But in this section we are referring to programs that charge you a great deal for your own self-improvement. To be fair, the value of many of these types of programs is dependent upon the attitude of the person attending the programs, because some programs can actually be of help to people. However, in the end, many such programs are okay but are generally not needed.

False success comes in many forms, and it is often a trap cloaked in the beauty and lure of money, riches, and prestige. Keep far from this trap because it is fleeting and dangerous! It commonly trips people up and leads them down a path of arrogance and self-destruction. "Get rich" plans always prey on the unfortunate and unknowing who desire to have success in life but who have come to perceive that success is about *status*, *money*, and *goods*—Success is not about status, money, or goods! True success has nothing to do with status, money, or goods. Those are all a *results* of true success!

In order to successfully pray yourself rich you must not be concerned about status, money, or prestige. And you must place your concern in bettering yourself and stepping into harmony with order and truth. It is when we do this and understand it, that our prayers will be answered and we will have true success in our lives.

True success is free, and it has no penalty or fee. It can be done by you at any time for free, and it is desired by your Creator that you do so.

Praying yourself rich can only involve what is true, and it will build up everyone around you. Including your enemies, even if they end up being torn down before they are rebuilt and renewed.

A clear sign that you have your heart in the wrong place with regard to prayer is when your focus is money. Focusing specifically on money makes it apparent that you worry about your sustenance, and doing so makes it clear that you are focused on shortage, or that you feel lowly about yourself and believe that your worth is based only upon status and money.

It is okay to ask for money or other good things, but *focusing* on money and status cannot get you the true success that you desire. Only embracing truth and order can accomplish true success!

Do Your Wants Require Harm to Others?

A simple check that you can do, which may help you in better understanding your motives, is to question: Does what you want require any harm to others? We live in a big world with many people in it, all of whom have their own goals, dreams, and desires. If our goal is not in harmony with the good desires of others, then the goal will cause the other people harm. Desiring harm and defeat for others so that *you* can succeed is not good or constructive in any way. In the long run it will lead you to your own destruction—It is a coward's way to live.

Everything we do should be built upon things that are good and true! When everything that we do is built upon things that are good and true, then truth is in us and in our true goals and in our desires. This will shine brightly for all to see and will bring blessings and goodness to many people.

Truth will always expose error. Be cautious not to confuse *error being exposed*, with *harming* others. If you are on a quest to defame another person by exposing their errors, then you are sorely headed down the wrong path and will most certainly be the maker of your own doom. Error exposes itself when truth is anywhere near it. If you are true and honest in what you want, and if you have been forthcoming in your plans and in your prayers, then expect that if you are utilizing the skills for which you were designed, that your prayers *will* then be answered.

When your goals are built with unselfish pure goals of truth, and those goals destroy the work of someone who lives their life based upon errors or lies, it is of no concern to you. Their destruction will occur naturally without your deliberate interaction and without any intentions to harm them. They will eventually fall because of their own errors and lies.

The Creator said "Vengeance is mine". We need not concern ourselves with trying to "get" someone who is living wrongly. They will destroy themselves and will be destroyed when the good and true is compared with them.

But, let us not confuse allowing truth to work its wonders, with protecting ourselves and other innocent people from injury. There's a difference between *aggression* and *protection*. You do not have to allow evil to harm you. It is okay to protect yourself and others from the harm from things that are not of truth.

"Allowing truth to work its wonders" means to allow others, who will not receive truth, to destroy themselves by means of their own folly. It also means that you do not have to let *them* destroy *you*. Realize the difference between *aggression* and *protection*.

It is always good to protect the innocent. Always keep this question in mind: If what you want requires harm to others who are living rightly, then why would your prayer be answered by the Creator? This is true whether or not you are aware of the potential harm of your requests.

Are Healings Real?

Healings are claimed to be happening everywhere, but we typically choose to believe that these accounts are not real. Our lack of ability to believe is largely because all too often false "healers" are cheaters and liars who make healings appear to be fraudulent, thus, causing us to doubt. When preachers take the stage and perform fake healings for viewership-ratings and donations, and then are later exposed as being fraudulent healers, it crushes our blind-faith due to the fact that we have wrongly placed our trust in these false preachers. This happens to us because we are led to believe that money can buy us financial freedom and healing. False preachers are appealing to us because of their words of acceptance and the *apparent* love that they seem to promote, similar to the lure of a gang who accepts an outcast youth. They themselves might even believe that they are in truth and that they are doing "God's work" as they promote their lies or errors. It is foolish to believe that giving money to them will make your troubles gone. Giving them your money is often confused with tithing (Tithing is giving ten percent of your income for temple services.)

If a preacher is wrong, then they are wrong and that's all that's to it. When a preacher is wrong about what they teach about the Bible, their error makes them a "false preacher". Parts of their messages are likely accurate because they typically read from the Bible, but *false* preachers manipulate the words of the Bible in order for us to open up our pockets to support their work. Some false preachers may even have a pure intention of good and may not seek your money, but if they are wrong, then still they are wrong. And in being wrong they are, in fact, false preachers. It's not wrong that we should give money to the service of a preacher to support their cause. In the Bible we are encouraged to do so by making our offerings in addition to our tithes.

The problem for us is the way in which some of the preachers are teaching us to understand things. The problem can also be in our own error of not properly understanding what they are saying or what they mean as they teach us. *True* preachers, and the *true* Church, **should** be financially supported by us.

Let us not be swayed in our understanding: true healing can come to us through prayer and understanding. It is a clear and concise promise stated by both the Creator and the Christ, that, if we understand and abide by the truth and then know that our needs will be taken care of, then "it is already done"—including our health. This is repeated to the people throughout the Bible in various ways, but seldom is it heeded by them. For instance, the effects of our thoughts on our bodies are finally starting to be proven scientifically, though many scientists do not read the data in this same way.

We have the power to heal ourselves and to heal each other, but this is only when we have come to understand what is true. Our believing any lie attempts to corrupt any truth within us and place our lives in a state of chaos even if we are unaware that it is a lie. Nonetheless, it is still our own choice. The unproductive thinking of believing lies sends shockwaves of negative chemistry and electrical impulses cascading throughout the entire body. This is a biological function, and it is the cause of much physical discord in the health of many people.

The twentieth century ushered in extensive knowledge about our bodies. Anyone who cares to take the time to understand these things will quickly see how accurate and upright the words of the Christ were with regard to healing. Just on a purely physical level alone, the chemistry of our bodies is greatly affected by the way we think. Destructive thinking will clearly destroy our bodies, and doing so is counterproductive to our prayers that we pray when requesting good health, just as eating poorly is counterproductive to our prayers for good health.

Since our thinking is a major contributor to our health as discussed earlier, one would think that it would be easy to heal ourselves and make cancer and disease vanish from our bodies. Yet, healing cancer and disease is not easy for us to do. This is because of our low levels of faith, which are mostly due to our focus on others and society. It's a difficult task for us to grasp the truths that we have failed to see for so long and have become proficient at ignoring. Then, additionally, a medical "professional" comes along and dictates that we only have a given amount of time to live, and sadly, we believe them.

Even if healing was strictly and only chemical, we would still be trapped because we typically fail to conquer our negativity. Few people will admit, or can see for themselves and realize that they are negative, that they think negatively, and that they live negatively.

Whenever you pray for something, set your focus on the Creator and make sure that you are not contradicting your prayers with your thoughts or in your actions.

The Answers are there for Those Who are Willing to See

The connections of the physical to the Creator are all there for those who are willing to see this beautiful simplicity. Because of the distractions of the noise and lies that surround most of us, we are blinded from seeing the simple beauty of understanding what is true. These distractions blind us from having the ability to embrace and hold understanding tightly and to never let it go!

Anything we do in our life that runs contrary to the order of truth places us in a state of chaos and adversely affects everything else in our lives, including our health and our circumstances. It should be our goal to teach truth to our children—our babies—from the moment they are born, to the day that either they or we breathe our last, and even beyond that through their memory of us and our words to them.

It is to be our hope, and then our trust, that truth and order are spread from one generation to the next to be the fresh green grass upon a fertile earth where pure joy rains down to refresh us all.

We must put behind us our focus on others and place it on the Creator. It is our choice—our own free will—to decide to choose such a path, and then to abide by it, to dwell in it, and to live abundantly in it. Truth is everywhere and it has always been there for us! But, it is our own freewill choice to choose truth for each our own lives.

Chapter 17

Unkindness and Negativity

As children, many of us did not understand unkindness because we grew up with it all around us. We recognized it but we did not understand it, and it did not register with us because it was a regular part of what I refer to as our "Hot Water", as noted in the cornerstone book *Hot Water*. Basically, Hot Water works like this: If you place your hand in hot water for a long enough time, eventually you will become accustomed to it; then immediately afterwards if you place your hand into lukewarm water, it will feel cold to you. Alternately, if you place your hand into ice cold water until you get used to it, and then immediately afterwards you place your hand into the lukewarm water, then the same lukewarm water will feel hot to you.

The same lukewarm water is *perceived* differently due to your relative perception. Your perception is based upon your past experiences with either the hot or cold water. The Hot Water effect in our lives, how it has changed our lives, and what we can do to stop it is described in detail in the cornerstone book *Hot*

Water, but for now, understanding this fundamental aspect of *Hot Water* is sufficient.

When we grow up in any sustained situation, we become immune and desensitized to the behaviors that surround us. For instance, when people from a rich nation look at those from a poorer nation, then we typically wonder, "how can they possibly live that way?" Since they have never before experienced anything other than what they are currently living in; their own hot water is conditioned in such a way that they simply do not understand that something better exists—the way they live is "normal" to them. Even if they were to somehow catch a glimpse of a more luxurious life, to them, it would be similar to when a wealthy nation's people watch stories of the rich and famous. We see it and admire it, but we give abundant wealth little thought with regard to our own lives because we believe it to be out of our reach. And so, we dismiss such abundance as fantasy when considering ourselves and our own lives.

There was a young woman who had *Hot Water* that was such that she was accustomed to arrogance, sarcasm, cruelty, and doubt. She did not understand unkindness because unkindness was mostly all that she knew. She was frustrated in her younger years and was excited when it came time to move on and go out on her own to begin her own life. However, she lived close to her birth family so nothing really changed for her during the early years of her independence.

Over the years, their families separated as families typically do with age and children, and with each passing year she became more and more at peace. When situations arose where she was required to interact with her birth family again, all of the frustrations that she felt in her youth began to reemerge. Because this was all so deeply rooted within her, she still could not place her finger on the problem. All she knew was that each encounter drove her further from those situations, and eventually she began to figure out that she needed to withdraw from those particular people. The more she withdrew, the better her life became. This continued until they were no longer a part of her life. Once she had reached full separation, everything began to come into sharp focus for her, and suddenly it was very easy for her to see how unpleasant those early years truly were. Her old Hot Water became cold to her, which caused her to become very aware of it. Cruel arrogance is no longer allowed in her life and is now very easy for her to spot.

This is Not About Crushing Your Enemies

Crushing your enemies is for the weak. In fact, if you still have enemies at this point, then you have entirely missed what this book is about. It is understood that an enemy is someone who is trying to bring you low and do you harm. But that is for them, *they* have made you an enemy of them—this does not mean that you should have them be an enemy of you. Nor does this mean that you should stand by and accept their vicious assaults on you or your family.

Not labeling someone as an enemy does not mean that you won't admit that others are trying to harm you. It means that you have come to an understanding that you cannot be defeated when you understand certain things such as your Hot Water. It also means that you can exercise your right to walk away whenever you desire. Just the same as they have the right to say and do as they wish, so do you have the right to turn and walk away from their vicious and unjust attacks against you and your family and friends. You have the right to protect yourself and others from those attacks.

The sooner we depart from unjust vicious situations, the sooner those situations will dissipate from our lives. The problem that we often face in our world is that we have allowed this behavior in our lives, societies, and cultures for so long that it is very difficult for us to eradicate it, such as is seen with terrorism.

Allowing terrorist type people to have their way in the borders of your own land becomes a very dangerous compromise later on when they lay threats upon your people, and doing so is quite deadly for the citizens of that land.

We, in our effort for kindness, with open arms, allow others into our lives, as we should. But our error is that we allow them liberties that we ourselves would never take upon others. If we will not allow ourselves to behave this way in our own home, neither should we allow others to do so in our home.

Unkindness is rooted in jealous-covetousness, and when adopted, this life-behavior becomes a noxious weed that is immune to all poison.

Our best effort and method to eliminate these noxious weed problems in our own lives is to stand by what is true and allow those around us to see our true intentions. Then eventually, they will stand with us. If they do not, then at a minimum, we now know that they will stand with those who have come to think of us as an enemy.

Make no false peace with these people. If you live in truth and compromise that truth in effort to "make peace" with them, then you will be living a lie and you will be taken advantage of by the un-peaceful people. We need only extend our hand once and keep it extended for peace. Beyond that it is for them to choose to reach out and accept our offer of peace—we cannot force them. Making any concession with regard to staying true is not an option for those of us who desire truth, order, and joy in our lives.

The Danger of Angry Passion

A person who has chosen to consider you as an "enemy" has done it of their own accord if you have not provoked their attack through unkindness or covetous-jealousy. There is little you can do, other than to offer your hand in peace—the rest is up to them.

Provoking a person who proclaims to be your enemy, with more vengeance, will only bring you to where they are and cause them to hate you all the more. Then you will be guilty of the same sin that they are guilty of. Staying in truth is your only protection, and there is only so much that is in our power—the rest is up to them.

When we try to "get back at them" for something, even if we are justified in doing so, we cause them to dig in and prepare for battle. People who see us as their enemies are looking to attack us and want to fight. Some will even try to provoke you into a fight.

This sort of provocative angry passion is misdirected passion, and it is sad that we waste so much of our energy with such negativity. Imagine if all of that energy was put into something creative and good. What a wonderful world it could be!

Through our hot water, many of those of us who behave this way have come to believe that we are not highly valued. In believing this lie, we often try to make ourselves appear better by tearing others down and trying to force *them* to comply with *our* desires.

Many people who choose to be enemies could be brilliant contributors to society. But instead, they have taken their genius and Creator-given gifts and have forfeited those gifts to distrust and incorrect beliefs. When we choose this path, then even when things are explained in a calm and rational manner, our defenses go up and we refuse to allow correction when we see it coming. When this is our case, there is little that can be done to help our condition.

It is our own choice to select what is true, and then to reflect upon the past days of our life to discover where we truly are. At that point, we need to make decisions as to where we want to be tomorrow and all the rest of our days as we adjust our voyage accordingly.

Protect Children from Naysayers

There is little good accomplished in allowing others to discourage your good efforts in life—this is especially so with children. Children are very sensitive with regard to negativity. Doubt and prayer *do not* mix. Doubt greatly damages prayer, and when children are exposed to incessant negativity, they will have many doubts in life. This same issue applied to *you* as you grew up.

If you have family members from your birth family who are bringing your own family down, then depart from them to protect your children from those poor attitudes. Anyone in your life who is negative should be removed from your circle of trusted friends. They can go their way and you can go yours. Even if it is only you who has contact with the people who have poor attitudes, but your spouse and children do not have direct contact with them, these negative people will still affect your family indirectly through you. The frustration that you feel because of the other people's bad attitudes follows through your every move while you are interacting with your spouse and children. In turn, this teaches certain negative attributes to your children. This is unfair to your children since *you* are the one who they are trusting to keep them safe from harm.

With our spouse and children it is different because we cannot separate from them. Rather, we need to teach them rightly and to be positive.

When naysayers are from the outside it's fairly easy to eradicate the problem because all that you need to do is to reject it and depart from them. However, it is more difficult to detect negativity and unkindness when that naysaying behavior is a part of your own family's hot water. Naysaying within your own family (your spouse and your children) is often hard to detect because it is a part of your hot water, and therefore, you generally are not aware of it—this is extremely damaging.

Become sensitive to your own words because those words have a profound impact on your children.

The importance of understanding the impact of your words cannot be understated. This problem can become even worse for a child when the children learned these habits from their parents. This is especially so when it is a deep rooted part of the Hot Water of the family as a whole.

Name calling and unkind negative remarks being tossed about from child to child is unhealthy, and it generally causes the children to lead less than excellent lives. This causes the children to hide behind fear and arrogance. This problem can become especially difficult if one child is targeted by more than one of the other siblings. If you see this in your family, eradicate it as soon as possible! Teach your children to disregard that sort of behavior and to ignore it. You will not regret your efforts in protecting your children from naysayers no matter who the naysayers are. And at a very early age, teach your children that it is wrong to behave in a negative manner—do not allow it.

If Only We Had Passion

All of the viciousness of unkindness that we receive in life often leads us to a great deal of anger that we seem to have no problem passionately expressing to those around us. Yet, when we pray, we pray in a monotone, lack luster, and passionless manner. Imagine how effective our prayers could be if we would only adapt that same level of energy that we have when we are negative, but instead do it in a positive manner, and then pray with excitement and expectation equal to that which we exhibit when we're angry.

Pray with the same *level* of passion and conviction as is used when you're angry and shouting at someone, but instead, use positive feelings in your prayer. Then you can be assured that if you have fully grasped the truth of what is written in this book by adopting what is true into your life, your good prayers *will* succeed in their proper time. And when you are in pursuit of your born-in gifts in effort to make the world a better place, then you will see great things occur in your own life as you move towards that end goal.

People sometimes have their prayers answered when they have finally reached their breaking point and they break down in tears in total submission to the Creator when praying to be delivered from their problems. Sadly for us, and at the same time good for us, this is highly effective. What is sad is that we must be broken and crushed from our own folly before we finally decide to have enough humility to overcome our arrogance and admit our errors to the Creator, and then finally submit ourselves to the Creator. It is also the time where something has actually affected us enough to make us passionate enough to have some noticeable emotion during our prayers.

Our denial of reality and truth is what causes our problems. We go on to complain to the Creator to rectify the negative circumstances that *we* have caused. In the Bible, the people are clearly told that if they turn their backs on the Creator, that the Creator will turn from them, which is the point where destruction always came to them—When you reject sound advice, then you get no more protection!

The Creator's forgiveness and acceptance of us, with open arms, is not necessarily because the Creator feels bad for us when we come crying with our problems in our prayers. But rather, it is the fact that we have finally tossed aside our arrogance and are praying with passion and emotion that finally is actually authentic and true. You could pretend passion on the outside, but it is what is in your heart and mind that matters to the Creator, and the Creator does not like it when we deceive.

If humanity ever did have the ability to pray in a positive and highly passionate manner in the past, it certainly has been forgotten.

We pray as if we are ashamed and unworthy. But, the only way we can be unworthy is if we have chosen to be so by disregarding truth. If we have chosen to be unworthy then we can still change at any moment *if* we choose to do so. But let us *not* be arrogant in our prayers.

There is a time limit for us to change our direction in life and that limit is our lifetime. But the longer we wait when we know better, then the more it counts against us. Live life robustly and pray robustly. Pray what you mean, and mean what you pray! Test the Creator in this! You will not be disappointed when you align yourself with truth. But, this does not end at you. If we fail to share this message with our children, then what have we gained?

It should be the goal of all of us to share this simple message of passionate truth with everyone—a theme that is repeated throughout the Bible. Unfortunately, we often only share these things with those who have already come to the same understanding as we have, while neglecting those who truly *need* to hear the message who are never allowed the opportunity to decide because no one has the courage to tell them or hand them a book like this.

We need to pass this information to those who need it: both to those who may already know it but could use a boost, and to those who are caught in the dark trap of embracing things that are not true. Be courageous enough to also get the message to those people who are caught in the trap of darkness! Though, they may attack you for trying, someday they will likely thank you for your gesture of kindness and love!

Chapter 18

Calling Down a Curse

Most of us don't pay much attention to the fact that we call down a curse upon ourselves and our children. But the truth is that many of us do this as a very frequent habit.

Because we were brought up in a world filled with lies and, typically, in a family built partially upon a foundation of lies, we live with a great deal of frustration. When the frustration becomes great enough, we burst out in anger often *cursing* everyone and everything in our path.

If the target of our frustration happens to be our home, our children, our spouse, our job, or anything else that is important to our lives, then we are truly doing ourselves a disservice when we do this. In our anger we often go about saying "god damn this thing!" or even "god damn you!", or just "god damn it!" in general. What is even more common is when we simply utter "damn it!" And to obscure this all even further, we have even created a word "goddammit" that is listed in many of our dictionaries.

The word "damn" is a base word that means damage or loss. The way of man is to believe a lie, and when we do so we are no longer as pure as we once were. We are reduced from a perfect state and are less than what we are meant to be—we are cursed.

Think about this: When you are calling down a curse upon something, you are asking that it should be reduced or made less than what it currently is. This counterproductive thinking might seem to be a petty insignificance when we are in our fit of rage, but it would do us well to realize that it serves us no purpose to utter such words. And more importantly, it potentially works against our actual goal, because, after all, we are asking God to damn the thing or person that we are dealing with.

If we're dealing with a person who is frustrating us, then we are frustrated with them because they are already falling short of our expectations of them. Will it do us any good to utter words to them that are requesting that the Creator or they themselves reduce them even further? Or if we are working with something and the project is not going our way, and we choose to curse the project and request it to be damned, then does doing this do us any good? Are we not asking for it to become even more difficult by doing so? After all, we are usually trying to create, not destroy. Even when we tear down an old structure we are typically doing it in effort to create something new in its place.

Our frustrations come as a result of broken expectations, or as a result of violations of our expectations. When we want something to live up to our expectations, one of two things needs to occur. Either we need to change our expectations, or we need to do something that helps the person or project meet our expectations. Damning them or the project is completely opposite of what needs to be done!

Can you imagine the look on someone's face if you were frustrated with them because they have violated you, but you shouted out "God bless you!" They would likely be very stunned that you would be calling down a blessing upon them after they have violated or failed your expectations. But that is what we should be doing rather than cursing them. We should ask the Creator to bless their understanding and open their eyes, rather than damning them

The Christ said that we should pray for our enemies; but we confuse this thought with the thought of wanting our enemies to have more power over us. If a person is harming you or violating you in some way, then you certainly don't want to add to their power over you by asking them to be blessed. However, it would be good for you, if somehow their eyes were suddenly opened and they saw their error with which they violated you. You need not call down a blessing upon them that increases their power over you, but it would certainly be to your advantage to call down a blessing of truth and understanding upon them that would make them aware of their errors against you, and pray to have them be repentant of that error. And you would certainly be better off saying nothing at all, than you would to curse the person, situation, or thing that you are trying to get to comply with your desires.

This doesn't stop at requesting that something be damned. It includes the intention of many other cursings or swearings that we so often do. Cursing or swearing is especially damaging to children who are under your care.

Any thoughts that leave your body in any form, that seek to harm anyone in any way, are technically an effort to damn them. To "damn" something is to reduce it. When you desire to harm anything in this way, then you desire it to be damned. Even if you are doing this out of blind habit, you are still saying to the other person that you want them diminished.

Take caution in not damning with your words and actions towards those around you—especially your children. There is nothing more powerful than the words of a parent to a child. Even if your damning words are unintentional, they still work to bring low whomever, or whatever, those words target.

If You Don't Want to Regret Your Mistakes Then...

Few people think of saying "damn it!" in any serious way during their fit of rage, but it is a common mistake and it matters. We even go as far as to say "god damn it!" about something, and then later will request for it to go well in our prayers.

It is important for us to realize our double-minded contradictions so that we do not make our lives more difficult than they already are. We often regret our mistakes, but don't realize that we have an option with regard to those mistakes. The option is as simple as this: If you don't want to regret your mistakes, then don't make regrettable mistakes.

It is very important for you to learn to be sensitive about things that seem simple and insignificant, such as saying "damn it!" If you let simple things like this slip by in your life, then the probability that you are making other similar seemingly insignificant mistakes is extremely high.

Take the time one day to analyze all of your words immediately after they leave your mouth. Think about those words and what was actually said. Most of us find that we often uttered nonsense or something that we regret or would have been better served to not say at all. You will find analyzing your words in this way to be a very effective method for you to learn to change your attitude. Doing so serves to reduce the mistakes that you make, while increasing your accuracy in everything that you do and say.

All too often, we spew cutting and cruel words from our mouths that are beneficial to no one. Words used in this way most certainly become a source of trouble for you when they come back around to you in their further developed and corrupted response. That response may be returned to you in the form of words, thoughts, or actions. Regardless of whichever it is, you can be assured that you will pay the price for those negative words that you initiated.

With regard to negative words, there is a difference between *correcting* words and *condemning* words, though many people cannot tell the difference.

Correcting words point to the error and describe why the error occurred and what can be done to prevent the error from occurring again.

Unjustified condemning words typically point out error or opposition in general and are usually delivered in a cruel and mocking manner. Condemning words are of no use to anyone, and they only serve to make a situation worse.

Condemning words are damning words. "Why is this?" you ask. Because the word "condemning" is an extension of the word "condemn", and *condemn*, when broken down, is *con* and *demn* or *damn*. Anytime you are condemning someone you are trying to bring them down or reduce them in some way—you are *damning* them.

Do You Give Negative Situations Power?

When we curse something, we place our focus on the negative aspects of the situation giving it power by doing so. It's good to briefly analyze the cause of a problem, but once an analysis is made then all focus should be placed on the solution and how to achieve it.

When we keep our focus on negative things, we forfeit all of our Creative energy to that negativity. A very good example of this problem is when a bully or terrorist type personality is frightening or threatening you and you succumb to them.

When you succumb to a bully-terrorist, you have forfeited your power to them and they now control you and have gained your power. Anytime a situation has power over us it is because, at some point, we have allowed it. All we need to do to regain our power is to reject the fear that the situation is attempting to burden us with. This is done by embracing truth.

If a person is trying to control you with forceful or manipulative actions, then you must realize that, in reality, the only way they can truly do so is if you choose to believe the lie that they are telling you. If you are afraid of them, then you are believing the lie that they have power over you. It is your fear that has been induced by their lie that destroys your power and hands it over to the person trying to control you. Fear is the result of the absence of Truth.

Anyone who is making any attempt to control anyone is actually condemning them. They are attempting to bring the person under their control and make the other people less than they themselves feel that they are. Do not confuse this with being in control. There is a difference between *controlling* someone and being in *control* of the situation.

Controlling people is an effort to get others to submit to your will, where being in *control* is the ability to understand all of the needs of a situation. Being in control has the ability to take clean and decisive action in effort to quickly bring a situation back into order. Being in control builds others up, where being controlling does not.

When we're afraid of someone or something, then we are focusing on that negative and on disorder. In doing so we are giving it our power. This means, of our own freewill, we have forfeited our power and we are decreasing our ability to be in control of our own situation. It also means that we have handed our power over to a person who is trying to control and condemn us with the power that we freely handed to them. This is not wise, and it was the fall of mankind in the Garden.

Wisdom Creates Favor

The word "favor" is often used in sermons, and it means *attention*, or to *revere*, or to show *friendly regard* towards someone. The word "wisdom" comes from the word *wise* and from the word *domain* or *dominion*; wisdom is wise-dominion.

The word *wise* means to see, but it is better understood as, to *see in advance*. If you have wisdom, then your dominion is to be able to see ahead, which allows you to understand what will occur before something actually occurs. The only way we can do this is when we use a scale that balances everything against what *is*—this scale is Truth!

Without truth you have no chance of being wise. By the very definition of the word wisdom, truth is *required*. When we understand how to determine truth, and when our prayers are well ordered, and when we make those prayer requests in purity, then we should expect favor in our lives.

Again, the word *favor* means *attention*, or to *revere*, or to show *friendly regard* towards someone. If we understand how to pray correctly, and are in harmony with what is true, then we can expect the Creator to give attention to us and to our request. And we can also expect that the Creator will likely show friendly regard towards us by granting us our request near to as we expected—this is why the word favor is often used by preachers.

For a lot of people, the word *favor* being used by itself is not particularly common. However, if we use the word with the ending of "-able" as in something is "favorable" then it might make a little more sense to us.

The Creator will be favorable to you when you understand and when you pray according to what is true and good. Pray in purity free from condemnation and doubt.

Chapter 19

Passion in Prayer

Many people are willing to fight to the death for their beliefs, for which they have no sound foundation, in an effort to force others to agree with their own matters of blind-faith. There is far too much misunderstanding in our lives to quibble about matters that have no need to be discussed within the concept of prayer.

Our doctrinal differences have caused so much bloodshed and pain over the centuries that it seems that we may have done ourselves more harm than good over all of those years with our blind-faithed "beliefs". All of our passion and anger have availed us only death and destruction, and condemnation and ridicule. And yet, mankind seems no closer to being able to explain our blindnesses in contemporary times than we were in any other part of recorded history.

Our zeal to prove our point at any cost has taken a heavy toll on humanity; such as the bloodshed, turmoil, and sickness and disease that we have caused, spread, and perpetrated onto our fellow man.

Our truly extensive damage has been to our own selves. The passions without substance in the hearts of the peoples of past centuries, not only caused their fellow man many deaths, but have caused many of their own deaths as well. But our passion, which all too often lacks substance, has blinded us from being able to ascertain truth. Some people believe that truth does not exist and that there are no absolutes. I contend that truth does exist and that it is the only thing that is absolute. What fails us is our human condition. Our desire to have things our own way regardless of truth causes a bitterness that we project onto those who we are able to persuade to follow our erred thinking; and it is often *forced* onto those who we cannot persuade.

Too much of our problem is our inability and our unwillingness to properly communicate to those around us. For instance, we can argue about the existence of a Creator, and we can rationalize—that because there is Creation, then there must be a Creator. We can also rationalize—that everything just happened without intention and all those changes spontaneously occurred in a gradual manner. Both arguments *appear* valid.

From a scientific perspective, everything must be explainable. But from a **true** Creation perspective everything must not only be explainable, but must be *scientifically* explainable with intent and purpose. In their passion, the religions have failed to properly deliver all three of *explanation*, *intent*, and *purpose* to their followers in a clear and comprehensive way. This is why many followers of the world's religions have fallen away and adopted non-creation beliefs. The failure to adequately explain Creation and the failure to be able to properly embrace science has left the Church congregation in an even darker scientific state than it was in centuries past.

With all of our modern technologies and vast amounts of research, we have once again blinded ourselves from open-minded research and are again quickly slipping into an abyss of religion with passion—only this time it's the religion of science and "reason".

Neither religion nor evolution can adequately explain the deeper aspects of human existence. Our passionate, and often baseless, discussions with regard to these things are typically a waste of our energy because of our attitudes. It's not a waste to study religion and its theories, or to study evolution and its theories. What is a waste is our vicious passion to the opposition. It is time for humanity to rise up and claim its rightful place in connection with the Creation.

We must drop our arrogance, fall into humility, and be as we are Created. "Religion", as *we* typically think of the word, is a lie, and it has nothing to do with whether or not there is a Creator. The Bible is an interesting document that, when met with any sort of religious fervor, be it Christianity or evolution, still has a great amount of historical significance. When we read it without the rose colored glasses of religion, or the opaque black glasses of naturalist-evolution, then its value is far more significant and its principals far more profound.

There is much understanding that can be gained through the words that are written in the Bible and the concepts that those words convey. But, so long as we bind our passions in the blindness of our own arrogance, we will continue to miss the true message that is actually being conveyed in the Bible and in all of Creation, regardless of the method of Creation. When we remove our arrogance and bind ourselves to truth and to the quest for truth, and then use the passion we once wasted on our arrogance and turn it towards joy and prayer, then the level of success in our prayers will be greatly increased!

Typically, we first pray in a lackluster and lowly way, and then we further go on to believe the lies that say we are of little value. This offers us little in way of persuasion when we pray. Plus, all too often, when we pray, we are focused on the negative.

Imagine if a salesperson came to your home and wanted to sell you a product by discussing all of the bad things about it and the things that needed to be fixed in order for that product to be useful to you. If he came to you and said "It's really not very good, but I really want you to buy it. Please buy it, but you'll need to fix it before using it." Then would he not be more successful if he himself fixed it and made it work, *and then* came to us and wanted us to buy it?

The analogy is not about selling your pitch to God. It is about your attitude and what *you* are selling. In asking the favor of you to buy what he is selling, a salesperson is asking you to make an investment in something. Do you want to invest in something that's broken down and must be repaired all the time? Or, would you rather buy something that enriches your life and brings joy to you and those around you? Always pray positive! Pray for future. Pray for what *can* be.

We need to get our minds in the right place, and then we need to pray for things that we want, rather than always praying for things that we do not want in life.

When we pray for those things that we want, we need to do so with passion and vigor. But more importantly, we need to live our life with that same truly joyful passion and vigor. Pretending will not work here.

Obsession, Reward, and Compulsion

All obsessions and addictions are filling a natural void in our being. If the natural void is not filled with *truth* and *love*, then it will be filled with an addiction that is both empty and bad for us. When we build these bad addictions, we need to remove them from our lives, but often we have nothing in our lives to properly fill the void left from removing the addiction. It is our ability to find something good to fill that void with that stops us from repeatedly returning to the bad addiction.

Addictions and obsessions are often thought of as bad, and for good reason: Typically, when we are addicted or obsessed with something it becomes destructive to us. For instance, when we become addicted or obsessed with religion or scientific theories to the point where we will defend those obsessions with violence, we proceed to ignore things that do not fit with what *we* want to hear and believe.

All of our decisions and actions become formed around and based upon our addiction or our addiction to our obsession. We become addicted to things that we obsess with and about. We obsess over things to make ourselves feel better or we hide behind the obsession, and possibly even both.

When we choose something like misdirected religion or misdirected science to explain away our doubts and fears, then we tread a very slippery slope and have, for the most part, trapped ourselves in that addiction. Our reward in following misdirected science and religion is in the easing of our own conscience. In a religious manner, if we accept the rosy view that all of our sins are forgiven no matter what we do, then our compulsion is to have the reward of—not having to go to the fiery pits of hell. Within the evolution theory, if we can explain away a creator, then we ease our conscience and our compulsion is to have the reward of having a mind free and clear of guilt and free of the penalty of—having to go to the fiery pits of hell. Both of these use the same rationale with a different approach. But are either of them correct?

When referring to the true sense of the words *addiction* and *obsession*, it is not wrong or dangerous to have either, provided that you are addicted to or obsessed with or to the proper thing. I suppose we could get into the splitting of hairs as to what these words mean, but when broken down into their basic root elements ("dict-" to *say* or *talk* about, and "sess-" to *sit*, or essentially *to be around*.) there is nothing wrong with being addicted or obsessed with things that are constructive and good, such as truth. Not our version of truth, but actual truth.

Our problem is that we obsess and become addicted to things that are very superficial. These superficial things help us to hide our problems, rather than causing us to face our problems head on and deal with them efficiently.

We hide our problems because we have a compulsion to want to feel better. This compulsion is driven by our mental biochemistry to achieve the reward of feeling better, via the "feel-good" chemicals spoken of earlier. What this means is that, when we think in certain ways, believe certain things, or do certain actions, it brings a favorable chemical result and we have a compulsion to obtain that chemical result again and again. It doesn't matter if the favorable chemical result is brought about by our thoughts and beliefs or by physical tangible items because all of it creates part of the feel good chemistry that we desire in our bodies.

When we have an obsession or addiction to money, it can *only* be for vain purposes. We have no need for money beyond our fundamental need for shelter and food. So what else could possibly be our reason for wanting to stockpile great quantities of money and buy things that are far beyond our actual needs?

It's okay to have abundant money and the things that money can buy, but we are discussing an *obsession* or *addiction to* money or anything else that brings us a false sense of status and security. This could include cars, homes, clothing, and even people of notoriety and/or people of wealth. It's when we believe that these things somehow make us better that our troubles come in to the picture. We get very passionate about our addictions and obsessions and we put all of our effort into obtaining *things* and are willing to forfeit truth with in us, and then we replace truth with the objects of our obsession or addiction, doing this does us little good in the long run.

All obsessions and addictions seek to duplicate the results of truth. Truth will *always* bring joy when you live in that truth. Joy will always bring good chemicals to your body and will typically bring abundance and wealth to your life in the long run. At the core, it is the abundance of life that truth automatically brings to people that we attempt to duplicate with our bad obsessions.

We incorrectly believe that if we can acquire the rewards that typically come as a result of being true, without actually being true ourselves, then we will have the same status and authority that those who exhibit and embrace truth have. This wrong thinking is the source of our bad addictions and obsessions.

Sadly for humanity, obsession or addiction for the purpose of obtaining status is a most fundamental component of feeling good where we place most of our passion. The resulting inability to achieve the desired goal creates a compulsion to repeatedly seek the rewards that we see others have, which is where the dangers of the obsession reside. You cannot have the same result with tangible items if you obtain those items outside of joy. A joyful person will be joyful with or without any items or status. Any attempt to obtain the abundance that often accompanies a life of joy, without first finding joy, will end in futility and failure because it lacks the proper foundation of truth and joy. All unhealthy obsessions are obsessions that follow the same model as arrogance and fear do, and it happens for the same reasons.

It Comes Down to Believing a Lie or Believing the Truth

You could take a person and force them, with threats of death, to say something they do not want to utter that opposes their beliefs. However, this does not change their will and underlying passion in their belief. Using such an approach to coerce someone to comply with our arrogant demands to see things our way, does not change their true underlying intent and passion.

As a graphic example similar to things that have occurred in the past, people who have subscribed to the naturalist theory of evolution could take religious church-going people and threaten to burn them at the stake if they will not admit that evolution is correct. And people who have subscribed to the belief that the Bible is our evidence of Creation could threaten to burn naturalist people at the stake unless they admit that Biblical Creation is correct. However, if this is done, it is likely that even if the confession is made, the persecuted *person's heart and mind* still has *not* submitted to those beliefs.

Everything, no matter which side you are on, comes down to believing a lie or believing truth, the strength of your belief indicates your passion level. The truth never changes, it is what it *is*. Truth exists with or without us, and we must receive truth deep within ourselves. If we evolved, then we evolved. And if we were Created, then we were Created. Nothing we think, say, or do is going to change whichever it actually is. But, in the end, if we all evolved then we simply die. Or if we were all Created, then we will have to answer for what we chose to believe. But again, what we choose to believe *will not* change what is true about *life* or *no life* after death.

The only thing that ever changes is our ability to perceive what is true. But often, the ability to perceive truth is derived from the evidence around us and the choices that we make with regard to that evidence. There is no avoiding this fundamental principle of our existence. The more wrong we are, then the more difficult it will be for us to see our way clear to finding truth. Often the more wrong we are then the harder we will fight to rationalize our unsubstantiated beliefs.

On our own, all of us must each choose what it is that we are going to believe. But, regardless of what we believe, we have either attached to a lie, or we have attached to truth—it really is that simple!

What is actually true has nothing to do with what we believe. Even if all of the people on the face of the earth believe something to be true, they will all be wrong if what they are believing is not true—We would all be believing a lie. The Truth is now, and has always been, right before our very eyes.

Our problem is that we *choose* to not see things. This is true for both the principles of Creation and for the theories of evolution. Regardless of how convicted you are, how loudly you shout, how rapidly the words flow from your mouth, how many college degrees you have on your wall, and how many big words and hypotheses or theories you present, the truth will always be the truth. And if you are not embracing the truth, you will simply be *wrong*.

With your statements, you may be able to get other people to succumb to your foolish arguments about what is true, but in the end, if your statements are wrong, then they are wrong and eventually you will be proven wrong.

It is not for each of us to force others to submit to our own belief. The only job that any of us has—is to do our best to reveal truth to our fellow man, and, more importantly, to reveal it to our own selves. If we fail to do so, we are accountable for our own lies and also for deceiving those who believed our lies and inaccuracies. It is important to be ever vigilant in seeking truth.

Whether or not you believe in Creation is of no consequence to what is true. You are still responsible for your own thoughts, decisions, and actions. Anybody who is deceived by your lies, or by your inaccurate assumptions, is being led astray *by you*. It does not matter whether or not you are a Creationist or an evolutionist, because you still carry the burden of being wrong, and nothing can or will ever change that simple truth.

Is there a consequence for being wrong while leading others astray? I suppose it depends upon your analysis of the word consequence. If by "consequence" we mean that something in the sequence of events following your choices to promote and believe the things that you have promoted and believed, will alter other people's and your own thoughts and actions, then yes, there are consequences.

With regard to Heaven and Hell and the potential blessing or curse that you would be subjected to, that is something which is a personal choice for you to believe or deny. However, it still does not matter what you believe because there is a truth that will become apparent and cannot be denied. When that time comes we will be held accountable no matter how vehemently we disagree with whatever is true.

If Heaven and Hell are a figment of our imagination, then it is of no matter. However, if Heaven and Hell are an actuality, then we will face the consequences of our own choices made here and now. Our choices are all up to each one of us, and no one and no thing anywhere, in any way, can force us to believe something that we do not want to believe. In the end, accepting truth is a freewill choice that is up to each one of us. To reject truth is to choose destruction. This is true regardless of whether we evolved, or were Created.

Our choice all comes down to either believing a lie or believing the truth no matter what the truth may be. The truth is unchanging—it is *what is*. Our speculations are not true because they sound good. If our speculations are true, then they are true because they are accurate and agree with truth. They agree with *what is*.

What we each believe is our own choice, and nothing can ever change that. This means that, regardless of whatever the truth is and whatever the consequences are, we are responsible for ourselves. It is true that if someone deceived you, whether intentionally or deliberately, that you maintain a certain amount of innocence in the matter, but you are still going to be held responsible for being slothful in your lackluster approach to life and in your failure to go out and investigate and understand of your own accord and freewill. Therefore we must always be seeking truth in everything in our lives. Once you have reached an age of reasonable mind, then your guilt and shame are upon your own shoulders. There is only one truth and it is wise to choose it. Be ever seeking to passionately understand truth.

Marriage Prayer Harmony

Prayer is often a big part of married life, and as discussed in the cornerstone book *Red Hot Marriage*, husband and wife become one and should work as a team. If a husband and wife are bound spiritually, but then they do not agree in direction with regard to their prayers, they could end up voiding each other's prayers. If you are married, you should be in passionate harmony with your spouse. This harmony should include your life's direction together, and your prayers should have the same passionate long- and short-term vision. It will do a couple absolutely no good to be praying for two different things that cannot possibly occur in harmony. You must think in terms of the Creator; how is the Creator supposed to grant a solution for your prayers as a couple if the two prayers are in conflict? If both desires are not harmful to anyone then whose request should the Creator grant when the two desires oppose each other?

Where are Your Strongest Emotions?

The problem we have as humans is that our fear and our fear's subsequent arrogance typically dictate our lives. When we are afraid, we often go so far as to put on an arrogant show to hide the shame of our own fear. Our emotions are tightly interwoven with the *beliefs* that we have each chosen to adopt.

A belief is something that you have taken into your heart that is subsequently shown in your actions and words. Our beliefs are what we base our lives upon. Our strongest most passionate emotions will always be attached to our beliefs. Our "beliefs" do not have to be a matter of *religion* versus *evolution*. The reason that the Creation debate is so heavily discussed in this book is because it has had tremendous impact with regard to people's faith, and subsequently their prayers and the success of those prayers.

Our beliefs can be our belief in someone or the level of trust that we have placed in them. If someone let us down after we have granted them our trust, then it will bring about a fair amount of emotional discord within us and our hearts. When we trust someone or something, we are believing it to be true, and we will confide in it and have faith in it.

Confide, *fidelity*, *faith*, *trust*, *truth*, and *true* are all the same, and they all point to what is. When we have chosen to believe that a person will not let us down and we have made that our trust and we have placed our faith in them, then when our faith or trust is broken, our emotions will typically pour forth in anger and/or sorrow.

We often feel violated by the Creator because we have believed wrongly about the Creator due to what we were taught and also due to our slothfulness with regard to taking the needed time and effort to actually find out what is true. Instead of seeking the truth, we typically listen to others spew inaccurate information to us that soothes our itching ears. Anytime we discover that whoever, or whatever, we have put our trust in has violated us, no matter what the violation is, our reaction will be emotional, and it will be rooted in lies, doubt, fear, and arrogance. Placing our trust in anything other than truth is a tremendous error because only what is true can be true. Anything else is empty and void of truth and simply is wrong.

Your strongest emotion and deepest passion can only come while you are thinking about what you are thinking about. Meaning that if you want **thing A** and are thinking about **thing B**, then your strongest emotion won't be about the **thing A** you wanted. Your strongest emotions won't come when you're thinking about something else. If you are angry at someone, then your strongest emotions about that situation will come when you are thinking about that person.

The same goes for joyful experiences; your strongest joyful emotion will be when you are thinking about those joyful experiences. This is something that we can use to our advantage!

We must stop wasting our energy and thoughts on negative and petty arguments that come about through allowing untrue or unjust information into our lives. Once we choose to eradicate the non-truth from our lives, we can focus on all things good and beautiful. And then we can welcome the good and beautiful into our lives and direct our prayers towards praying for good constructive things that will serve to build up humanity and bring us all to a better place.

Our emotions are a wonderful gift that we can utilize together with our passion and desires in order to enhance our eagerness to accomplish wonderful and great things. Let us not pervert this wonderful gift with lies and doubt, rendering it worthless, or worse—harmful!

We have been granted a very special gift in our emotions. Our emotions should always be used for our own good and for the good of those around us in order to reveal our true selves. Always pray using *true* and *strong* emotions.

Making Your Prayers Work with a New View

Take a few moments to absorb what truth is, and the potential blessings of our emotions and desires. Use your new perspective to review everything that surrounds you in your life and prayers. If you want to have your prayers be effective, then stop pretending that air opportunities are answers to your prayers.

Get your thinking right and align your life with what is true. Have a clear picture of what you want and where you're going in life, and then make your request with passionate emotions of joy, and expect and be ready for those prayers to be answered in the most peculiar of ways—ways that you will likely *not* anticipate.

When you get this right, your prayers will likely be answered through other people, but often in an unexpected manner: Someone will randomly come to you and say they felt like helping you. Word will somehow get passed to someone about you and you will be offered a job from an utterly unanticipated source. Someone may randomly give you something that fits perfectly with your needs with regard to your request in prayer. A long-time hostile friend or member of your family may come to you with an authentic sincere and heartfelt confession and apology that you have been waiting on for decades. Someone will say something that triggers your mind and gives you a brilliant idea that solves your problem. It is these sorts of seemingly impossible "coincidences" that are the answers to your prayers.

Since we often attribute such occurrences to mere happenstance or coincidence, it is a good idea to break down those words.

"*Coincidence*" is an extension of the word *coincide*, which means to *fall together*.

"*Happenstance*" is an extension of the word *happen* and happen is an extension of *hap*, which means occurrence by *chance*, or *random*—typically not being able to be reproduced on demand.

When something "coincides", it occurs together with synchronization at the same time or in response to something else. But when something "happens", it just happens, there is no connecting thread or coincidental nature about it—It's just a random thing occurring.

When trying to make your prayers work, truthfully you need not try to make them work, it will simply occur when you get it right in God's time. But what you must understand is that you will have to stop attributing the appearance of seemingly coincidental air opportunities to your prayers. "Air opportunities" are all around us all of the time. Pure prayers of truth with pure passion will bring about the promises mentioned in the Bible.

It's true that when we pray for something, we ourselves open our eyes to those air opportunities. Then often, when we see those air opportunities, we feel as if they are a result of our prayers being answered, but often they are not. They are not "coincidental" because they do not coincide with your prayers as it appears. Rather; they are closer to "happenstance". Prayers of a happenstance nature appear to be answered randomly because what you believe to be an answer is actually an air opportunity. Until you free your mind enough to realize that the air opportunity was always right before your eyes, it will be missed by you. In this case, the seemingly random nature is the random nature of the awareness of your own mind and its ability to see what was always already there for you. This is a typical Red Car Effect before you bought the red car.

Since air opportunities always exist all around you, they cannot be attributed to happenstance because they just are there—always! They are *what is*. They are part of the order of things. Not specifically each individual opportunity, but rather air opportunities in general, and they coincide with *everything* because they are always there. When you have a realization that you need something, then you pray for it. That's when you begin to have a realization that allows you to see the air opportunity that has been sitting before your eyes for many years.

Once you have broken your mind free of this inhibiting error in your thinking, then you will be able to see a real answer to a prayer when that answer actually coincides with your prayer.

While answers to prayers can come in the form that is in our own day-to-day life, the best answers come in those unexpected places where a person who normally is never in your life, and maybe, who you have never met, seemingly "happens" across your path in a peculiar and unusual way. This allows you to progress via meeting the person, which is actually the answer to your prayers.

If such a happenstance occurs once in your entire lifetime it is of little consequence and can be attributed to pure random chance. However, when you learn to order your life properly and bind yourself to truth and pray for good things in your life so that you can share truth with the world, then the things that you pray for will more regularly cross your path and the *coincide*nces will become more frequent for you. At some point, you will be forced to admit that this goes beyond mere happenstance and that it is direct and distinct and often is a peculiar response to a particular request that you made in prayer!

Are You in the Zone?

Most people who pray on a regular basis have probably felt closer to the Creator at various times, and likely felt a substantial connection at those times. Being able to bring your mind into a substantial connective state is an important part of prayer.

Having a strong connection goes beyond prayer and into your everyday life. Our regular day-to-day contributions to our world should share a very common practice that passionately successful people do regularly but not necessarily deliberately. It is their *level* of focus that brings them their successes.

Great singers, writers, athletes, scientists, philosophers, and patriarchs (founding fathers) all share a great ability to immerse their minds in their work. They become engrossed in doing something that they feel will be a benefit to those around them. To share in each their own special way, their deepest thoughts and most wondrous ideas with the world, is what makes them special!

The rest of the people are too afraid, both to think on their own, and to release their own thoughts to others. This comes from the fear of ridicule and condemnation and shame for being potentially wrong in those thoughts that they fear to share.

Truly creative people do not wish to be wrong, but they do not care if they are wrong in that way. It is of no consequence to them because they will stop immediately upon finding their error, and then they will make adjustments that will put them back onto a path of truth.

The focus of passionate people is so intense that if the rest of the people could step into their passionate brain during those moments of focus, the others would likely feel as if the lights were so bright that they would be unable to open their eyes.

When we free ourselves from the lies that try to invade our thinking, we can more readily get in the zone and achieve the goals that we each have that are best suited to the gifts within each one of us.

It's true that it is natural and easy for creative people to get in the zone quickly. This gives them the ability to be free of all the negativity that surrounds them. The ability to get into the zone is within each one of us. "The zone" is not some meditative state that you should try to achieve. The zone is a result of your ability to free yourself from the negativity that surrounds you while you embrace truth with passion.

The only way to be able to get into the zone is to free yourself from "cannot" and to embrace the truth of creativity, and then to let your gifts flow from you so that you can share them with the rest of the world.

This same ability *that we all have* to get into the zone should be used when praying as well. An intense ability to free yourself from all negativity and then to focus while praying, because you have chosen to disregard lies and untrue things, will enhance the effectiveness of your prayers for several reasons: First, it gives you the clarity of mind so that you can see exactly what you need to pray for. Second, it intensifies the passion with which you will be praying. And third, it cleanses you of the lies and untruths that inhibit you in your life and during your prayers.

Attempting to get into the prayer zone through meditation, or any other means to cloak or hide, is similar to buying a car when never before having driven one or not even understanding how to operate one. You will own the car and you can sit in it, but you are not going to go anywhere with it because you do not understand how to start it and operate it.

You can attempt to drive your new car, but you will likely get things wrong until you figure it all out. Depending upon your capacity to understand how it all works, it may take you a while to learn to use it, and you might die in the process if you crash it.

The ability to properly get into the zone is like wanting a car, but you realize that you must first come to the understanding of how the car operates or else it will be of little use to you. Sure, without that understanding you may feel "cool" or special when you're in it and the neighbors see you sitting in your new car when they pass by your driveway. But it is of little use to you if you don't know how to use it properly, other than maybe it being a place to go sit and relax. This is similar to copying people who meditate so that you *appear* enlightened.

Relaxing in a new car may bring you some enjoyment, but to have a real effective tangible use for that car, as it was designed, you must understand how everything on it works and that it is all there for you to utilize these designs for the benefit and joy of yourself and those around you. If you know that you have to start it with the key and push the gas pedal, then you will get somewhere, but you'll end up in a place that you do not intend because you have failed to learn to steer the car.

It's when you know all that your car is designed to do for you that you are able to utilize the powers that it offers you. When you realize this truth, then you and your car become a very effective team, allowing you to come and go as you please, to and from wherever you choose. Plus, you get to do it in comfort while experiencing the pleasure of your favorite listening, all while being protected from the weather—provided you understand how to use it all.

Don't try to get into the "zone" through vain means such as meditation. You understanding what is the cause of the zone, is what will get you into the zone. When we can practice the cause of the zone, which is to reject lies, then misinformation and things that are untrue will quickly vanish from our lives and prayers. Then we can see how easy it is to release the gifts that reside within each one of us in the zone, thus enabling us to use that zone and the cause of the zone within our prayers.

Not understanding prayer is troublesome for people, much like trying to drive a car if you have never before driven one. Some people get lucky and end up close to their destination, but others will cause themselves great pain and remain lost. But, when you are able to get into the zone, then you can access the promises that are there for *all* of mankind.

The Creator is not handicapped and in need of our assistance. The Creator Created us as companions to share Creation with. Sure, offerings to the Creator are appreciated, but the most effective offering is a pure heart that seeks only the truth of the Creator. The pure heart theme is subtly repeated throughout the entire Bible. Our Creator wants to bless us with abundance, but can't because *we* typically will not allow it while we hold onto all of our impurities.

Do You Pray with Passion?

Accept only what is true to get your mind into the zone of truth. Live your life with the same level of passion that you use when you're angry. Do not use the same *type* of passion as when you're angry, but rather, use the same *level* of passion!

Your level of passion within your prayers and your ability to be in the zone relate directly to the level of the result received in the answer to your prayers.

If your prayers are at all in doubt, then you are not in the zone and you should not necessarily expect an answer to those lackluster prayers as you desire. People who get angry at the Creator due to the troubles in their life will pray for deliverance from their trouble, and then often receive an answer to their prayer, but it might not be the answer that they wanted. Compare this to a child unfairly shouting at his or her parents: The parents will not take kindly to the child's disrespect towards them, and it will not go well for the child. It is no different with us in relation to the Creator. The possibility does exist that we may be spanked, so to speak, due to our bad attitude towards the Creator, just as our parents may have done to us while we were growing up.

I do not believe that we should blindly follow the Bible without verification, just as I do not believe that we should blindly follow the Church or theoretical naturalist sciences without verification. However, the Bible, for those who choose to take the time to adequately do the research in reading, you will find to be robustly full of truths, even though it is filled with many examples of death, destruction, and sin.

We are not told to follow the errors of death, destruction, and sin in the Bible. In fact, we are instructed to steer clear of that sort of behavior all throughout the collection of all of books in the Bible. All of the horrible behaviors and accounts of vicious and violent behavior are there as our measuring stick and as an example as to what we should *not* aspire.

In the Bible, we are clearly, and repeatedly, told to love each other and to turn away from bad things. We are instructed to accept, with all of our strength and with everything in our body, the things which are true.

We often hear people who have turned from the Creator complaining that their prayers were not answered. The reason some claim they have turned away from the Creator, is that they say they have seen contradictions in the Bible and/or because their prayers were not answered. The problem with this is that the likelihood is very high that they were full of doubt and were angry and frustrated, which is generally evident in the stated reason for turning away. Being caught in this state of mind is problematic for us because we have been caught in a reciprocal trap of negative thinking that was cast on us by those who surrounded us throughout our past.

We can say that there were promises made in the Bible with regard to prayer, and technically breaking down the word they are "promises". However, as we arrogantly use the word "promise" with regard to the Bible, it is thought of more in terms of "Hey you told me something, so you better deliver on what you said!" And thus, our negativity pours forth causing damage to our prayer efforts and our mental disposition. When we are caught in this trap, then the worse it gets, the worse it gets!

Think of a "promise" in terms of: Being told the truth that we must come to understand and accept *truth* deep within every fiber of our body and being, and *then* utilize that truth for the greater good of ourselves and of those around us, and for the greater good of all of mankind.

However, even though we have been given these truths (promises) we still find it difficult to thoroughly accept them within our mind and heart. You must understand that I am not speaking of *your* interpretation of what is written in the Bible. But rather, I am speaking of the truth of what is written. It does not matter what you or I think about the promises made in the Bible. What matters is making sure we are in accordance with what is true in our understanding of those promises.

If we *fail* to understand the promises of the Creator, then our prayers are virtually useless and the best we can hope for is that, in our ignorance and hopefully innocence, our lowly prayers not be ignored by our Creator; and also that, maybe, we will get lucky once in a while, and get things right by pure chance.

We should strive to eventually come to the proper understanding of prayer and obtain utter and absolute acceptance of what is true. Of all things to pray for, *proper understanding* will be best for you and will allow you the best results in your prayers!

Chapter 20

Your Brain and Its Connection to Prayer

Anyone who was around any time during the start of the twenty-first century had a distinct advantage over all people throughout all of prior recorded history with regard to understanding the reality of the effect of our minds over the state of our bodies. This advantage is due mostly to our collective technologies and scientific equipment.

Our prayers are affected by our thinking and our thinking is affected by our prayers. When we put ourselves into a negative mental state, our prayers and our bodies suffer from that negativity. Negativity feeds on itself.

We humans are chemical beings who are made of tissue, and the tissues' subcomponents—cells. And their subcomponents— molecules. And their subcomponents—atoms. In contemporary times we have the ability through our technology with microscopes, electron microscopes, PET Scanners, and other such devices, to gaze into our live bodies without having to cut our bodies apart. And as far as historical evidence reveals to us, this has never before been possible.

We can now see and monitor live, real-time action that takes place as our bodies function. The detail known about how these micro-systems function within us is fairly deep and proclaims loudly of the order by which we and all things are made.

It is not so much the understanding of the technical aspects of chemistry that has value; rather, it is the understanding of the basic aspects of how that chemistry is utilized in our bodies that is of value to our understanding. How that chemistry is used is simple and important for you to know. You do not need to understand the detailed technical inner workings of the body systems and chemistry to understand their fundamental and underlying concepts. It is the simple and fundamental underlying concepts that we should all strive to grasp.

Earlier in this book we spoke of how our thinking can affect our bodies where when we hear a word, then the sound waves (or air pulses) have come into our ears, which in turn makes the inner-ear parts move causing chemical signals to be sent to our brains. We process our thoughts about what we heard, and then our thoughts react based upon our being's (or soul's) disposition. This causes our brain to begin to emit electromagnetic impulses and chemical chain reactions. Nearly instantly, both the chemical means of communication and the electromagnetic impulses cascade throughout our entire body causing us to move and speak etc. In turn, this causes our senses to receive more stimulus, which in turn sends signals to our brain and the cycle starts over again.

It's difficult to determine if the things that we sense with our bodies, that are received by our brain, can have a negative effect on us during the period of time that the signals are on their way *into* our brain. However, we understand with a tremendous amount of certainty that once those electromagnetic and chemical signals are received, that the corresponding output is greatly affected by our perception of what was just communicated to us.

If we think bad thoughts and become angry about the communication we just received, then our brain will react in a certain way, producing very specific chemistry in our brain and throughout our entire body. If we perceive the communication received as *good* then it pleases us and brings us joy, and the electromagnetic signals and chemical compositions are greatly altered to that end.

The understanding of the level of effect that our thinking has on our biochemistry is, in itself, evidence enough of the need for paying serious and close attention to what we allow in our senses via what we allow in our lives—our thinking seriously affects our health.

The heavy impact that our thinking has on our bodies is becoming so evident with every new level of scientific discovery, that, as a society, it seems we are finally beginning to conclude that our condition doesn't dictate our thoughts, but rather our thoughts dictate our condition. Yet, there are still many who will debate the overwhelming evidence in this regard. This is a different issue than believing that you can make things come to be just by thinking or believing something. What we are discussing here is the real connection of the chemical effect of our thoughts on the well-being and health of our chemical-machine bodies.

The twentieth century brought about a great deal of research on the brain, which near the end of the century mistakenly concluded that our behavior was affected by the condition of our brain. This may be partially true, but lacks a great deal in explanation.

There's a certain level of accuracy in realizing that there is connection between our brain's condition and the thoughts of our mind, but the condition of our brain is more a resultant effect of our thinking. When we place ourselves in a situation that is of a negative nature, then we will be receiving a tremendous amount of undesirable stimulation through our five senses of touch, taste, smell, hearing, and sight.

When we receive messages that do not please us, then our mind gets out of harmony and becomes frustrated, angry, and possibly sad. The moment the undesirable messages are received and realized and accepted as true in our mind, the resulting response instantaneously activates our brain to correspond to the various interpretations of the message received in our mind (our mind being the essence of us).

Your senses are your interface to your brain and your brain is *your* interface to the world. When your brain activates during receiving negative messages, it puts out great amounts of the various negative chemicals, causing negative results.

It's interesting to note that science has been indicating, in general, that the chemicals that accompany any negativity are damaging to your brain and body and inhibit it, and, inversely, the chemicals that are associated with good things, such as positive desire, ambition, joy, and love, increase your brain and body and make them stronger, healthier, and more robust.

Don't let all this talk of chemistry and electromagnetic signals reduce the respect for the intricacy of our bodies. Believing that our brain just magically does things, and that our arms just magically move because we said so, is like going to a magic show and choosing to believe that the magician actually made his assistant vanish into thin air. We understand that magic is only an illusion and that there is something we didn't see that occurred in the magician's act that allows his illusions to occur.

Spoiler alert!—the assistant is certainly no longer visible, but she has likely escaped through a hidden trap door or is hiding behind a secret panel. Let us embrace the mastery of his illusion and how he did it, rather than wanting to pretend that it is all magic.

When we understand *how* our brain works, we come closer to understanding *why* it works. An elusive part of humanity is understanding exactly what it is that makes us human.

Biblically speaking, the Creator made us in the Creator's image and then breathed spirit into mankind. Some people understand and accept this, while others will refuse to accept this as the answer as to what differentiates us from the animals. Yet, the answer they seek still eludes them.

We each have our own reasons why we believe what we believe. And what we believe is all choices that we have made of our own accord. But even these choices affect our biochemistry and electromagnetic output.

I want you to realize that, no matter what you do, what you do is a result of your thoughts. And your thoughts are an action, just the same as moving your hand, screaming in anger, or smiling with joy are also actions.

Intense and specific brain activity occurs just by thinking about situations that make you joyful, sad, frightened, angry, etc. Our brain may not specifically understand the concept of joy, sadness, or anger, but our body does have the ability to create specific chemicals in varying quantities that correspond to each of these emotions when they are felt or experienced by us.

Is Your Thinking Organized?

When researchers study the brain they often fail to understand *cause* and *effect*. In other words "What came first, the chicken, or the egg?"

"What came first, the chicken, or the egg?" is asking: Was the chicken there first and then laid the egg, or was there an egg made which brought forth a chicken? If you think deeply about it, this is sort of a philosophical question. But, with most other things, cause and effect is very simple to grasp.

If your finger is bleeding and at some point a hammer had hit your finger and then someone walks in and sees the bloody finger and the hammer:

Will they assume that your finger was bleeding so then you hit it with a hammer, or will they more likely take the obvious choice and assume that you hit your finger with a hammer and *that* brought forth the blood?

When we use our brains by thinking, we are taking action with a mental hammer, and our body's chemicals are the result from that action. Stating that chemicals are there, therefore we think and are thus taking actions, does not quite hit the mental nail on the head.

It is true that if we hit our finger with a hammer and are in instant pain, which we caused using the hammer, that we may, in our sudden fit of pain, take a second swing at the nail and miss it and once again hit our finger. This is the same way our brain works—if we think negatively then we produce negative chemicals and, in turn, those chemicals will likely cause us to think more negatively, which will then cause our brain to create more negative chemicals and so on.

So long as we continue to voluntarily swing the negative mental hammer, we will continue to miss the head of the nail, and continue to cause ourselves pain by hitting our finger, causing it to bleed more and more profusely with each successive blow of the hammer.

We are told by the gurus of self-help to organize our thoughts, and this is a good thing. However, it is similar to the cause and effect of the chicken and the egg; or in our case, a mental hammer and a very sore finger. When we organize our thoughts, we are saying, "Whoa that hurts, I better not hit my finger anymore because it will bleed. I will be more careful in the future making sure to hit the nail squarely on its head." And we are also understanding that it is a good thing to remember, and that it is certainly better than repeatedly smashing our finger for no specific reason.

Do not create an incalculable multitude of rules for yourself that have to be remembered, such as don't poke yourself with the screw driver, don't hit your finger with the hammer, don't pinch yourself with the pliers, don't cut yourself with a knife, etc... Rather, organize the way in which you think. Too many of us have been trained by family, society, and the school system to learn trivia, with seven steps for this and ten steps for that, to succeed, etc. It has become a multitude of facts and rules that must be specifically applied to *each particular* situation in order to successfully navigate through life.

While it is not a bad thing to know such trivial information, it is our dependence upon that trivia that becomes our problem. In order to organize your method of thinking, instead of organizing your thoughts, you need to forget about what you think you know, and then learn how to focus on trying to understand what is true and good.

Understanding what is true is the one simple thing that is required of us all, and it is the only thing that is required of us all. With this secret mystery, or better understood as—simple truth—we need not memorize many rules because it becomes obvious as we each ask ourselves the question about what we wonder. Our true knowledge is only a small portion of infinite truth.

If someone goes about lying and we later find out that what they said was a lie, then in general, if we don't have an irrational personal agenda, we will quickly disregard the information and remove it from further concern and consideration. It is our ability to do this that is important to each of us.

This is how you should organize your thinking: Organize it into *true*, and *not true*. Doing so allows you to free your mind in more ways than you can imagine!

The *true* or *not true* technique allows us to walk away from bitterness, fear, hate, arrogance, lies, doubt, and just about any other negative attribute you can imagine without really having to process them to a point of harboring contempt. Once we learn to do this, it becomes an immediate decision to disregard foolish attributes and memories. When we organize our thinking in this *true* or *false* way, then we need only think of people in terms of their trustworthiness. If they are not trustworthy then we need not index them in our mind other than to stay clear of them.

It's certainly okay to remember things, facts, and people, but we need not bog down our brains in remembering petty meaningless rules that serve us no purpose until we run into that one single rare situation where we may actually have an opportunity to apply that particular and rarely needed rule.

When we understand the reasons *why*, in conjunction with what is *true* and *good*, then that same pattern can fit any analysis that we will ever need to make in life. Truth is the perfect one-solution-fits-all-situations rule.

Image of a Brain and Body

Using imaging equipment to monitor and watch a live image of a brain or body functioning, helps us to understand our Creation and the intricacy of our bodies. I have a great amount of respect for the work done by archaeologists, paleontologist, cosmologists, and scientists of all sorts. The *data* gathered by these people has been, for the most part, of immeasurable value to humanity and is our best attempt at better understanding our origins and Creation.

However, we should not jump to conclusions in reference to agreeing with *their conclusions* of the data that they collected. We certainly owe them respect for their efforts to search out and retrieve the data. Much of the work done by scientists and engineers has allowed us the wonderful privilege of being able to peer inside of our bodies to see these incredibly complex electrochemical machines in action without injury to anyone.

With every level deeper we are able to see into ourselves and our biological makeup, the more simple complexity we see. In other words, there is more stuff the deeper we look but it is much more basic. The building blocks look more and more basic with every step deeper that we investigate, but there are more of them doing more things at each deeper level. As we learn and discover, it has all only been increasing the number of questions we have about our origins.

It is difficult to ignore two particular components of our existence—*order* and its *truth*. These two fundamental principles are seen throughout everything we have ever been able to observe. We can't always explain it, but we have certainly witnessed it. Our inability to be able to grasp or explain something does not mean that it is not so.

Take our understanding of gravity as an example: Just because we do not fully understand gravity, does not mean that we cannot utilize it. Just because we cannot see it, does not mean that some force is not causing us to be able to walk on this earth without floating out into space. Similarly, just because we cannot see a Creator, does not mean that a Creator does not exist. Think of it in terms of, we are Created in the image of the Creator. Approaching our own image with this understanding brings a whole new understanding to the complexity of the Creator.

Going on the assumption that everything was Created with purpose and intent, it becomes much easier to see and explain why some chemicals are harmful to us, when others are not. We can break things down and see all of these chemicals react with each other. We can also see that certain chemicals cause *problems* within our brains and that other chemicals serve to *enhance* our brains. We can even explain many of the technical aspects of how all of this occurs. And with technology we can monitor these functions in action—but that does not explain *why* it occurs.

Adopting a blind view that "That's just the way it is, and that it was all done by a Creator" is an easy route to take in order to not think about the vast intricacies of our bodies' functions. Similarly, choosing an entirely naturalist view, with a creatorless evolutionary model using only chemistry to explain everything, is also an easy route to take for those who do not want to answer the question "Why?"

We often confuse *how* with *why* when we research things with our "scientific method". Science does not answer *why*, science serves to answer *how*. Philosophy and religion search the "Why?" Science may look at something and see that it is a result, and then ask, "What caused that?", but the "why?" is thought to be an entirely different area of study.

In observing people, including yourself, you are likely to notice that when any individual reaches their personal limit of desire, they tend to shut down and stop progressing. This is because our personal limit is typically bordered by the question "Why?" "Why" infers *purpose*, "how" infers the *method*. As in, *how* you organize your thinking versus *why* you would organize your thinking.

You organize your thinking by choosing to differentiate what is true from what is not true, that is the *how* part. The *why* part is purpose or reason, and you do it because it is the most expedient way to use your mind and it allows you to be able to make distinction between harmful and helpful. It is a *conscious* choice.

When we understand that we need to know the *why* when looking into our brains, we begin to see the *why* and the purpose behind that *why*. And we do this all while using the wonderful gift of technology we have given to one another that we have created using our own gifts. When we begin to grasp the purpose behind the *why*, then we begin to understand our minds, our thinking, and the depth of "Created in the image of".

Your Good Addictions and Your Bad Addictions

With the understanding of "purpose", we begin to see why there is a difference between good and bad addictions with regard to our thinking. The "how?" that we see when we peer in to our brains, is a good example of order or the way things are. What happens in our brains is an excellent indicator of the result of truth and our response to it.

The *why*, in the case of addictions, is a deeper subject, so in pondering the "*Why?*", we need to make the assumption that there **is** a Creator and that we were made in that image. And thus, we must follow the Creative nature of constructing and building up rather than destroying and tearing down. We can accept that as the "Why?" There is no shortage of opinion as to the "Why?" in Creation; even many "experts" do not agree with each other, so *you* too should also ponder this further after considering what you read in this book. All rational thoughts should be welcomed into the discussion, yours included!

Using the assumption that we are Created for the purpose to—construct and build up—we can then see why *not* following what is true would be destructive to us.

It stands to reason that anything that violates the order of Creation would not be able to survive. This is because violation steps outside of what is true. This is not done as some form of punishment by a mean and cruel megalomaniacal god. Rather, it simply is a bit of true or false logic. If it is true, then it survives. If it is not true, then it does not survive and it eventually goes away.

All negative experiences are the result of things that are not good and true. All negative experiences come from a failure of thinking, or a failure of systems that did not abide by the expectations that we have of those thoughts or systems. If we trusted someone and they failed us, we have placed our trust where it did not belong, which in turn caused us pain and frustration. Pain and frustration result in the production of chemicals and electromagnetic output that are potentially damaging to our bodies.

Over the years there have been studies with regard to the brains of nuns who are regularly at peace and at prayer. The nuns' brains show healthier brains at an older age than is seen in the general public. Yet, some researchers have been unable to ascertain, and seem to be perplexed, as to what the difference is with nuns.

Setting aside the terror that unruly school children believed they experienced at the disciplining hand of some nuns, the likelihood that the nuns have much higher rate of having brains free of disease because of their good mental attitudes, is incredibly high. They do not experience the same day-to-day bitter anger towards them or the strife that most of us do in our day to day lives. Also, nuns typically dedicate a higher than normal amount of their time in thinking of prayer, praise, and the Creator. It doesn't surprise me at all that their brains would appear healthier than most other people's brains at older ages. When we lose the truth with which we were born, and subsequently our ambition, we corrupt our bodies and they begin to malfunction and decay prematurely and unnecessarily because losing truth is a violation of Creation and causes our bodies to produce harmful chemicals.

This is where, as we talked about earlier, good addictions versus bad addictions begin to become apparent. Most nuns are addicted to the Creator, that is what they do and kindness is their purpose. They have made it so deliberately, and they have deliberately chosen that path. When we become addicted to bad things, it is not the fact that we are addicted to these particular things, but rather, it is the reason "why" we are addicted to them that has become our problem.

It is not addiction that is the problem. The problem is the reason and the emanating attitude that emotions the chemicals from within our bodies. It is our emanating attitude that causes each specific helpful or harmful chemical to be released. This means that much of our health is up to us and is based upon our very own personal "Why?"

Believing that you can *pretend* to be happy by doing wonderful things through having good addictions will not change what's really going on within your own personal "Why?" Doing the *result* to achieve a *cause* cannot work in the long run, though it may deceptively appear to work for a short time.

It is possible that through doing good things, it may snap you out of your bad attitude, but short of that, it will do you little good to lie to yourself about the *why* part of why you are doing something. Doing so will potentially make your situation worse. Your situation occurs and becomes worse because you are further lying to yourself; and you are adding yet another erred premise upon your previous lies.

Tap into your deeper "Why?" and understand your reasons and motivations. Do not be afraid to admit to the reasons to yourself. Do not be afraid to change your reasons and actions in order to redirect the rest of your life to a life of truth.

It is not the addiction that is the problem. Rather it is the reason behind your addiction that causes your body to produce the damaging chemistry.

Most of your reasons are caused by your past experiences in life, which are all based upon your five senses of hearing, sight, taste, touch, and smell. What you have experienced has come through those forms of communication and has altered everything in your perception. In the same way that what you experience affects you, the way that you behave towards others and your words affect them *and* you.

We hold a great deal of power in being able to build up or tear down those around us. When we tear others down, we also tear ourselves down, but when we build others up we also build ourselves up.

Brain Waves and Mind Reading

As mentioned earlier, our brains and our bodies emit electromagnetic energy or signals, and our brains can also be affected by strong electromagnetic pulses.

When someone's brain is exposed to high levels of focused electromagnetic energy, and while they are being pulsed with this energy, they momentarily lose some ability to use certain functions of their body with any efficiency. Those functions, such as handwriting, become jumbled. This is a repeatable experiment, and it clearly demonstrates that our brains are sensitive to such energy.

Alternately, much of the imaging and sensing equipment that we use to examine our live and functioning human brains, while they are still safely tucked away in our heads, utilizes similar energies and chemistry in the imaging or monitoring processes.

The fact that we can affect our brains with electromagnetic energy such is done with TMS (Trans-cranial Magnetic Stimulators) and the fact that we can get computer images and data recordings of a live brain via electromagnetic energy emanating from the brain such as an EEG (Electro encephalogram) or FMRI (Functional Magnetic Resonance Imaging) clearly demonstrates that our brains can be both, affected by the energy, and can radiate the energy outward to be detected by sensors. To take this a bit further, this means it is highly likely that a human is able to sense, in their own head, these electromagnetic brain signals emitted by other people, which can come from the brain of another nearby human.

The probability that we detect variations of these emitted positive or negative electromagnetic signals from other people is extremely high. These signals potentially alter our own physical brain chemistry along with the electromagnetic signals that we emit to others from our own body.

The ramifications of emission and detection of such signals are critical and far reaching with regard to our attitude and health and in relationship to prayer. This explains a great deal as to why we seem to have an ability to sense tension even when we may not be seeing visible signs within the room. It also explains why we seem to feel another person's sorrow or joy by us feeling sad or feeling euphoric while we are around them or thinking about them. This electromagnetic ability (for lack of a better description) that we have, can affect us in the same way that our five senses do. This is because when we feel good or bad, regardless of why or how we feel it, it causes our body to produce the feel-good or feel-bad chemicals. However, this does not necessarily explain how someone comes to have strong emotions about someone who lives clear across the country as the distant person experiences something traumatic. This occurs even though we know nothing about the person's traumatic experience occurring, yet often something is felt by the connected person *not* experiencing the trauma.

We humans are far more capable than we have been given credit for over the last several hundred years since the time when the age of enlightenment ushered in the low aspirations that have resulted from the human-evolution-theory's fundamental principles. These low aspirations are equally, if not more, damaging than what some Church leaders had caused prior to the age of enlightenment. To its credit, the study of evolution has brought about helpful scientific advances to humanity. And to the Church's credit, the Church funded much scientific research over the years, especially during the enlightenment period, much of which ultimately led to the thoughts that brought about the naturalist evolutionary theories.

We can't somehow get in the head of someone and control their behavior, but it is certainly worth considering that we need to get ourselves into the habit of thinking kindly and lovingly about those around us, for our own good and for their own good.

As an example of the interpersonal effects of brain function and thinking: If your job is to be a salesperson, where you alone are solely responsible for connecting with your customer and getting them to like you, then if you do emit some sort of electromagnetic output that is detected by them as negativity, it may turn the customer away from you for no particular apparent reason even if that negativity is not specifically directed at them.

Changing your heart to a heart that is always trying to help other people will be beneficial to you. Not as a reward, but as a result of your attitude. This change of heart must be internal and complete, and not merely an outward act. It must be real and *not* forced.

An additional thought to remember is that, you do not need to specifically have these negative feelings towards the particular person who you are dealing with at the particular moment in order to have them sense your electromagnetic-negativity emissions. In fact, you can have good feelings towards them, but in the back of your mind you might be processing the negative information about a bad situation with someone else who you are trying to deal with. Even though you have put on a happy appearance, the person who you are currently with will subconsciously sense the negativity that you are silently processing in the back of your mind, and thus they may reject you for no apparent reason.

If your deeper emotions can affect people, then those negative thoughts that you are processing in the background of your mind could be emitting both negative chemicals and negative electromagnetic energy. The energy, which will be subtly perceived in the mind of the other person as *dislike*, will be reflected back to you in their attitude towards you by their unwillingness to do business with, or associate with, you.

If you had a bad day at work, but come home with a smile on your face, you might *appear* to be in good spirits, but if you're processing the negative information from work in the background of your mind, then you are emitting the type of electromagnetic energy to your family that is subsequently sensed by them and felt as *negativity* or *strife*.

Be careful to check your thoughts as you leave each situation, and then strive to completely remove those situations from your heart and mind when you are in other joyful situations. Failing to do so will have negative effects on those who you are with at that point in time.

The likelihood that we possess the ability to communicate on this unseen electromagnetic level gives us good confirmation of why the Ten Commandments were given, why they are good, and why the Christ told us to love our neighbor as ourselves. It is also a good confirmation as to why we are instructed to place our burdens in the hands of the Creator.

Understanding that it is likely we communicate to some extent in this way, does not mean that this is done outside of a Creator. This only stands to support the point that deliberate Creation actually took place. The construction of our bodies is an analogy of the essence of a soul. Because so many people doubt the idea of a Creator who purposefully Creates, I like to try to keep things as tangible as possible. But, in addition to our electromagnetic communication abilities, there is also the idea of spiritual communication, or communication of the soul.

Body Drugs

Since our brain is key to our central nervous system, it is the initiator, second only to our thoughts, for causing our bodies to produce their various chemicals. Our brain causes the production of serotonin and endorphins and many other such chemicals, both good and bad, which are said to be the reason that we "feel good" when we're in a euphoric mental state and the reason that we "feel bad" when we are feeling down.

If we become frightened, adrenaline is one particular chemical that's produced which allows us to boost our strength for self-preservation and self-protection. We risk our health when we artificially substitute this or other chemicals with outside drugs whether they are prescription, illegal drugs, or simple alcohol. Anything that alters our chemistry in this way should be the subject of much scrutiny.

Our bodies are susceptible to atrophy in just about every aspect known about our bodies. This means "Use it or lose it!" It's important that we keep our thinking organized properly. Consider this: If we are using outside drugs to prop up our physical and mental well-being, then those outside chemicals are artificially exercising those parts of our bodies for us.

If you take something that causes your body to not have to produce this chemistry on its own, then you are risking atrophy of the chemical function of your ability to produce that chemistry without the help of external chemicals. You can think of it like lifting weights, but instead of you doing it, you have somebody else actually doing the lifting for you. Eventually, you will lose muscle mass, and then later on, no matter how hard you tried, the weights will be too heavy for you to pick up.

In addition to the potential problem of mental atrophy, you may lose other abilities that are tightly connected with these chemicals. Certain chemicals, such as serotonin and possibly endorphins, are believed to aid in the healing process when you are injured—this is incredibly important to us all! If this is correct, it means that your ability to heal will be slower if you are in a constant state of doubt and depression or if you are in a constant state of stress, frustration, or anger.

Evolution or Creation, Creation, or evolution, no matter how we look at this, we keep arriving at the same conclusion that there are real and true physical real-world ramifications from having a bad attitude that is not in harmony with what is true.

We can try to dispel a Creator and you are welcome to do so, but when all is said and done it's going to it come back down to that question of your own personal "Why?" And your *why* is a very philosophical question indeed!

Your *why* is outside of the realm of evolution, and it is outside of the realm of the cosmos and of the big bang theory. Your why is the ability to ponder self and to reason. Our why has been the point of contention in the lives of mankind for thousands of years.

We each have a personal choice to decide what information we will believe and follow. And through our choice of what we each believe, it becomes our own choice of the quality of life that we will live. Regardless of what we choose to believe, in the end, there is only one truth, and at some point, we will come to know what that Truth is. Regardless of what it is, what we think it is, or what we hope it is, **we all will face what is True.**

Our prayers will bring us closer to what is true when we put away negativity and place our thoughts upon joy, especially while we pray. Living in a negative state of mind only brings you lower with each passing day and inhibits the true power of your prayers.

When we choose to remove the negative from around ourselves and to always seek truth, then joy is the natural result, thus, causing us to be more joyful, healthier, and most importantly, doing so strengthens the power of our prayers!

Chapter 21

True Faith is Not Surprised

The biggest hurdle that we face in regard to our prayer is our understanding of the word "faith". In fact, the word *faith* has implications all throughout our lives and in everything we do.

We often think of the word faith as a set of beliefs. While that is one usage of the word, it is really not the proper usage. The reason that a particular religion is termed as a "faith", as in "What is your faith?" is because the word faith indicates a sharing of what you know or promise.

The word *faith* and *fidelity* are from the same root word which means *truth*. If we say that someone has *true faith* we are saying they have *true truth*. But since we use the word differently it is important that we throw the word *true* in front of *faith* because, often, the word *faith* is accompanied by the word *blind* as in blind-faith.

The term "blind-faith" is contradictory. It is like saying "I want my lights *off-on*" or "I want *bad-good*." When we think of it in this manner it seems incredibly nonsensical to use the two terms together. But to be more specific in this explanation, we will look into each word separately.

The word "blind" means to make *cloudy* or to *conceal*, and it has the obvious meaning of not being able to see. The word "*faith*" means *truth*, or what is true, which has a meaning that it is clear and in the open and not hidden. To use the words *blind* and *faith* together is like saying *unclear-truth* or a *hidden-truth*.

When we think of it in terms of a *hidden* truth we might imagine that we are seeking truth that is hidden away. But that cannot be the case. Truth is something that is obvious, apparent, and out in the open. So if we are going to fully convert the term blind-faith then we should really say that it is hidden-obvious. It might not seem obvious to us at the moment, but once we see it we wonder how we ever missed what had always been out in the open just waiting for us to notice it.

Blind-faith hides the truth. When we accept blind-faith, then we are believing something that we do not understand and which is possibly altogether wrong.

This might seem good on the outset, but it is actually a recipe for disaster! If you do not understand exactly what and why you believe what you do, then you are subject to the errors of the person who is guiding you.

Many of us look at blind-faith and think "Well that's fine, because I follow Jesus. After all, He *is* the good shepherd." It's understandable and admirable that we want to follow Jesus. The only problem is that the Christ is not here before us in person at this moment. I can imagine that this statement ruffles some religious feathers, but with the following information you will understand what this comment is getting at.

The Christ discussed the concept of "The blind leading the blind" and requested for the people to "Come follow me" and discussed being a "Good shepherd". So it would make sense that people would choose blind-faith and then follow the ways of the Christ.

Following Christ with blind-faith would work well, and for a couple of thousand years, for many people, it has. But there is one glaring problem with this sort of blind-faith: If you are blind in your faith, then you will miss some of what the Christ was saying. Seldom do we, on our own, actually take the time to stop and read the words of the Christ. If we do read the Christ's words, it's rare for us to actually contemplate the actual meaning of those words, and, when we do, we do so with bias, twisting the words to suit us rather than us changing ourselves to be in accordance with the words. But more typically, we rely upon a preacher to do the interpretation for us, and then we must further *blindly* interpret the preacher's interpretation that we heard. And too often we select a preacher who has an interpretation that *we* like, thus allowing us to continue in our poor habits and behavior.

In our blindness and unwillingness to do the work on our own through our own reading and thinking, we instead go to a church service or listen to a preacher who may not understand the Christ's words accurately or fully. This is not wrong, but it does mean that if the preacher gets it wrong, and some of them do, and you use blind-faith and listen to what the preacher is teaching, then if what he is teaching you is wrong, it is a case of "The blind leading the blind".

I do not believe that the Christ wanted people to have blind-faith. But sadly, that is our condition. The Christ healed the blind so that they could see. Healing the blind was not done as an entertaining special effect. There is a message in this for all those who hear about it.

The most admirable thing that any human can do is to try to know and understand the Creator. We do not live long enough to know everything about the Creator, but we do live long enough to know any particular thing we are insightful enough to seek about the Creator. However, without truth, we will know nothing. There is a message interwoven throughout the entire Bible, and that message is nothing more than for us to open our eyes and to stop believing lies.

Truth is What Builds Up

Truth adds to understanding and strengthens anything that is exposed to it, with the exception of a lie.

A lie is not something. It does not exist and it is made up. But it is believed or accepted as if it does exist, which is done through blind-faith. Truth is the only thing that can expose a lie. Something either *is*—or—it is not. Lies will be defeated by truth. A lie does not have order and therefore cannot exist, and anything attached to the lie will degrade until it is destroyed, including you—Unless of course, you stop believing lies.

When we choose the scale of truth, and we live our lives based upon the reading of that scale, we will build ourselves and those around us up with a strength that no lie can contend with.

Truth is eternal. Truth creates. Truth makes better. Truth builds up. Truth is everlasting. And Truth will always be—no matter what. What *is*—is *what is*—this cannot be denied. It is a clear and simple piece of logic that all of mankind is born understanding. Anytime the truth is next to a lie and is seen with open eyes, the lie becomes apparent and is discredited and cast aside.

A lie is corrupt and short-term and will defeat itself through the corrective nature of the order of truth. Something that is not—is not. In other words, it is not there and it will eventually be forgotten or disregarded. When you believe a lie, doing so corrupts you and alters your mental and physical state.

When we think of lies and truth in this context, then we get a clearer picture of what occurred with Adam and Eve in the Garden. They chose to believe the lie that was offered to them by the serpent, and in doing so, they were corrupted and could not live forever because they could no longer stand in the face of pure truth.

In a real physical sense, they corrupted their bodies and subjected their bodies to destruction. Whatever we choose as our foundation determines the strength of our own self. If our foundation is destroyed, then we will be destroyed along with it. Eve, and then Adam chose, of their own freewill, to ignore the truth that was told to them, and they paid with their lives.

Truth Is a Choice

Truth is a choice that we make. Truth exists—a lie does not exist! It is up to each one of us to make this choice on our own and no one can force us or do it for us. In the end, we will be weighed on the scale of truth and our value will be determined by the truth that we each choose to keep within our heart—or choose *not* to keep within our heart.

Blind-faith is asking someone else to make the choice for us. The Christ was **not** saying, "Close your eyes and follow me." The Christ was saying follow me by doing what I do.

Unfortunately, since we have an inclination to believe lies, we have become subject to laws. A law is a man-made rule that we record in an effort to create a guide by which we should live. The laws of our lands are exactly like those that the Pharisees imposed upon the people but did not always completely abide by themselves.

The Christ was telling us to abide by what is true, as did the Creator while the people were wandering in the desert. Not long after the people finally settled after wandering for forty years, they promptly demanded a king to be appointed to guide and protect them.

We humans seek to be guided. We desire to have somebody tell us exactly what to do so that we can behave rightly, but in doing so we have believed a lie. There is only one thing that any one of us needs to concern ourself with—and that one thing is Truth!

When we seek order in our lives, we can break everything down into simple choices of *yes* or *no, good* or *bad, true* or *not true*—everything follows this simple logic. Anytime we get something wrong, we are set on a path of error and we will pay the consequence of our choice at some point. That cost will be proportional to the choices we make and to the length of time we deceive ourselves and others with our bad choices.

Truth is a personal choice. We do not get to decide if something is true, we get to decide if we will agree with or admit to what is true.

Our freewill choice is a part of the order that we are Created with, and without order we cannot exist. But there is a catch for us in order for us to be able to live abundantly and thrive, and the catch is that *we* must *choose* what is *true*.

The consequences of choosing what is not true, is to be ignorantly blind or to have blind-faith. Meaning that, you ignore things and choose to believe what you *want* to believe because you are too lazy to do the research on your own. Or you want the instant gratification offered by a lie and/or you want to hide your own errors or the errors of those around you.

Truth is a choice that is only yours to make, no one can make it for you. And no one can take the choice from you.

Through threats of violence, someone can try to force you to believe a lie and deny what is true, or someone can force you in the same way to reject your lie and accept what is true, but in the end, the choice remains within your own heart, mind, and thoughts.

You can be brought to the point of death and still deny what is true even though someone is trying to force you to see the light, or in the case of the Christ, using threats of death, they requested that the Christ deny the truth unto his death—He declined to do so.

The message for all of us in the account of the Christ, was that nothing, not even your life, exceeds the value of Truth!

It is not worth sacrificing truth that resides within you in exchange for anything, because *Truth* is the only thing of real value in any person's existence.

What is True Love?

Our misunderstanding of the concepts beneath the words that we utter is humanity's mental stumbling block that bars us from being able to see, with any clarity, things that are true. In the realm of Creation, whether done by a Creator, by a big bang, or by some other theory, things that are not true cannot be seen because they do not exist and therefore they are not there in a physical sense or in a spiritual sense.

If we lose sight of the most basic of words, such as Truth, then we are surely left in the dark. The word Truth is a fundamental principle that cannot be any further dissected with fundamental language. If we fail to grasp the concept of what *truth* is, then we are bound by the lies that will enter all aspects of our lives, and this will affect the success of our prayers.

"Love" is another fundamental word that cannot be any further dissected. We can all only *try* to convey love's meaning. Love is an ability to *give* and *receive freely*. It is the ability to reveal yourself or to give yourself to others. And it is the ability to receive others when they offer themselves to you. Please note: to receive someone who has corrupted themselves without them repenting, will corrupt the person receiving them. Even the Creator will not receive unrepentant hearts. In fact, it is humanity's biggest error that, in our supposed "love" for someone, we allow and receive their bad behavior, thus indicating to them that what they do is okay. Such behavior issues are further detailed in the cornerstone books *Red Hot Marriage* and *Hot Water*.

When we fail to be able to grasp the fundamental concepts of these fundamental words, we are left without hope of ever being able to see what is real and true.

Not being able to define the words *true* and *love* places humanity in a very dark and dangerous place. All relationships of mankind are based upon our ability to understand these two principle concepts. Not understanding their basic essence will bar you from being able to detect deception in your life, and more importantly, in your relationships. If you allow these simple words to be undermined within your understanding, then you have lost your ability to see and you will pay a very dear price for doing so in everything you do.

Your primary quest should always be to grasp these two words—*truth* and *love*—over any others so that you have the opportunity and skill to make proper decisions and choices throughout life.

When our understanding of truth and love is wrong, we have lost a very important index that would have allowed us to understand both a physical world and a world of thoughts and emotions. This index is our only true measurement, and it gives us the ability to judge other things with the index. Without a strong ability to make sound judgment, there is no index. Your life and aspects of it will be chaotic due to your own choosing to not embrace and properly understand these two simple concepts—*truth* and *love*.

In the beginning of this book, we discussed the importance of definitions and standards. We also discussed how governments have index units of volume and weight measurement that are vaulted with a great amount of protection and preservation. The reason that these units are protected is because, if we do not have a consistent standard, our economy will become chaotic and will quickly collapse due to deception and cheating for nothing more than the selfish benefit of those who cheat. To an extent, we are all guilty of inconsistent personal index, and it must be eradicated from our lives if we want successful prayer.

Changing weight index in commerce is a common form of deception with regard to cheating. This is sometimes done in commerce because you can sell customers less than you are claiming you that are actually selling. Using dishonest weights was common in the past and only in recent centuries have we come to a civil international agreement in regard to enforcing accurate weighing. This dishonest sort of behavior is illegal the world around but it still occurs. If we collectively, via our governments, did not hold tightly to the fundamental unit standards, then our societies could not function well. Societies would break down because the parts that are made would not fit from one manufacturer to another. Formulas and recipes would change from one batch to the next, and you would not be able to depend on anything made with human hands. This deceit does happen, but thankfully, when done intentionally it is illegal and the index is typically well enforced.

The words *Truth* and *Love* are no different, they are standards and they must be protected and preserved. Without their consistency we cannot depend upon anything that involves humans. And what is worse is that if we do not understand these two words properly, our expectations of nature will also be wrong and our prayers will greatly suffer as a result.

If you believe wrong things about nature and the constraints by which nature functions, then if your changing index indicates that you can fly without an apparatus, and you proceed to jump off of a cliff, then your index will prove to be a problem for you when you plummet to your death at the base of the cliff.

These two words—*Truth* and *Love*—in specific, are the most important for you to determine and understand their actual underlying meanings.

Truth and Love are both forms of revealing. Truth reveals physical existence and more, and Love reveals mind, spirit, or thought existence. They are both the same thing within a different form, realm, or authority. They are embodied in every person and they are to be protected within us. But too many of us allow them to be corrupted, causing them to be forced out of us.

Anyone proposing to alter these terms by assigning more than one definition, or by assigning alternate definitions to them, is trying to usurp the supreme authority of the two concepts.

Anytime someone is attempting to change the standard, they are then violating the original standard. With mankind's rules we can change a standard so long as we all agree on what the change is to be. However, when it comes to truth and love, everything breaks down when an attempt is made to change these two standards. The standard of truth is a natural master-standard, and it mimics the standard of love, but they are both the same in function. Love is a non-physical standard that we often see in a physical way, but is detected in a non-physical experience in our heart, mind, or soul.

The term true-love is a bit redundant, but it is certain— unless you have allowed a redefinition of these terms into your thinking. Due to each of our own life experiences, most of the people in the world have a differing and skewed, or crooked, understanding of these two words— *Truth* and *Love*.

Many people misperceive love. Consider that if we are told by people that we are "loved" by them, but instead are regularly experiencing something that is **not** love, then our perception of the word *love* is skewed, and our perception of the word *truth* will then also become equally incorrect.

We are the protective vault for *love* and the standard for *truth*. If we have allowed the love within us to be corrupted or changed, then nothing in our life is able to be accurate or dependable. We might be able to function, but we will be functioning by chance and will have unpredictable results in all areas of our lives, especially in our prayer lives. And all of this is due to our skewed definition and understanding of *Love*.

We attempt to demand things to be our way, and, for a time, others will comply with our selfish demands. But at some point, our distorted index of love breaks down in order to correct itself, causing you to be caught in the fireball of correction. True Love is to reveal ourselves, just as the Creator reveals through all of Creation—it is our standard! But when we live with a skewed standard of love, then our truth is perverted and corrupted. We then go on to pray with our corrupted version of truth and expect that our prayers should be answered. When our prayers are not answered, as *we* see fit, or when we miss the answer to our prayer, we then go on to further corrupt ourselves by rejecting the Creator.

Why We Cannot be Healed

"Faith-healing" would be far more common if we only understood the power of the truth in our bodies. From a strictly physical perspective, the evidence is obvious that we are in a great amount of control over our health. We might not be able to control everything we encounter, but we can certainly control our thoughts.

In an earlier chapter, we discussed the connection of our thoughts to the chemicals produced in our bodies as a result of those thoughts. When we think about this in relation to the idea of being able to heal ourselves, or others, it becomes very real.

No matter what you might choose to believe, the chemistry that occurs in our bodies is directly connected to our thoughts. These chemicals can have harmful or helpful properties. And, as best as science can tell, it is our thoughts that determine the release of the chemicals. This brings a tremendous amount of validity to the words of the Christ and the Creator with reference to healing and being protected from disease.

If a person can bring their thoughts to a pure and full understanding of what is good and true, then that person can control, at will, their biochemistry just by choosing the correct thoughts. Or better put, the correct mental disposition. This gives anyone who can conquer their thoughts an ability to, at will, cause the production of good chemistry, which in turn allows for better health and more rapid healing.

In the Bible it says "My people perish for lack of knowledge." We must ask, what knowledge do they lack? Often, when people get very sick they visit their doctor and are told their disease is progressed too far and that they will die in a short amount of time. Sadly, people blindly accept this and are then given excessive amounts of painkillers in effort to ease the pain that is believed to be a result of their disease. It is a futile prayer effort to pray for healing for a person who has been given a death sentence by their doctor(s) *and accepts it*, and is then subsequently prescribed strong painkillers to "manage the pain" until they die. When this is the case, the best that you can do is to pray that the person quickly comes upon the realization that the doctor is wrong, *before* their body is damaged beyond reasonable repair from "painkillers".

Such medication given in these situations is intended to end the person's suffering by prematurely taking their life in a literal mind-numbing way. Praying for the healing of someone who has accepted the lie of a death sentence, and is willing to take strong painkillers, is like praying that someone will not be hurt if they deliberately injure themselves. In the case of someone deliberately harming themselves, it is obvious that our prayer is being sabotaged. We also do this in other more discreet ways, but we typically are not aware of it with regard to healing.

If you say that you believe in healing, and then have any doubts that you will be healed, then you are in a state of conflicting-oscillation that will harm you. It is a case of being double-minded. By accepting that you are going to die because, "the doctor said so", places that doctor as your own personal god.

It is the double-minded "lights on-off" situation mentioned earlier. When we truly believe truth, it is *all* or *nothing.* There is no in between. Know that it can be done and do not conflict in your mind by thinking or doing such contradictory actions. Doctors and medicine have their place, but therein abuses do occur. And it is the *abuse* that is being referred to in this section. Anyone who is given such a death sentence is far better served to believe that they will live, rather than believe that they will die as prescribed by the doctors. This does not mean that they refuse treatment, but it does mean that they change the beliefs in their heart.

What is The Faith of a Child?

Blind-faith is frequently mistaken for having the faith of a child. We discussed blind-faith in-depth earlier, but to recap, "faith" ultimately means *truth* and "blind" means to *hide, conceal,* or *cloud*; so "blind-faith" means *clouded-truth* or *hidden-obvious.*

We often confuse blind faith with the faith of a child. The Bible records that the Christ said "Truly, I say to you, whoever does not receive the kingdom of God like a child does cannot enter it." This simple phrase is quite misunderstood, and it has caused many people to become blinded. This quote is often believed to support the concept of blind-faith, but it has nothing at all to do with believing something that is not evident.

> The faith of a child statement is not about *what* you believe it is about *how* you believe.

Very few people have true conviction about their beliefs. We might act as if we have conviction to a point where we will even fight or argue about our convictions. But few of us can actually explain those convictions. Not being able to explain is the blind-faith part. And because we cannot explain our convictions, we fail to be able to think and believe them with our whole heart to a point of absolute utter belief and understanding. Though, it is true that, in the purity of innocence, some people do achieve a full belief, with their whole heart, in something that is true because they have childlike faith. However, these same people could just as easily be wrong if they had chosen to believe *incorrect* information with their whole heart through their blind-faith.

Believing with your whole heart has nothing to do with being correct or incorrect. It is about the capacity to receive something with utter certainty to a point where your mind and body are convinced in absolute certainty that it is correct in what it is thinking. When a person has reached this level of belief, they then won't be in oscillation in this regard if they follow truth. This is why blind-faith is so dangerous. With blind-faith we receive something with utter certainty to a point where our minds and bodies are convinced with absolute certainty. But when we have latched on to something that is wrong, then our blind-faith has failed us. *Real* faith *always* checks the information for truth, where blind-faith doesn't think to ask. The faith of a child statement is not about *what* you believe it is about **how** you believe.

Many of us believe things, but then go about entertaining contrary thoughts, or we struggle to dismiss contrary evidence. This is doubt, and it is a form of cross-checking or correction. If we, as humans, did not contain this ability to doubt things, then we would be able to be completely deceived about anything— and very quickly so—Think Eve in the garden.

The only thing that we should doubt is *lies*, but our problem is that we do not do that. We have become very proficient at doubting truth. This is because liars are masters of disguise and they do all that they can to make their lie appear to us to be true.

Our ability to look at evidence and decide, *what is* and *what is not*, is based upon truth. When we forfeit truth, then we cannot easily "receive like a child". A good illustration of this is the "Santa Claus Effect" where parents tell their child that a jolly fat man from the north brings presents on Christmas Eve. The child initially believes this *without question*. They have no reservation about it and accept it as readily as they accept everything else that they see before them, including the ground beneath their feet.

A child's level of acceptance is unrivaled. Few adults have the same capacity of innocent acceptance that a child does. This is very close to blind-faith in that *how* a child believes allows them to believe a lie. They believe it because they trust *you*.

A child's acceptance of Santa Claus is blind-faith, but the *way* in which they do it is *childlike* faith. Believing in Santa Claus is accepting something without self-verification, but for a child, they are deceived by their own parents who they freely trusted. The mysterious appearance of presents under the tree is evidence enough for the child because the parents are in on the hoax and have lied to their children. The Creator does not do this and the Bible is very concise about this sort of deception. And yet, many preachers deceive countless people because these preachers insist that faith is blind and we should all just follow the Bible as *they* interpret it. I agree that we should follow the Bible, but the problem for us comes in with *whose* interpretation we choose to follow.

With the Santa Claus effect, the children later go to school and find out that they were lied to by the people who they trusted the most—their parents. Because of this betrayal at such an early age, they become somewhat incapable of being able to fully accept anything as true no matter what confirmations are presented to them. This is due to their lack of trust initiated by the parents' violating their childlike faith. Such violation crosses many boundaries and is not limited to Santa Claus. This problem includes Easter bunny, tooth fairy, religion, evolution, as well as most relationships a person encounters throughout their lifetime. There are many people who do not practice the Santa Claus hoax but have other areas in life where they practice other similar functioning deceptions and inconsistencies, and then perpetrate them onto their children causing the same blind-faith problem.

Every instance of this Santa Claus Effect type of fundamental deception in our lives erodes our capacity to completely accept correct information as *absolute* and *true*. Our ability to receive information in absolute trust is a primary language that is learned at very young ages.

To some extent, children begin to sense disappointment almost immediately in life. If you care to learn more about its effects on your family, the cornerstone book *Strong Family* discusses this further.

The Bible quote from the Christ, "Truly, I say to you, whoever does not receive the kingdom of God like a child shall not enter it." is specifically speaking of the ability to *absolutely* accept the truth of the kingdom of God without harboring any doubt.

We do not need to know something is true, provided that it *is* true. So long as something actually is true and we have absolutely accepted it, then we could "enter it" if we "receive the kingdom of God like a child". The problem that occurs for us is that corruption exists, and all too often, some Church and scientific leaders have led the way with "The blind leading the blind". This is why there is a "Good Shepherd" to lead the blind sheep. But, in reference to the Church, when we follow the words of the clergy without properly checking those words in comparison with what the Bible *actually* says, then we are at risk of not following the Good Shepherd, because instead, we follow the preacher or teacher. This same checking system must also be applied to what the leaders of the scientific community teach.

The words of Paul in the Bible are a tricky bunch of words that are legalistic and have deceived many people. Preachers spend more time talking about what Paul said than they do discussing what the Christ said. This is a tragic error on their part, and it has caused many people to be deceived. If misinterpretations of Paul's sometimes confusing words are taken as true over the Christ's words, then a preacher is, without a doubt, choosing blindness and is the instrument of "The blind leading the blind."—They have become false preachers.

This is a beautiful world in which we live, and *we* get to choose to make it even more beautiful, or to further corrupt it. Blind-faith has no place in a world filled with lies, and having blind faith eventually causes us shame because, at some point, we will follow the wrong shepherd, whether that shepherd is from the world of science or from the Church.

Investigate and understand, and then when you get a good grasp on what is true. Accept it with the same amount of certainty that a young child accepts whatever their parents tell them. Step outside of the Santa Claus Effect and learn how to once again believe in something that is true with every fiber of your being—have the faith of a child and follow the **good** shepherd.

Truth is a Dangerous Double-Edged Sword

Truth is a dangerous double-edged sword that will cut you to pieces if you have been living a life based upon what is not true. Truth cares nothing of our lies or error. Truth's purpose, and our purpose, is to correct error and to reveal *what* **is**. Truth has no consideration with regard to lies or anything that is untrue. Lies will be cut low and disposed of in truth's awesome fury.

Truth harvests the ripe crop and pulls out the weeds of lies and burns them in its awesome fury to destroy them. If you have chosen to be a weed of lies, then truth will uproot you and you will eventually feel the burn of your errors. This is why so many people run from truth and are afraid of truth, because they know they are embedded with the dry prickly weeds of the lies that they have embraced, and they realize that they will be burned in the path of truth's awesome fury. We cannot expect our prayers to be effective when we're in such a state. Remove the weeds from your Garden of Truth.

Truth seeks and destroys all false things with its intense light, causing truth to flow into the place that the false things once held in your heart.

Choosing to accept truth is our only requirement, and it is done by admitting our errors and by repenting of, and restoring, as best we can, the damage we have caused, and then ceasing all lying ways in our future. Once we have done this and follow truth, we are no longer subject to the vicious double-edged sword of truth.

When we have chosen truth, then truth is no longer our enemy and instead becomes our protector. It strengthens us and lights our way to all things good. Truth exposes all lies and brings about the destruction of all bad things in your life when you are absolute about truth.

Be careful how you handle this double-edged sword or it is sure to cut you. If you have been living a life built upon lies, then approach truth quickly but cautiously. Do not fear truth because truth is there to protect *you!* You will cut yourself with this double-edged sword if you do not put away all lies and double-mindedness.

Truth has no enemies, it just **Is**. *We* make truth *our* enemy when we choose lies. Truth wants to protect us, but cannot without our permission. We often choose to be the *enemy* of truth with our lies, where with wisdom on the other hand we can instead choose to be an *ally* of truth by *rejecting* all lies.

When We Choose to Deny What is True and Good, Then We are in Error

When we choose to deny what is true and good, we are in error. Think about this: If you are choosing something that is not true, good, or correct, then there is no choice other than for it to be incorrect and wrong. This is very important for you to understand for yourself, but equally as important to understand for when others are trying to harm you.

All too often, we want to hurt those who hurt us. Others will continue to try to cause us harm, but what we must understand is that we need not fight them. All that we need to do is speak the truth, not about them or what they are doing to us, but merely speak the truth about the topic. They will automatically be exposed and forced into admission of error. This will result in an attack towards you, but standing strong in choosing what is true keeps you in an undefeatable position in the long run.

When we depart from lies and embrace truth, others, who are as we once were, will feel judged by our new truth. Even if we say nothing, they might still feel attacked and will proceed to attack us in effort to protect themselves.

If you slip away from what is true and sink to a level of selecting what is not true, it will cause you to err because you have chosen what is not true. When you do this, then your attacker can use your error to discredit you and harm you.

A liar can use truth to harm another liar, and when they become proficient at it, they won't cut themselves very often because they will only draw attention to the truth in connection with others, but never with themselves. But usually their hypocrisy eventually catches up with them.

This sort of thing has happened in the Church on a somewhat regular basis over the years. Church leaders and the congregation often believe things that are not true, and then when they are caught in their erred blind-faith by others who are trying to accuse them, they are then made fools by their attackers. However, their attackers will not be able to do this for long if the others choose to not continue to believe wrong or incorrect information through blind-faith.

When we choose wrong information and are called out on it, or are accused with it, we technically cannot explain our actions and are thus discredited, causing us to not be well regarded when trying to expose the real lies in our lives and in life in general. Liars try to paint truth as if it is a lie.

All of this puts us out of harmony with what is true and it negatively and severely affects the level of success of our prayers. We get caught in this trap until *we* decide to embrace only things that are true.

When We Accept the Truth We Bind Lies, and then the Lies are Held Captive

We all make mistakes, and that is the human condition. But, to continue to make the same mistakes over and over binds us in our own stupidity and in lies. The sooner we accept truth, then the sooner we can be in control of our own lives and increase our lives, through our own diligence and prayer.

> Truth is so powerful that it will destroy destruction from your life!

When we pray, it is common for us to wrongly pray with blind-faith, not truly understanding what *is* real and what *is not* real. We do this, and then we become angry when our prayers are not answered. Eventually, when some compelling, but inaccurate, information is presented to us, we believe it in a manner like the Santa Claus Effect and we reject the Creator and live negative and doubt-filled lives. This is *not* the approach we need to take.

We also accept air opportunities—those opportunities that are as abundant as air—as the answers to our prayers. If we want to live a life that accepts the *mediocre* as if it is successful, then *we* have chosen our own lackluster path. If we accept these air opportunities as actual answers to our prayers, then we are deceived. When we live in deceit we are bound to a level of life limited to only that which the deceit is capable of offering us— this ranges from very limited to outright destructive. It's certainly okay to take advantage of air opportunities, but we should not accept or attribute them as the answers to our prayers. They are a longstanding gift from truth.

Chapter 22

Clearing Your Mind to Pray Properly

Recorded historical accounts of various cultures show us that as far back as it is recorded, humanity has struggled with the questions that we have been discussing, "Is there a Creator?" and "What is the value of prayer?" Though, historically it may not have been stated in those specific terms.

In recent centuries we have seen, in any time contemporary to each of us, where people who were overwhelmed with the trappings of the world would give up everything they have and then choose a life of a more relaxed nature, often entering into a life of meditation and relaxation. Yet, even with a profound life-shift of this nature, far too many still failed to find what they were truly looking for, as can be witnessed in writings or in speaking with some of them if they are still alive. Of those who are already gone, many died at younger than average ages and some others fell away from their new-found ways in the later years of their lives. Clearing our mind of lies and untruths is really what is being sought when we do these things.

This not being said to condemn those who choose a path free from the trappings of life, but we must realize that our frustration and confusion are not caused by what we have, or by what we do. Our frustration and confusion are caused by the way we think and by how we perceive these "trappings" of life. It is the way that we perceive those things that makes them trappings for us.

Seek to clear your mind of inaccurate information, thus freeing yourself from all lies. Our ability to clear our mind of inaccurate information is our most precious gift—it is the way to truth!

Do You Know How to Weigh Information Properly?

The reason that most of us cannot readily clear our minds is because no one has taught us the simple art of weighing information properly. When we lose our ability to weigh information properly, or we are not taught to do so, then it creates an oscillation (a back-and-forth) in our thinking, ultimately causing us to be unable to truly make up our mind about a situation. This mostly remains quietly in our own head unknown to us and others.

In an earlier chapter, we spoke of being double-minded versus being single-minded. The oscillating that we do in our thinking is part of being double-minded. This is something that we were warned against thousands of years ago by the words in the Bible.

We are instructed to be single-minded and to believe and have **expectation**. When we forfeit our ability to properly weigh information, we trap ourselves in the web of other people's deceit. Since almost all of our problems have to do with our relationships with other people, our relationships are an area that is most important for us to be able to control in our own lives.

While often not realized by ourselves, when people around us who we have trusted proceed to violate our trust, there is a part of us that denies that this is so. This denial is subtly done by us in order to keep the peace between us and them. We do this because we want to feel loved and because we do not want to be rejected, but we are choosing to *not* weigh the information accurately when we do so.

In our quest to have things feel as if they are in order and in harmony in our lives, we overlook things when our expectations are violated. It's good to give people or a situation another chance, but not if we are ignoring what actually occurred. Closing our eyes to anything and ignoring it, has a tendency to work like a magnet to bring it right back into our lives to occur again and again, tormenting us until we choose to properly and fully address the problem.

We confuse *ignoring* violations against us, with *rejecting* violations against us. Frequently, when we are violated, we close our eyes to the problem and wish it would go away. Then, the moment we open our eyes, the problem comes right back to us to violate us once again. Ignoring a violation allows it to be repeated again and again, but rejecting violation gives you an altogether different result.

Rejecting violation stops it in its tracks causing it to flee from you—but doing this can cause some existing relationships to become strained, distant, or even nonexistent. In general, this will be good for you and for your family if those strained relationships have been damaging to your family.

You will see the relationship changes coming when you embrace truth. Some relationships become stronger and better, and some relationships will disappear altogether.

Stop Believing Lies

Our ability to accurately weigh information is directly connected to our ability to stop believing lies. Anytime we choose to believe a lie, it's like having a scale that is specifically designed to be out of balance so that the lie appears as if the lie is true. There is no other way out of this trap other than to make a personal and conscious choice that you will no longer accept an inaccurate scale.

The flurry of chemicals produced by our bodies and brains when our thinking is out of sync from truth are very damaging to us. We can control a great deal of our health through our thinking and beliefs when we understand the real-life connections of how our brain, body, thinking, and prayer all work and connect. We do not need blind-faith to see how our electrochemistry affects us. *Blind* faith is a danger to us and it is different than *true* faith.

Our choice to believe lies is a *choice* that may not readily appear to us as a choice, but it is a choice nonetheless. Our inability to weigh information accurately is due to our choice to believe lies. Let's imagine that you're walking into a store to buy a scale on which to weigh all of your choices. When you get to the store, you see that there are three scales to choose from: One of the scales weighs things in your favor so that no matter what anyone around says, the scale always balances in your favor. We can call it the "me" scale.

Next to the "me" scale you see another scale that balances everything as it truly is; if the weight on the left side of the scale and the weight on the right side of the scale are not the same, then it will be out of balance making it sometimes look like things are in your favor and other times it will indicate that things are not in your favor.

And finally, there is a third scale. The third scale weighs everything so that no matter what you do, or what you put on it, it is never in your favor. We can call this scale the "them" scale.

**Before reading on, think about the
three scales for a moment.**

**Which of the three scales will you choose
to weigh your decisions on?**

If you chose the first scale, then you are very arrogant indeed! You do not care about anything but yourself because you have chosen a scale that is going to agree with you—*even if you are wrong.*

If you chose the third scale, you are likely afraid of everything and feel lowly and undeserving about yourself. No matter what you do you feel that you will always be falling short of having that scale balance in your favor.

If you have chosen the second scale, then you have chosen rightly and wisely. The second scale weighs things for what they actually are, and it shows you who you truly are. The only real choice in life that we need to make is which of these scales we will use to weigh and make all of our own decisions with.

Many people's misunderstanding of the enlightenment movement has worked at slowly deteriorating the hearts and minds of mankind over the centuries. A few of those who were the initiators of freethinking truly grasped what we are talking about here, but many of the followers of those people often misinterpreted what was actually intended by their leaders. This is similar to what happens with the Bible and the words of the Christ in the New Testament.

Various preachers and even certain Church leaders had taken the information in the Bible and twisted and manipulated it to serve their own purpose. Then they used those words as weapons of arrogance and bondage to enslave the congregation to their manipulated interpretation. They perverted the beautiful simplicity of what was written, and they used it as an advantage for their own gain because the scale that they purchased was of the first kind that weighed everything in favor of them— regardless of what harm it would cause others.

Using a lying scale, clearly was not the message that the Christ was trying to convey. Nor was it the message that the Creator was trying to convey. In order to stop believing lies, we must first make a choice to use an *honest* scale (the second or middle scale) of truth that ignores bias and does not change its accurate true judgement.

Negative and Cruel People

Choosing the right scale is the only good option! If you choose a scale that always favors you no matter what is being weighed, or if you choose a scale that always dis-favors you no matter what is being weighed, then you will either be arrogant, or negative, and likely both.

Because they are using the wrong scale, negative people and cruel people believe that they are not good enough. All of us have a natural understanding about which scale we *should* be using. When we choose the wrong scale we know that we are doing so even though we won't admit to it. This is why we have feelings of not being good enough, which we compensate for with negativity and/or arrogance. Thus we foolishly choose a scale that we wrongly believe fits us or gives us advantage over others.

> **The scale of "me" and the scale of "them" is no challenge for the scale of Truth.**

When we choose to weigh our life upon the "me" and "them" scales—the *first* and *third* respectively, then we become subject to a great deal of error. There's a problem that is inherent to these two scales. When we use these scales, if we are told that we are good or did a good job, then it goes to our head in the wrong way and adds to our arrogance and/or fear and feelings of inadequacy.

Our quest is truly to seek truth, which is why we're all here! When we use a lying scale and are praised for something that we happened to get right by chance, then we feel good. And due to our using the wrong scale, we have come to misunderstand the real meaning of the compliments and praise. The compliment became misdirected in our minds, causing us to think that we are somehow above those around us.

When we choose to judge our life-understanding based upon an inaccurate scale, we have then chosen a lie and our mind can no longer be clear and pure.

> **We all seek what is true
> until we have chosen the wrong scale.**

Once we have chosen the wrong scale, we seek the rewards that come with choosing what is true, but we do not deserve those rewards. Yet, in our arrogance, we still take credit that does not belong to us, and then we steal from others and do our best to hold them down below us. Even when we choose the "them" scale, we are trying to be loved by someone by placing them above us and being subservient to them, in essence, trying to be credited "love" by someone who we see as more important than ourselves.

The three scales that we imagined are actually only two scales: one scale measures truth, and the other scale measures lies. The scale of lies is a mirror reflection of itself; it is the same scale that both the arrogant and a fearful use; and that scale always tips in favor of the arrogant.

Arrogant people want everything to lean in their favor, regardless of what is being weighed. It is on the other side of that same scale where the fearful live, always being controlled by the arrogant. When we look at the scale of lies, the one side will always be weighed down in favor of the arrogant, and the other side will always be left wanting by the fearful, thus causing the fearful to succumb to the demands of what has become their arrogant task master. The fearful will falsely believe that their taskmaster raises them up, much the way the balance scale raises them up when they give their value and power over to their master's side of the balance scale. When we are left wanting, we are falsely raised up because we are outweighed by those to whom we have forfeited our power.

Being negative, through doubt and fear, forfeits all of your power to the cruelty of arrogance. Doing so allows the arrogant to have an ever-increasing power over you and puts you under their control and steals away your abilities of creativity and joy.

Those who are controlled by arrogant people would likely do the same as their arrogant taskmaster if given the opportunity to be in power over others. Choosing the side of the scale of arrogance blinds you from ever being able to do any serious amount of self-improvement because you have chosen a scale that always tells you that you are great—even when you are not. Cruel people and negative people are *us* until we choose the correct scale. Our prayer will not thrive when we choose the wrong scale—the "wrong scale" is the scale of lies.

Giving up Riches is Not a Requirement

When you think of prayer in terms of service to mankind, rather than service to yourself you can see the difference in benefit that you might receive from an identical answer. In this same way, one man can be rich and also be a joyful person. And another man could have an identical fortune of wealth and be in an unhappy and miserable condition. The difference between these two has *nothing* to do with their money. If you stripped everything from both of them and they only had the clothing on their backs, then the joyful rich man would likely still be joyful, and the unhappy rich man would likely still be in a miserable condition. The only difference now is that they are poor.

This common problem is not exclusive to wealthy people— it affects us all! When we have chosen the wrong scale, we believe that the things we have, and our status, are what makes us special. In doing so, we lose our creativity and become competitive and try to be like or above other people. *Like* or *above* will depend upon first or third scale ("me" or "them").

Those who feel low want to be like those who are arrogant and who want to be above other people.

When you have chosen the proper scale, then nothing that you have matters, and everything is only a bonus to you to make your life more comfortable. This is why the Christ said "It is easier for a camel to get through the eye of a needle than it is for a rich man to enter the gates of heaven." This might not seem to make much sense in this context, but what is being conveyed is that riches are not the way. Often, this is taken as meaning we must sell everything and have nothing. While this is okay to do, it is not necessary, nor is it the secret to get to Heaven.

Your possessions could be your—not so tangible—religion, or your beliefs in general, which is something that can far outweigh your financial status. If you sell everything and still believe that your religion is the way to heaven, then you are in for a horribly rude awakening.

If you think that your beliefs are superior and that you should be respected because of your religious beliefs, then also you are in for a horrible awakening. This includes belief of science and reason, as well as religion.

If you have given everything up, and you are still an unhappy and miserable person, then giving up your possessions has been of little help to you. Though, it may be *slightly* to your credit if you have actually helped others with those possessions when you gave them up.

The reason to sell your possessions, as suggested by the Christ, is because the wealth of a rich man hides his errors from himself and it blinds him from being able to see those errors. If a rich man thinks that his wealth is of any lasting purpose, then he is deceived by that wealth. If he is stripped of that wealth, then he has a far better chance to become aware of the fact that there is no real value in his financial wealth or social status and that it is his real inner-self that is important and matters. Money and status cannot gain you anything regarding your entrance to Heaven.

If the rich man was a miserable or cruel person *with* the wealth, he will likely be a miserable or cruel person *without* the wealth. But he will have a better chance of seeing his error when it is not hidden by his former riches. If the person has wealth and is happy **because of** *that wealth*, then will he be happy when his wealth is gone? If a person has prestige because of his wealth, then will he have prestige if his wealth is gone? He will have neither prestige nor happiness when his wealth disappears; this is because his prestige and happiness are dependent upon that wealth.

The Christ did not say you *must* sell all that you have; he said that "It is easier for a camel to go through the eye of a needle, than for a rich man to enter the gates of heaven." Giving up your riches is not a requirement. However, selling and giving it all away will help some rich people overcome their arrogant greed and reliance upon those riches because they will be stripped bare and can no longer hide their errors behind their money and status, thus, possibly removing their blindness. So, for most people, giving up riches is a necessity in order for them to be able to see that their wealth is not their joy. It is important to note that this is not the case with all rich people. There are many people who have great wealth *because of* the truth which they have embraced!

Do You Hold on Tight so You Don't Lose It?

World culture is based upon the scale of lies, and often that scale offers its takers tremendous amounts of *apparent* success. Arrogance feeds on fear and becomes stronger with every fearful submission to it. The fearful, seeing everything slipping through their fingers, try to hold on tightly to the little they have while at the same time others take it away from them.

The arrogant hold on tightly to what belongs to others, believing it to be something that will make themselves be more respected by the others. The appearance of respect shown to the arrogant is not respect at all. Rather it is actually the fearful person's self-doubt and their fear of the arrogant one. The only thing that allows us to escape this horrible trap of self-destruction is when we choose to balance everything on the scale of truth.

In prayer, we ask the Creator for us to be released from our difficult situation, but then we hold on tightly to the little that we believe we have. We do this because we are afraid that we will lose the little we believe that we have. Holding on to everything around us busies our hands and minds. Holding on also blinds us from being able to see the good that awaits us. And it stops us from being able to grab on to the new and better blessings that come to us.

The only personal thing we have of any true and lasting value is our own selves—the very fact that we exist. It is not the body we are in that is of great value, it is our ability to think and seek the order of truth that gives us value.

Without our ability to think and seek truth, we render ourselves corrupt and worthless, and we have lowered our position or status via our own freewill. This is why, when we choose lies, we feel we must try so hard to regain our status in vain attempt to look better to those around us. But no matter how much financial and social whitewash we paint ourselves with, underneath it all, we are still corrupted with lies when we use the wrong scale—We hold on tightly to the little we have, so that we do not lose the stolen status that we do not deserve to begin with.

Pray Properly and Clear Minded

Mentally release everything in your life and pray with a pure mind and a pure heart—pray properly and with a clear passionate mind. Think of blank empty space and cast away your worries, fears, doubts, and lies. Then think of what good or good things you desire in your life in clear and vivid detail. Ask the Creator for it, and then offer thanks that it is already coming to you. Then request an open heart and an open mind. And finally, request guidance and awareness in order to be able to see the true answer when it stands before you.

As you pray, consider that it should be within the goodness of Creation and to the benefit of all of mankind. If you were a servant of a very wealthy person, you would receive an agreed upon wage. But would you not *also* see many other benefits in being in the company of your wealthy master?

We always want everything for ourselves, or for a specific person in our prayers. But if, instead, we were to use our skills to serve Creation, which includes all of those around us, will we not be blessed in that service?

Many people take this to suggest that they should go out and become some sort of a preacher, but that is not at all what is meant. Your skills may be a gift of design where you are able to design or create beautiful works of art, or stunning architecture, or making and serving great sandwiches, or even collecting the weekly trash, all for your fellow man. It is sharing, not for your glory, but for the joy of all mankind that will earn you true respect amongst your fellow man and with the Creator.

You can be a designer and design a building for your own vain glory, or you can make it to benefit others. The same identically designed building can be built, but with two different attitudes. When we understand this, then when we are praying, we obtain the ability to clear our mind and see our way clear to truth that belongs to each one of us.

All too often, the motive in our hearts while praying, even though we may not be aware of this, goes something like this: "Lord, let me design a building that people will like, so that I can feel cool and loved, and so that I can be rich so that people will respect me."; rather than the way it should be: "Lord, inspire me to design a building that will serve my fellow man and you. I am at your service."

The end result could be the exact same building, but with one of these attitudes your credit is the praise shown to you, and that's all that you will get out of it. With the other attitude, your credit is the joy that many others receive from what you have created for all people, and in addition to that, you'll also be praised for your fine work!

Don't waste your time praying for petty selfish credit that does not belong to you, and don't waste your time praying in doubt always being afraid of everything you encounter. Release all of that and pray with confidence and Truth!

The Creator is not our servant to do our evil bidding. What we ask for from the Creator must be good for all good people. A prayer must serve the good of mankind, not just you. If it has any intent to bring anyone low, then it is worthless and corrupted. Your prayer might benefit mostly yourself, but it should not do so at a cost to others who abide in truth, otherwise it is not likely to be answered as you would imagine.

Accept only what is true into your life. You need not understand everything today, but some things are obvious to you today, and it is those obvious things that should be accepted immediately. When more becomes obvious to you, also accept it.

Be wary of believing that which runs contrary to what seems logical. Some creationist Church leaders, and some scientific single-trunk-evolution theory proponents, and those who preach single-point-universe-big-bang-expansion, have been masters at distorting truth, thus clouding the eyes of those of who have blind-faith in those theories.

Do not believe blind-faith, it is a dangerous lie. The real evidence is there before our very own eyes, waiting for us to realize it and uncover it all from our own blindness, and then to shout our findings from our rooftops.

Embrace this truth and you will quickly begin to see what *is.* When you pray, pray in truth and with purity of that truth, and know what you want in your life.

Remember to ask yourself "What caused this?" Understand the root of a problem and do everything in your power to make the needed corrections.

Know what you want and what is needed to get it. Have these ideas clearly formed in your mind when you pray, and then ask your request—make your prayer. Your prayer is your hope! Hope is your ability to imagine what is not yet.

After you have purified your life with truth and you have understood your errors, and after you have made and understood your plans and requested those plans in prayer, then you need to believe with the faith of a child. Know with every fiber of your body that an answer to your prayer will come to you, and, possibly, it will be in a surprising and unique way. You must set your intent upon your request, knowing and intending that it will be. And then be ready and take action for the answer to your prayer to occur in your life. These are all *your* parts of the request and are required of you for successful prayer—they are *your* part of the responsibility.

After you have accomplished all of that, you must understand that a real answer to a prayer is typically not something that you expect day-to-day. The answer is very likely to come to you in an unexpected way. If you do not understand this, you will probably not see the answer to your prayer when it is right in front of your face because you will not recognize it and therefore you will not be able to benefit from it.

Unique, special, and unexpected opportunities will come knocking on your door when you are seen as **favorable to the Creator** because of your acceptance of that which is true, and because of your understanding of why prayer works!

Blessings of Successful Prayer and Joy!

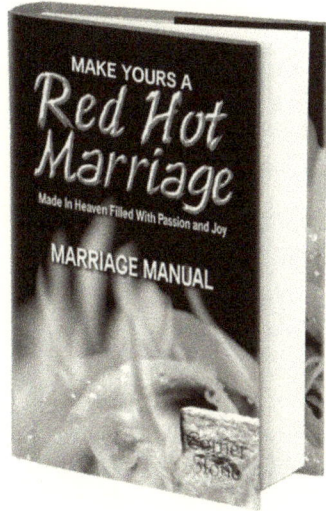

When You Dream...
DREAM THIN™
The Weightloss Repair Manual

Learn How to Lose Weight While Sleeping

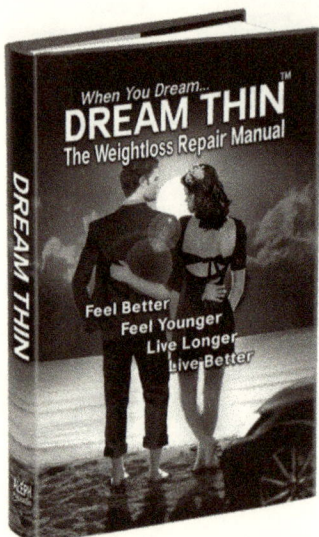

How many people do you know who exercise and still can't seem to lose weight? Has that ever happened to you? As a matter of fact, because we don't know the vital secrets that are shared in *Dream Thin*, many of us actually end up *gaining* weight when we exercise.

Do you hit your weight loss goals? And does your weight stay off when you do actually lose some weight? Even many doctors miss the *real* answers to weight loss. If you doubt this, then simply look at the waistlines of many medical doctors and nurses.

Weight loss is easily mastered when you understand a few basic principles. We often go on fad diets or follow the orders of our doctors, only to put the weight back on even faster than we lost it. Many of us suffer from unnecessary disease, and some of us will die too young.

Dream Thin does more than simply share answers to weight loss mysteries. *Dream Thin* explains the important details of *why* and *how* weight loss connects to mind *and* body. The information in *Dream Thin* allows you to make weight loss permanent without having to try so hard. Don't make more of the same empty promises to yourself each New Year's Day. Instead, quickly and easily change things today and make all of your tomorrows better with *Dream Thin* while still enjoying all of the foods you eat today—and yes, even fast foods!

Only you can choose if you want spend your hard-earned money on medical bills and funerals, or if you would rather spend your time and money looking great while being out and about and enjoying life with friends and family as intended!

Search: Dream Thin Book
SayItBooks.com

The Science of God
The First Four Days
Volume 1 - The First Four Days

Is there a God? Did we evolve? Did everything start from a big bang? These questions have been plaguing our minds for many years. Only science-minded people and clergy seem to have the answers. But do they really have any true answers?

Is what we are told by science true? Is what we are told by the Church true? Or are there other better explanations for everything? Did we hitch a ride from Mars, or is that all fantasy science? Was everything Created in six twenty-four hour days, or did it all take billions of years to happen? Few people are willing to even fully consider these questions, and even fewer have any coherent answers. *The Science of God* challenges your current beliefs while asking tough questions of science and of the Church.

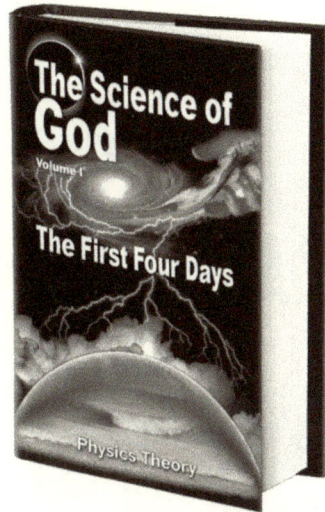

For years, Christian after Christian has attempted to argue for God and the Bible's Creation only to fail miserably. Why is this, why is it that Christians cannot seem to win this debate? Often Christians think they are winning the debate only to find themselves at a loss to answer the real questions, and then they get mocked for their poor answers.

Whether you are a scientist or an average Christian and want to discuss the Creation debate, *The Science of God* is a mandatory read for you. *The Science of God* takes you through the thought process to enable you to speak intelligibly about Creation, the cosmos, evolution, and astrophysics.

Search: The Science Of God Book
SayItBooks.com

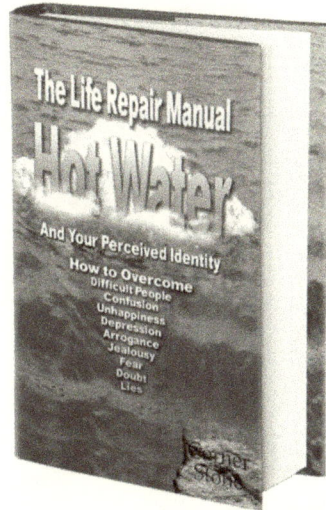

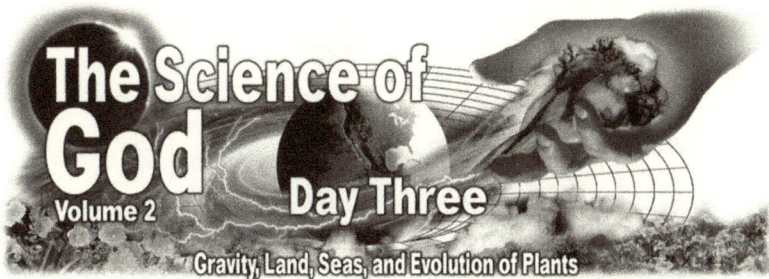

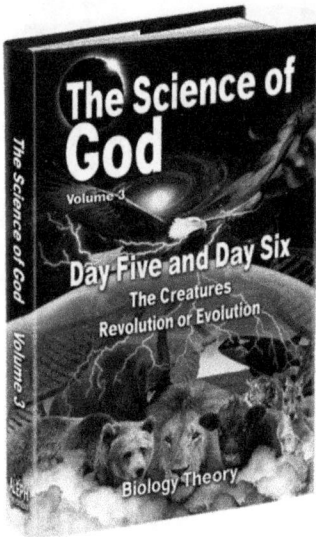

The Science of God
Volume 4
Day Six
Evolution versus Man
In Our Image

Rocking the Cradle of Life
A Decent Account of Descent

Have you ever wondered if humans actually did evolve from apes? Or maybe, if we were specifically created, then how might have that occurred? There sure are a lot of opinions on the evolution versus creation topic. And too often these views use confusing technical jargon that few people care to learn or have ever even heard.

The answers to the questions you might have are, in many cases, the same answers that many other people seek. When you have solid answers that are difficult for someone to thwart, it's good to share those answers so that others can also feel confident with their own understanding of the arrival of mankind and the level of importance that it has in their own lives.

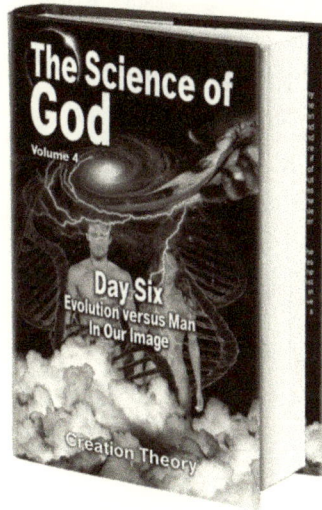

The Science Of God Volume 4 - Evolution versus Man – In Our Image takes a deep but simple dive into the human evolution versus human creation debate using simple language that everyone can understand and enjoy!

If you have thoughts that you have been reluctant to share, then suspend your thoughts for a bit and open your mind to consider the perspectives and evidence presented in *The Science Of God Volume 4 - Evolution versus Man – In Our Image*. You will acquire a much clearer view of the subject as you read the various points made in this engaging book about the arrival of mankind.

Search: The Science Of God Book Volume 4
SayItBooks.com

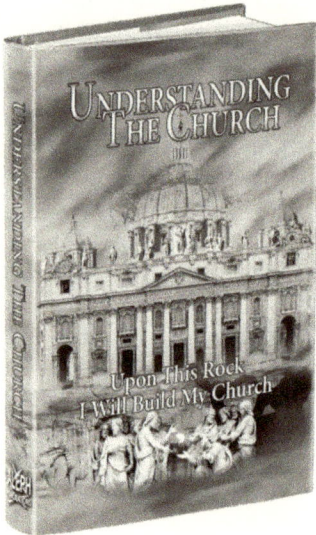

Thank You GOD
Finding Gratitude in Hard Times

How to Win When You Think You've Been Beat

Feeling grateful is a bit of a struggle when we face tough times in our own lives, and avoiding depression during those times can be tricky. The world cares little of us when we face our own personal struggles, in fact life kicks us when we're down. You've probably experienced the world caring little of your past or present problems, so looking to "The World" for rest and peace is typically of little help.

It doesn't have to be this way! You can change your disposition, and thus, change your future! It's no big secret and it's not difficult, but "The World" won't tell you that, so very few people ever get to hear or understand this simple "secret".

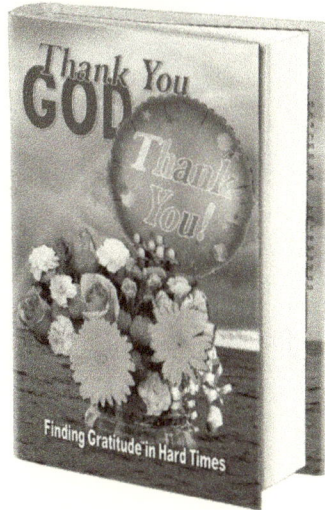

It's amazing to see the people and situations you can attract into your life when you find your own proper perspective, and once you find it you will not want to let it go! Days that test you to your limit become far easier to overcome, making every future test easier than it otherwise would have been.

Simply understanding a few key basics can change your direction in life in short order and can make life a whole lot more peaceful and Joyful! Let *Thank You God – Finding Gratitude in Hard Times* be one of your keys to peace and Joy!

Search: Thank You God Book
SayItBooks.com

Notes

Notes

Notes

www.ingramcontent.com/pod-product-compliance
Lightning Source LLC
Chambersburg PA
CBHW030715110426
42739CB00030B/398